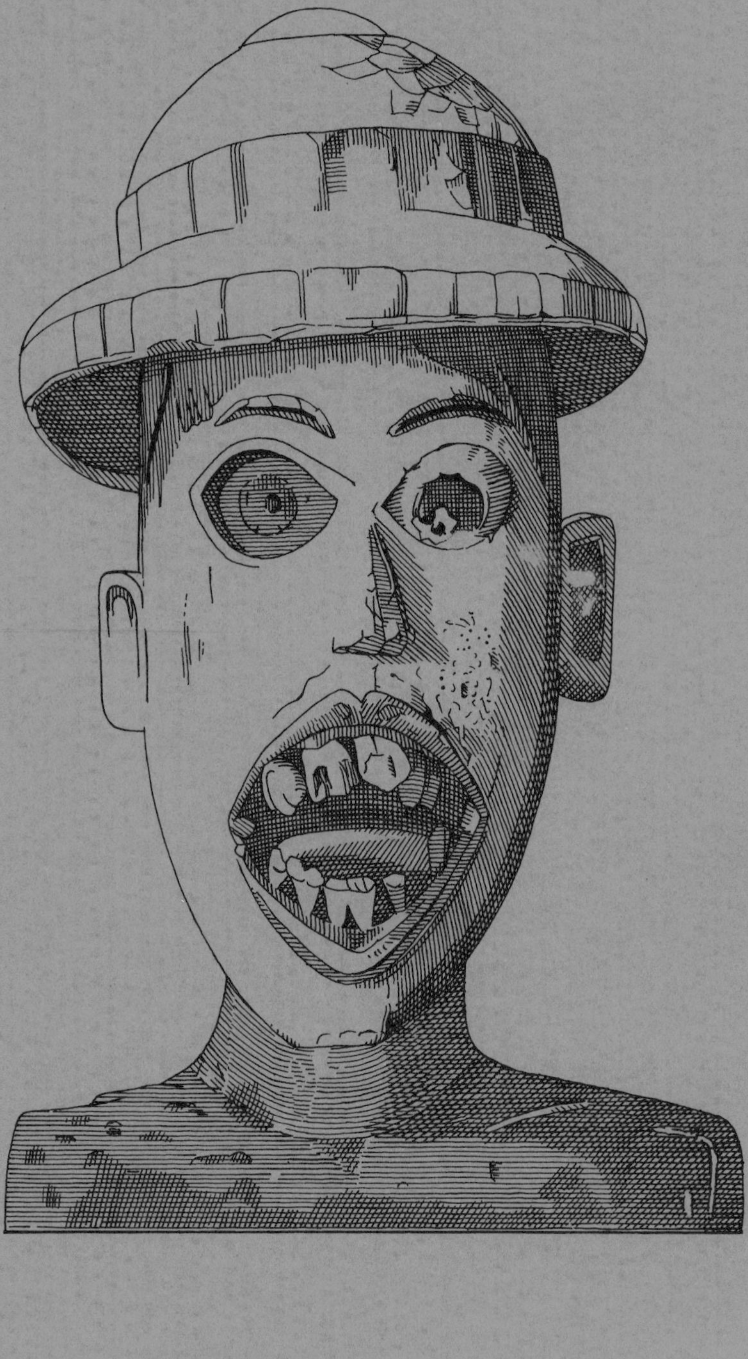

AF478603

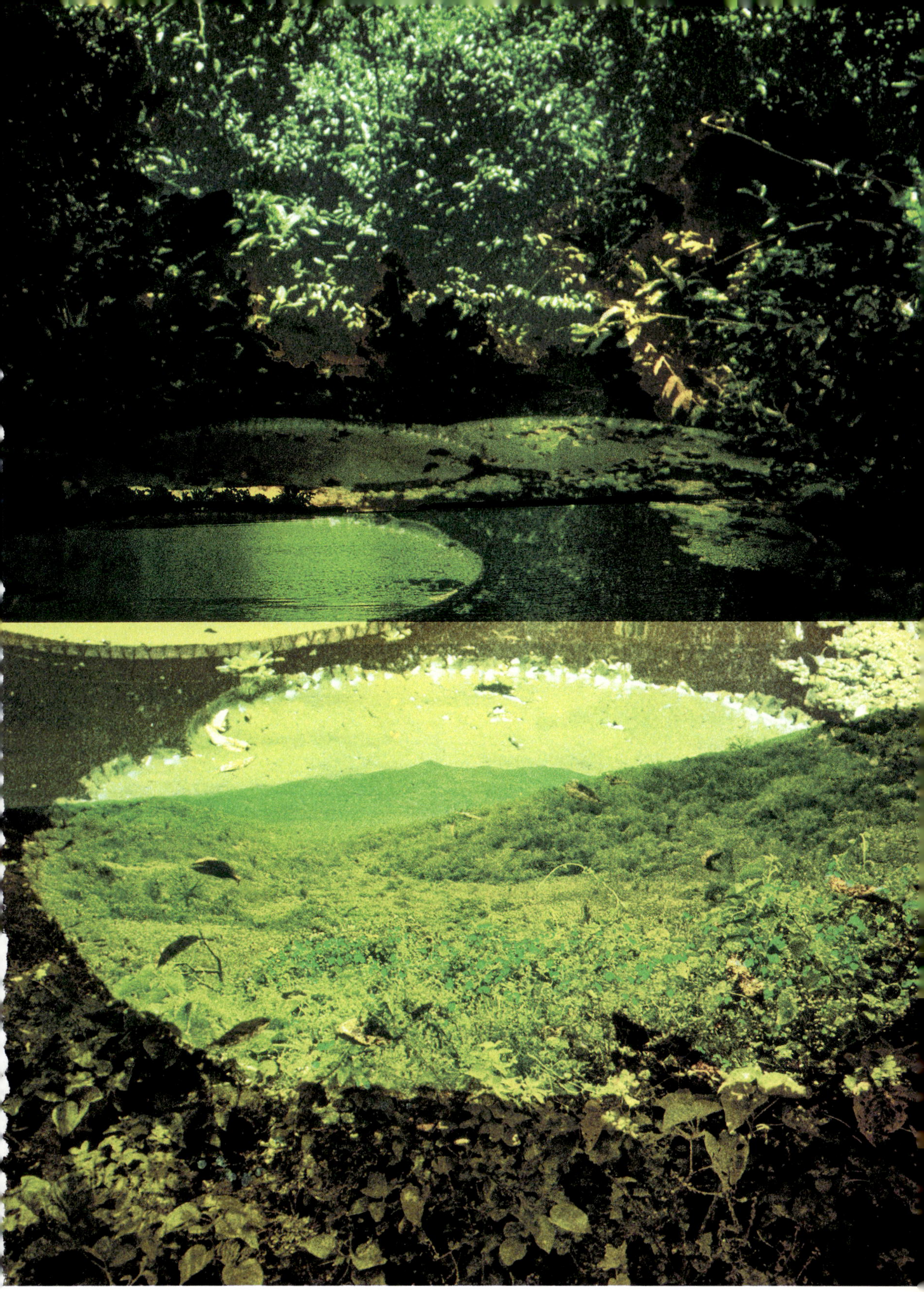

stagnant and shadowy and glassy-green, where mammoth milk-white blossoms floated, and strange high-shouldered birds with curious bills stood gazing sidewise without sound or stir. Among the knotted joints of a bamboo thicket the eyes of a crouching tiger gleamed – and he felt his heart throb with terror, yet with a longing inexplicable. Thomas Mann, *Death in Venice* And the best part about it is that I have the whole story told by someone who has never even been to the Tropics. That's the joke. It turns out that he, the Northerner, has the Tropics within him. Robert Müller, *Tropen* The tropics are less exotic than out of date. Claude Lévi-Strauss, *Tristes Tropiques* An Exot is a born Traveler, someone who senses all the flavor of diversity in worlds filled with wondrous

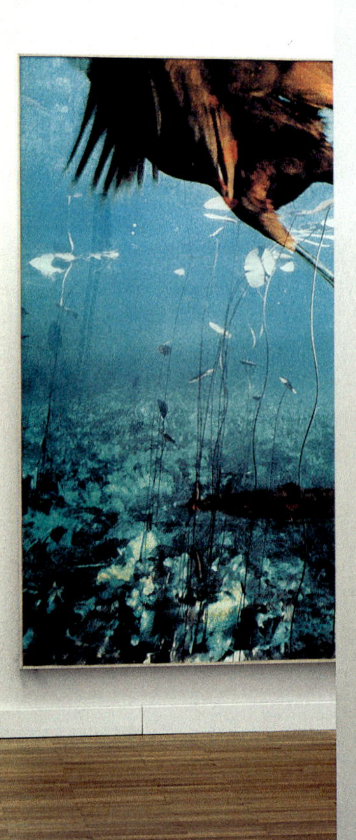

diversities. Victor Segalen, *Essay on Exoticism* It is not worth the while to go round the world to count the cats in Zanzibar. Yet do this even till you can do better, and you may perhaps find some "Symmes' Hole" by which to get at the inside at last. Henry David Thoreau, *Walden* It is always a squalid affair when someone writes a book, especially on the Tropics. After all, the Tropics are humankind's infancy. Whosoever has outgrown that infancy would be mature, and not write about it. The Tropics are a young European's puberty. Robert Müller, *Tropen* There was something languorous and velvety about the heat. A stifling fragrance came from the inflorescences of *Vallieria mirifica*, mother-of-pearl in color and resembling clusters of soap bubbles, that arched

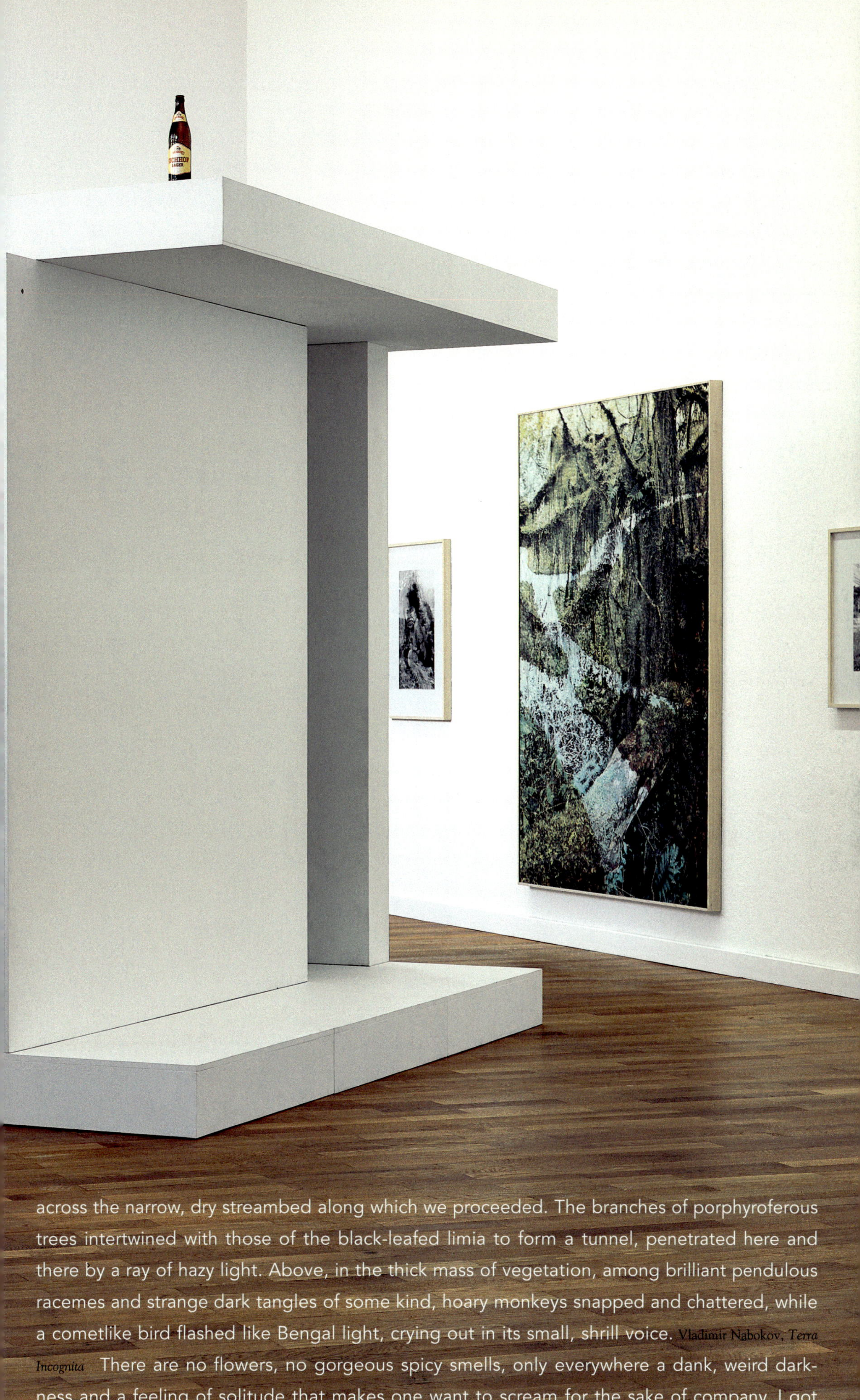

across the narrow, dry streambed along which we proceeded. The branches of porphyroferous trees intertwined with those of the black-leafed limia to form a tunnel, penetrated here and there by a ray of hazy light. Above, in the thick mass of vegetation, among brilliant pendulous racemes and strange dark tangles of some kind, hoary monkeys snapped and chattered, while a cometlike bird flashed like Bengal light, crying out in its small, shrill voice. Vladimir Nabokov, *Terra Incognita*   There are no flowers, no gorgeous spicy smells, only everywhere a dank, weird darkness and a feeling of solitude that makes one want to scream for the sake of company. I got back soaked with sweat, and in the evening had my first touch of fever. It was very nasty, but I

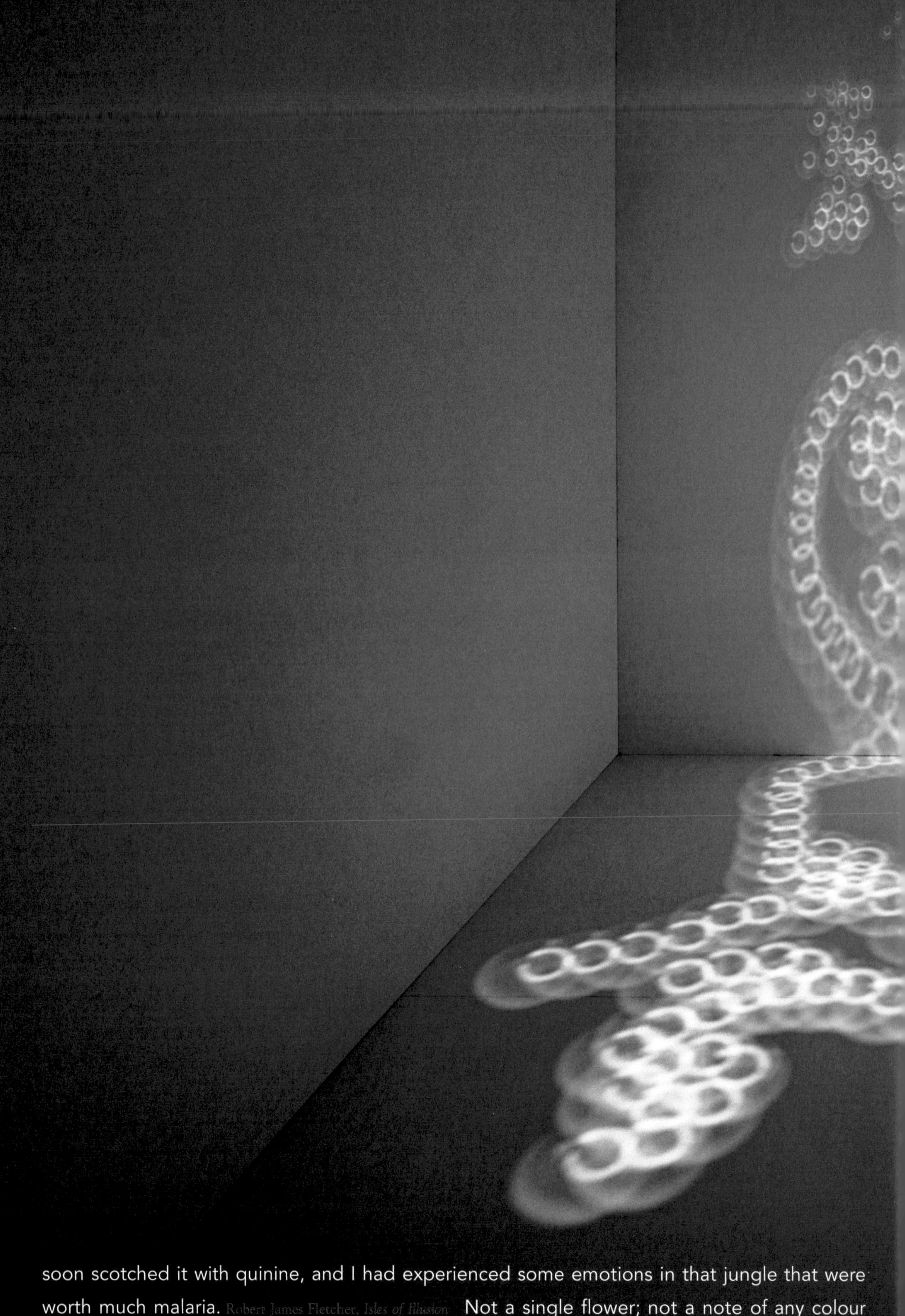

soon scotched it with quinine, and I had experienced some emotions in that jungle that were worth much malaria. *Robert James Fletcher, Isles of Illusion* Not a single flower; not a note of any colour but green, a very dark, monotonous green, which gives the landscape the solemn tranquillity of the monochrome African oases, and makes an impression of dignity unapproached by our northern landscapes, with their diversity of tones and shades. *André Gide, Travels in the Congo* But what did poetry, nature, indeed the world, matter to me? I had the fever, that African fever which, in less than an hour, fells the most tried and tested man, undermines all his springiness and energy, makes him insufferable to his dearest friends, inspires him with ideas of suicide and, in

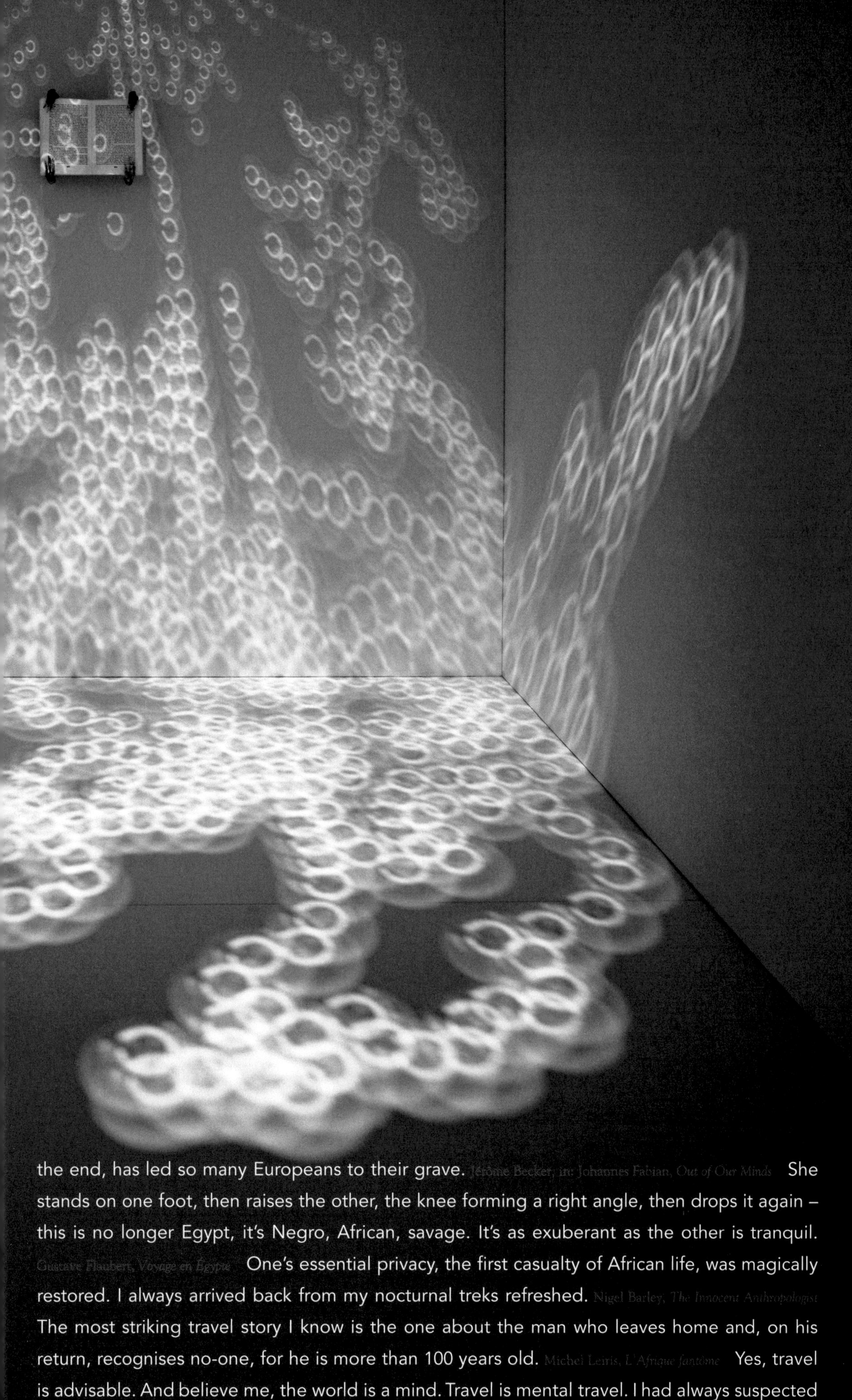

the end, has led so many Europeans to their grave. Jérôme Becker, in: Johannes Fabian, Out of Our Minds   She stands on one foot, then raises the other, the knee forming a right angle, then drops it again – this is no longer Egypt, it's Negro, African, savage. It's as exuberant as the other is tranquil. Gustave Flaubert, Voyage en Égypte   One's essential privacy, the first casualty of African life, was magically restored. I always arrived back from my nocturnal treks refreshed. Nigel Barley, The Innocent Anthropologist   The most striking travel story I know is the one about the man who leaves home and, on his return, recognises no-one, for he is more than 100 years old. Michel Leiris, L'Afrique fantôme   Yes, travel is advisable. And believe me, the world is a mind. Travel is mental travel. I had always suspected

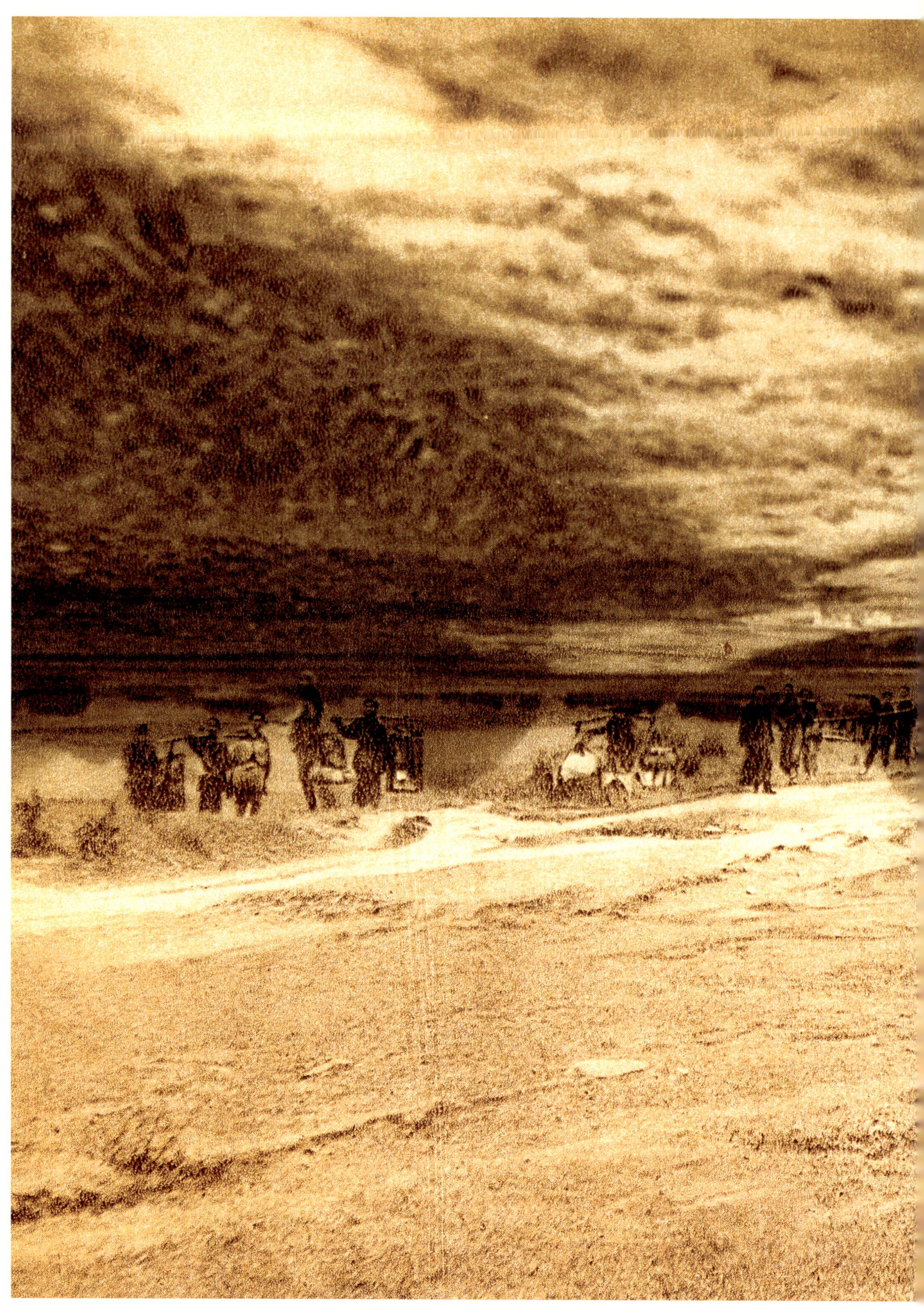

this. What we call reality is nothing but pedantry. I need not have had that quarrel with Lily, standing over her in our matrimonial bed and shouting until Ricey took fright and escaped with the child. Saul Bellow, *Henderson the Rain King*   The traveller who has fled the spirits – having seen how the Earth opens wide her maw and how the Heavens weep with stars – that traveller refuses to journey on. Victor Segalen, *Le fils du ciel*   It might be useful in this connection to point out the etymological origin of the German word *reisen*: The word *reisen* is derived from the Old High German word *risan*, which roughly translates as "to rise" (there is no doubt that the German word *auferstehen*, which means to "rise up" in the sense of "resurrect", is related in meaning).

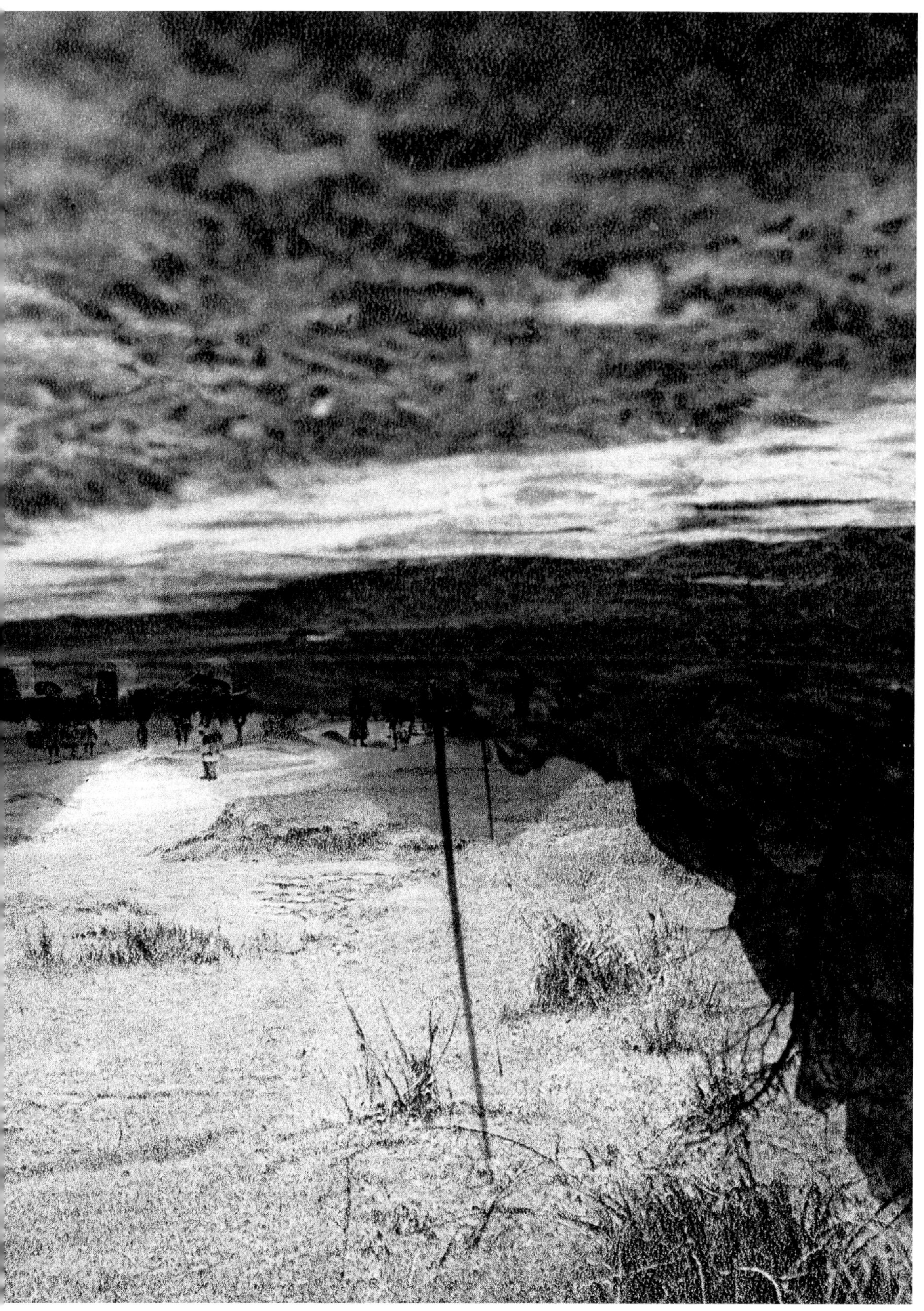

It also means "to rise up" and "to start out on a warlike venture". The English word "uprising" clearly has the same etymology. So the German word *reisen* is derived from a term that evidently bears the connotation of "war", "campaign" and "conquest". Christina von Braun, *Der Einbruch der Wohnstube in die Fremde* We stopped, and the silence driven away by the stamping of our feet flowed back again from the recesses of the land. The great wall of vegetation, an exuberant and entangled mass of trunks, branches, leaves, boughs, festoons, motionless in the moonlight, was like a rioting invasion of soundless life, a rolling wave of plants, piled up, crested, ready to topple over the creek, to sweep every little man of us out of his little existence. And it

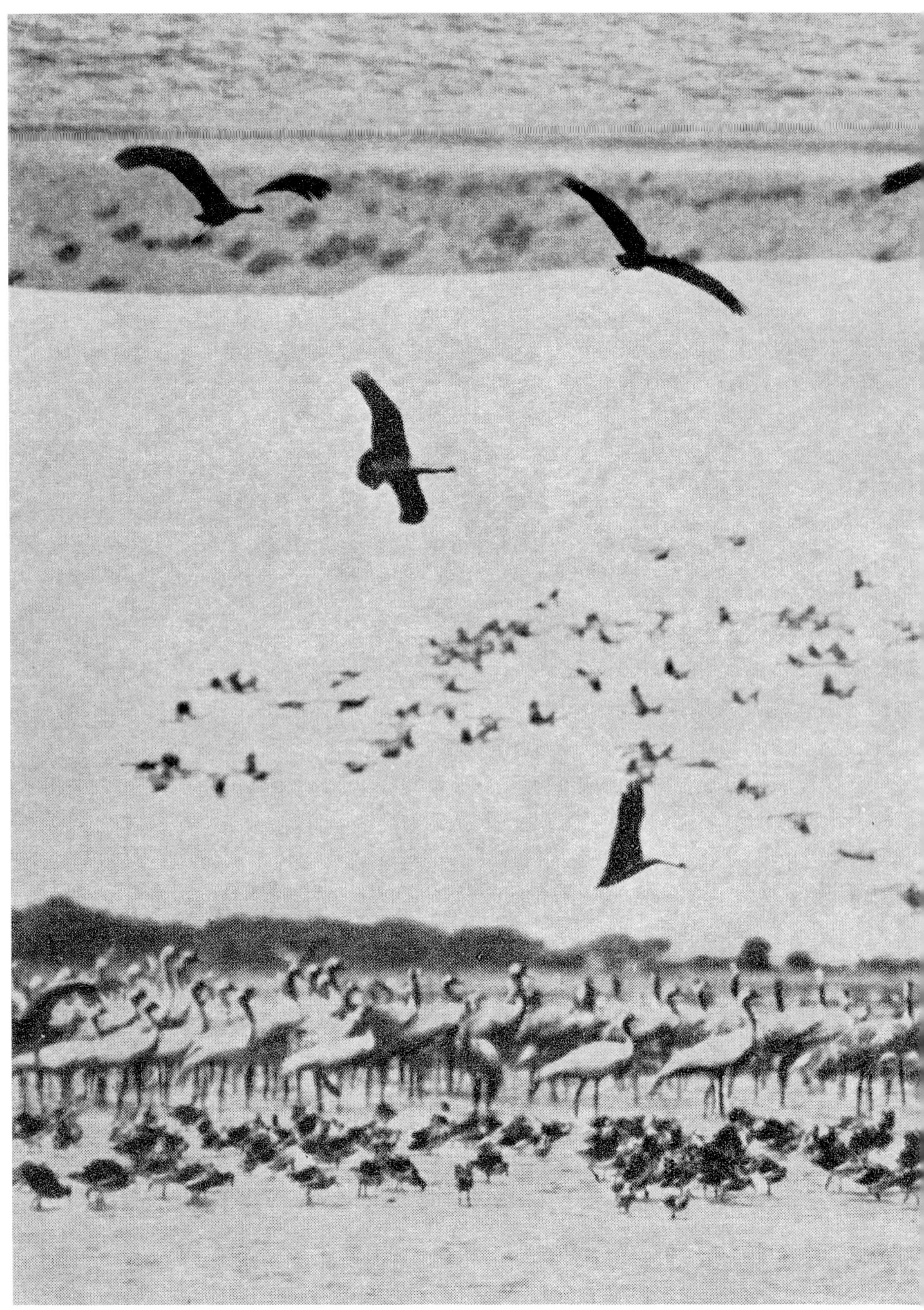

moved not. Joseph Conrad, *Heart of Darkness* He was drawn to the Pole, relentlessly, but not because he wanted to start anew from there. Everything had already started! The goal had been important so he could find the way. And now he had found the way, the way on which he walked, and the Pole once again became a geographical concept. His only desire was to keep moving, just like now, on a journey of discovery, until life was over. A Franklin System of living and journeying. Sten Nadolny, *Die Reise ins Eis* Travelers suffered from depression (or, in contemporary terms, "melancholy"); a few cracked and had nervous breakdowns. Johannes Fabian, *Out of Our Minds* Who am I to go on about the Tropics? The savage has no knowledge of them; only the

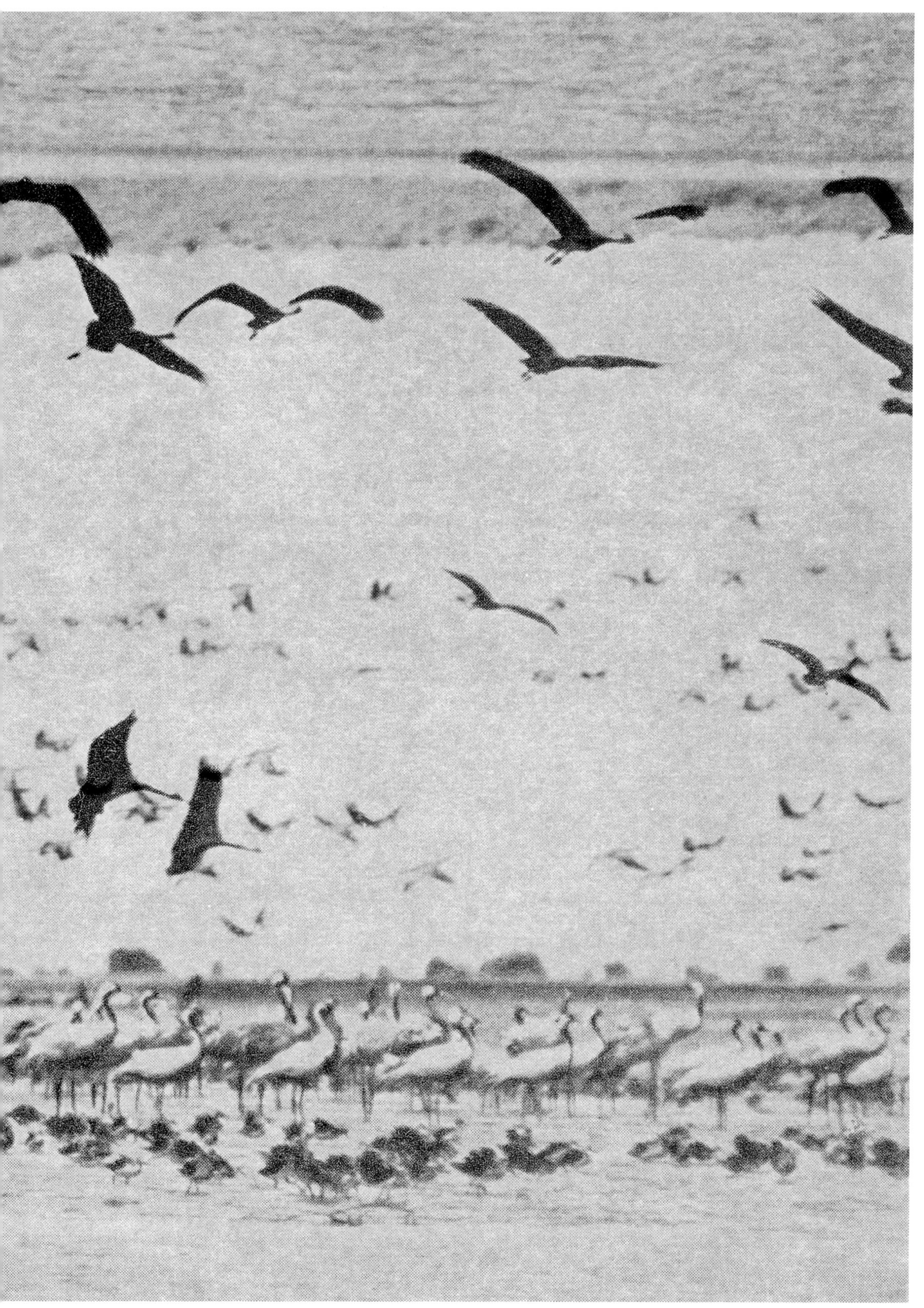

Northerner does, they are a trope for him and his fervour and the consuming fever in his nerves. He invents them to set himself an image. But they do not exist; they are merely a boring monotonous phase of growing up. Robert Müller, *Tropen* In the long-forgotten time when piety still mattered on the Island, when parakeets spontaneously broke into sutras, you wouldn't often have seen a bonze taking to the road. They used to move around by magic, tucking up their robes, mounting the winds, spinning like crimson cannonballs towards the Golden Isles or the Himalayas, unless they chose to plunge into the earth with a terrifying bang. Nicolas Bouvier, *The Scorpion-Fish* Novalis' *Blue Flower* comes to symbolise this yearning for

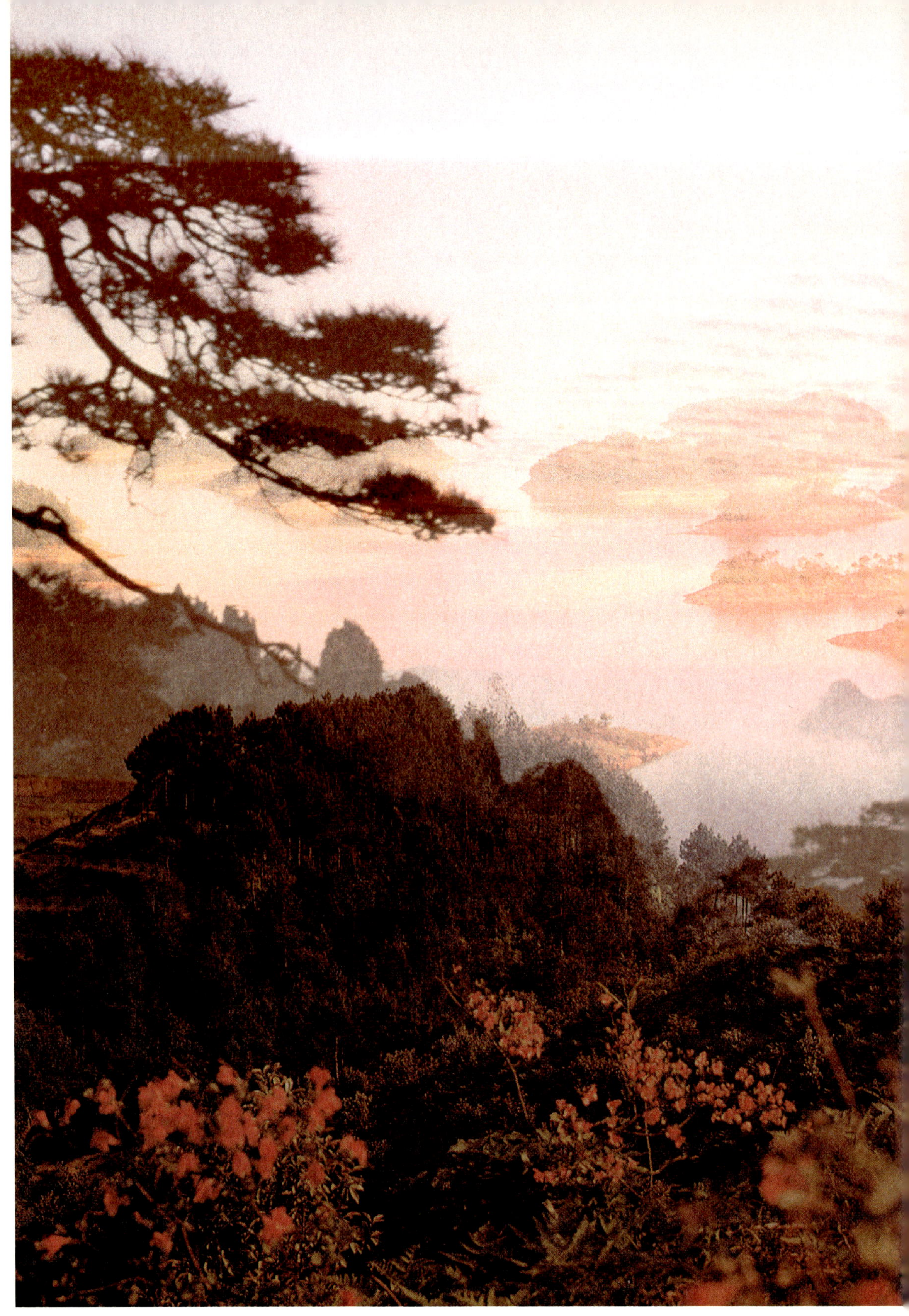

faraway places, which begins to take real shape in other respects, too. Particularly among writers and artists. They venture to the remotest corners – supposedly to encounter that which is foreign but in reality to conjure up that which is different. Christina von Braun, *Der Einbruch der Wohnstube in die Fremde* I remembered, too, the girl who sold pineapples at Dassa-Zoumbé station. It had been a stifling day, the train slow and the country burnt. I had been reading Gide's *Nourritures terrestres* and, as we drew into Dassa, had come to the line *Ô cafés – où notre démence s'est continuée très avant dans la nuit* … No, I thought, this will never do, and looked out of the carriage window. A basket of pineapples had halted outside. The girl underneath the basket

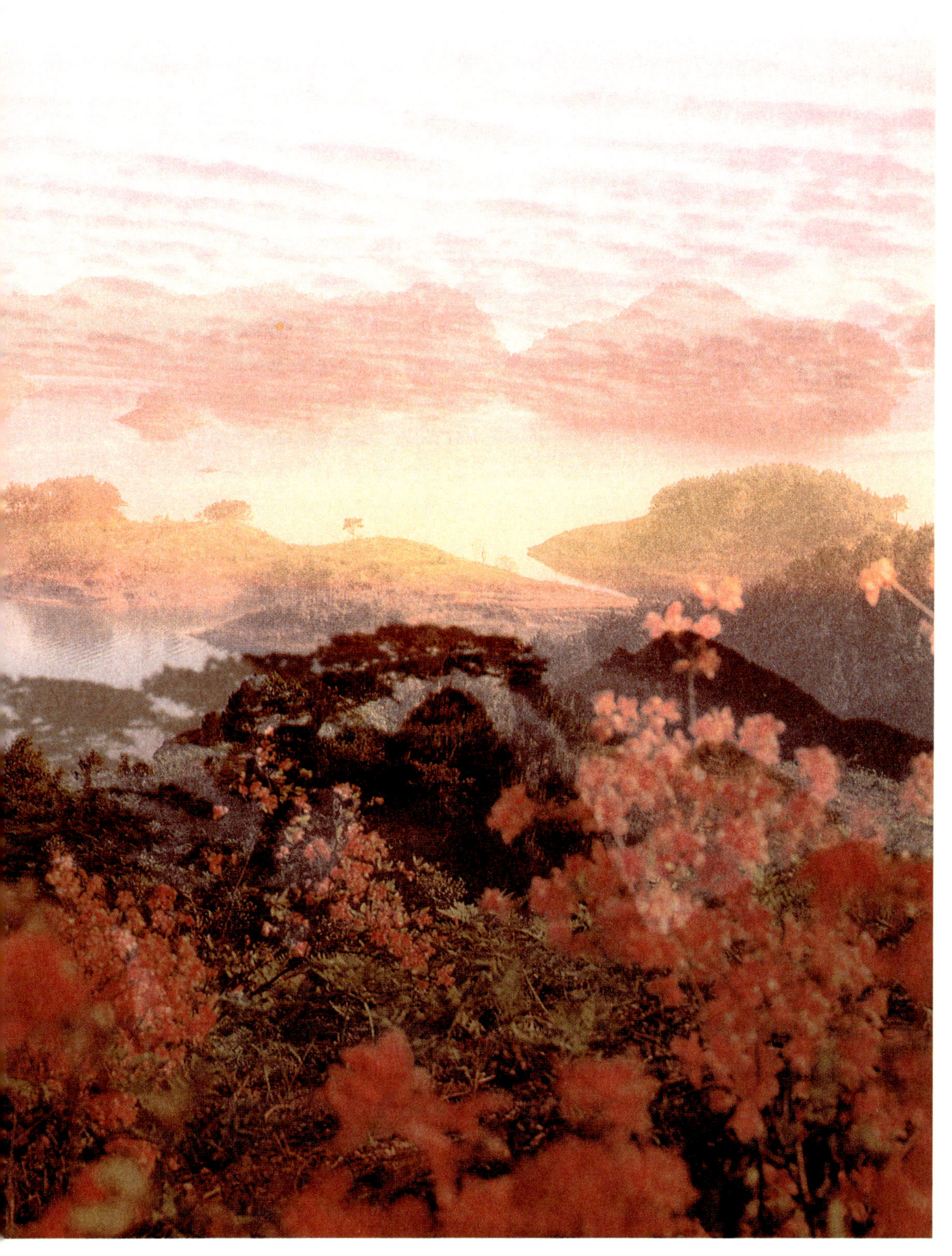

smiled and, when I gave her the Gide, gasped, lobbed all six pineapples into the carriage, and ran off to show her friends – who in turn came skipping down the tracks, clamouring, "A book, please? A book? A book!" So *out* went a dog-eared thriller and Saint-Exupéry's *Vol de nuit*, and *in* came the 'Fruits of the Earth' – the real ones – pawpaws, guavas, more pineapples, a raunch of grilled swamp-rat, and a palm-leaf hat. Bruce Chatwin, *What Am I Doing Here* But when we were married and I wanted to spend our honeymoon camping among the Copper Eskimos, she wouldn't hear of it. Anyway (still on the subjects of books) I read Freuchen and Gontran de Poncins and practised living out of doors in winter. I built an igloo with a knife and during zero

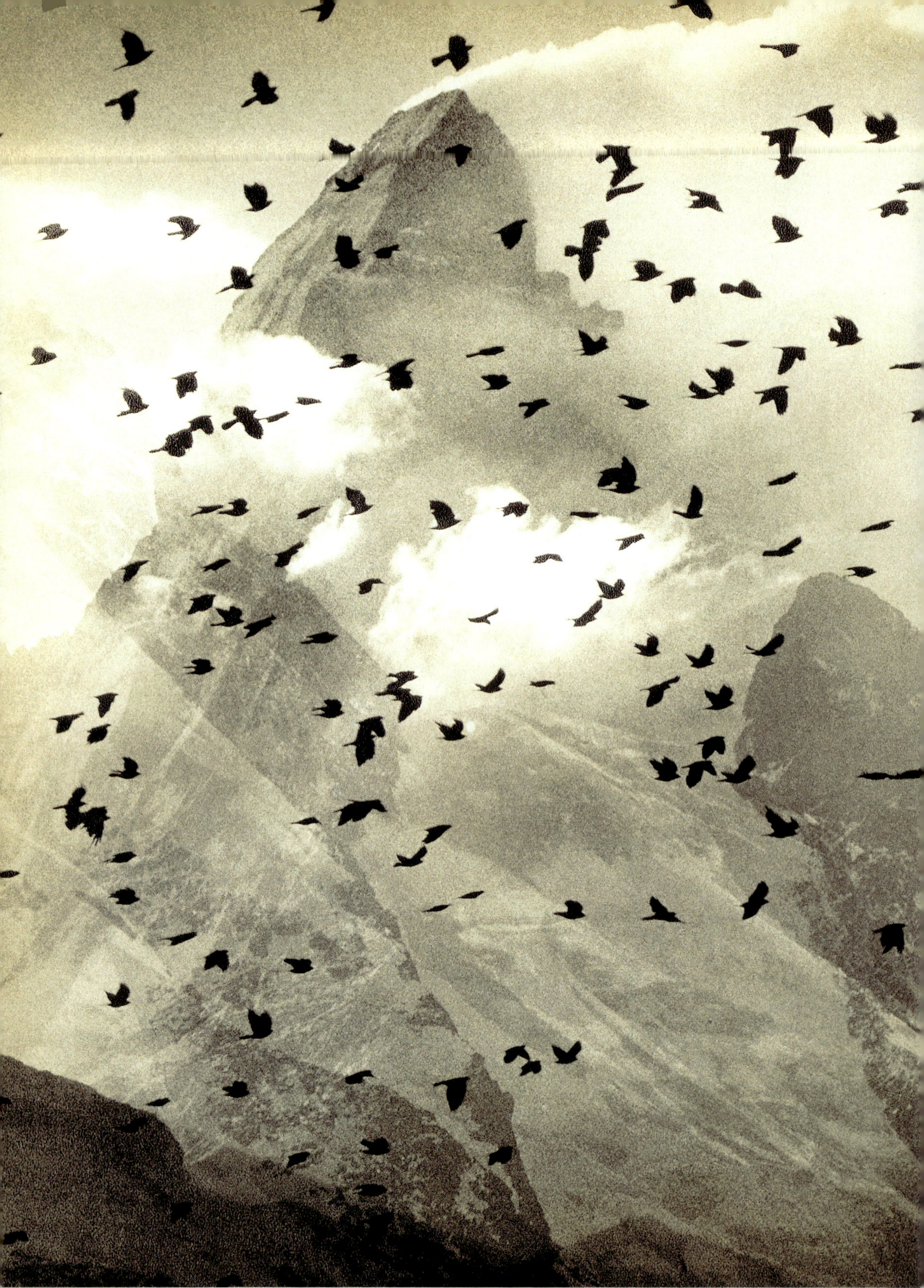

weather Lily and I fell out because she wouldn't bring the kids and sleep with me under skins as the Eskimos do. I wanted to try that. *Saul Bellow, Henderson the Rain King*   In 1933 I returned, having killed at least one myth: that of travel as a means of escape. I have subsequently gone back to therapy twice, once for only a brief period of time. *Michel Leiris, Manhood*   While the mistaken notion of wanting to breed human beings "racially pure", like race horses or dogs, prevails more than ever in our old world, for centuries the Brazilian nation has been established on one principle alone, that of free and unrestrained intermixing, the total equality of black and white and brown and yellow. *Stefan Zweig, Brazil: A Land of the Future*   We slip Asia and Europe and America over one

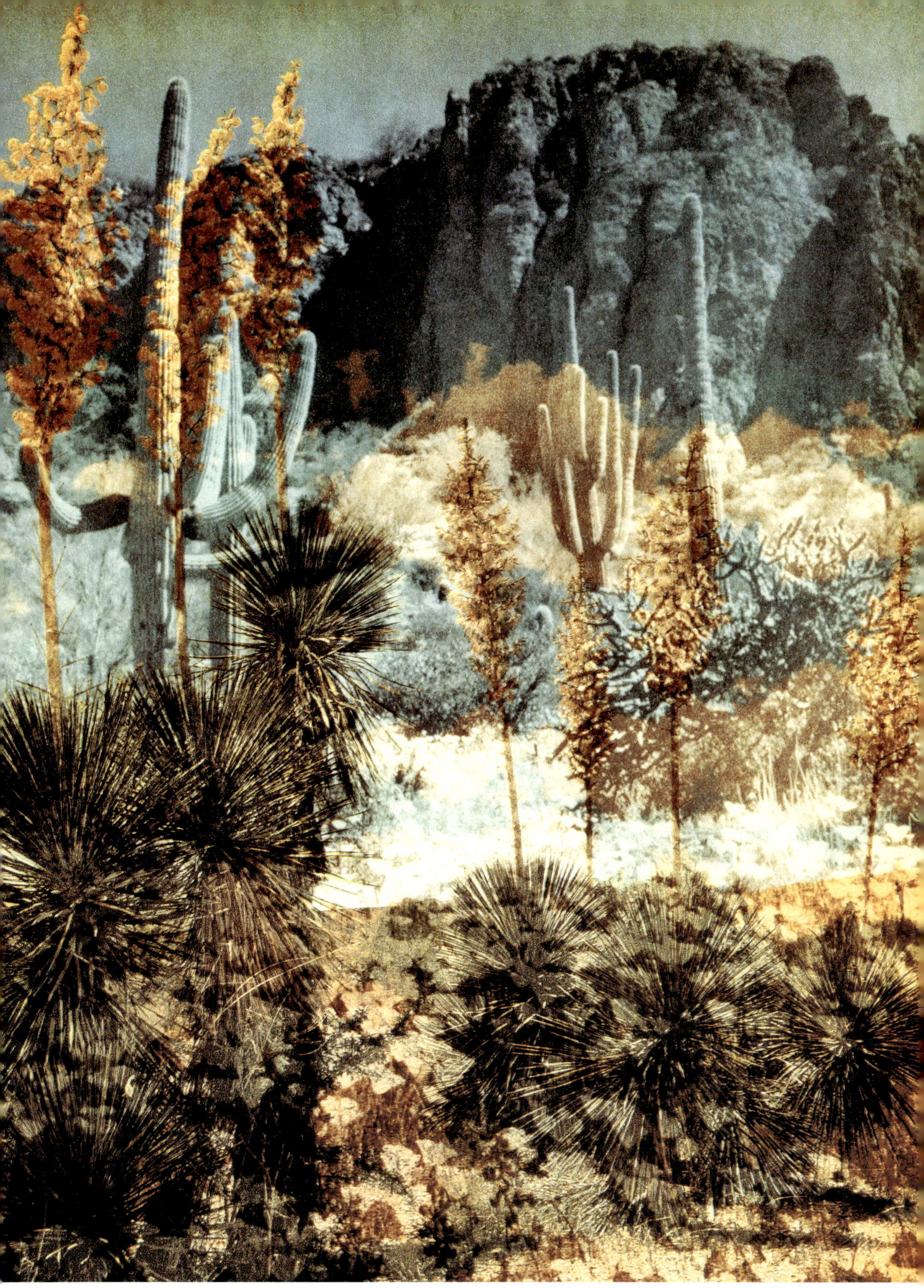

another. And what emerges is a humanity. It is not just America that is young; Europe is much younger still; much younger and stranger! They should launch voyages of discovery to Europe! You see, we who have overcome our longing, we do not know the faraway either. For us it is a question of courier. It is only by imagining the jungle as a somewhat antiquated boulevard that you will find your way about it. Robert Müller, *Tropen* The word Europe comes from a Semitic word that simply means "darkness". Sven Lindqvist, *Exterminate All The Brutes* In Europe everything ends tragically. There has never been any philosophy in Europe (at least since the Greeks … and even with them it is questionable). The French with their social tragedy, the Greeks with their

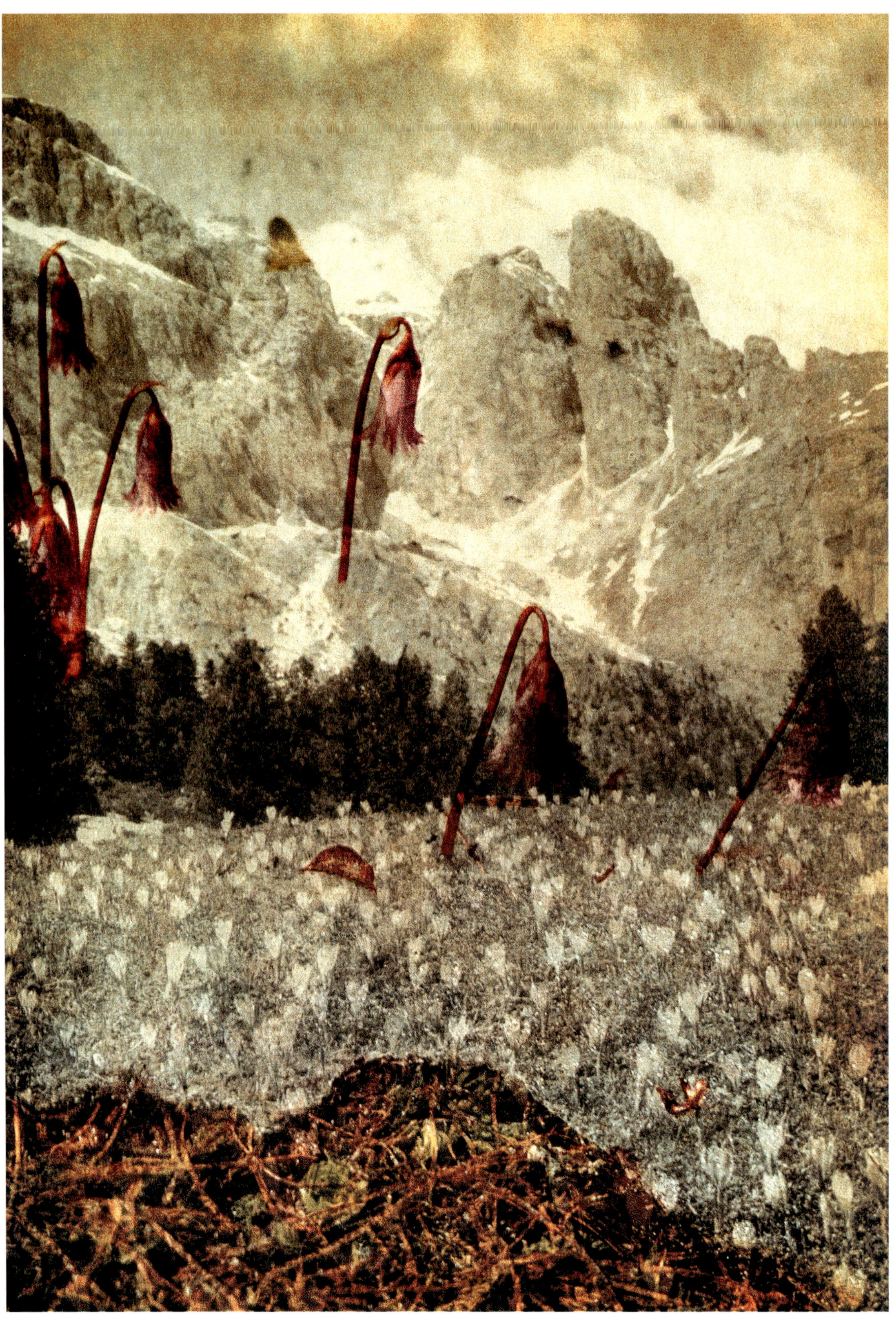

Oedipus, the Russians with their love of misfortune, the Italians with their pride in tragedy, the Spanish with their tragic obsession, Hamletism, etc., etc. If Christ had not been crucified, he would not have had a hundred disciples in Europe. His *Passion* is what excited people. Henri Michaux, *A Barbarian in Asia*   One of the striking curiosities of British colonial rule was the insistence of expatriates on constructing fireplaces even in the hottest tropical climate. This was clearly an important cultural need. Nigel Barley, *Native Land*   There is nothing more pleasing to a traveller – or more terrible to travel-writers, than a large rich plain; especially if it is without great rivers or bridges; and presents nothing to the eye, but one unvaried picture of plenty: for after they

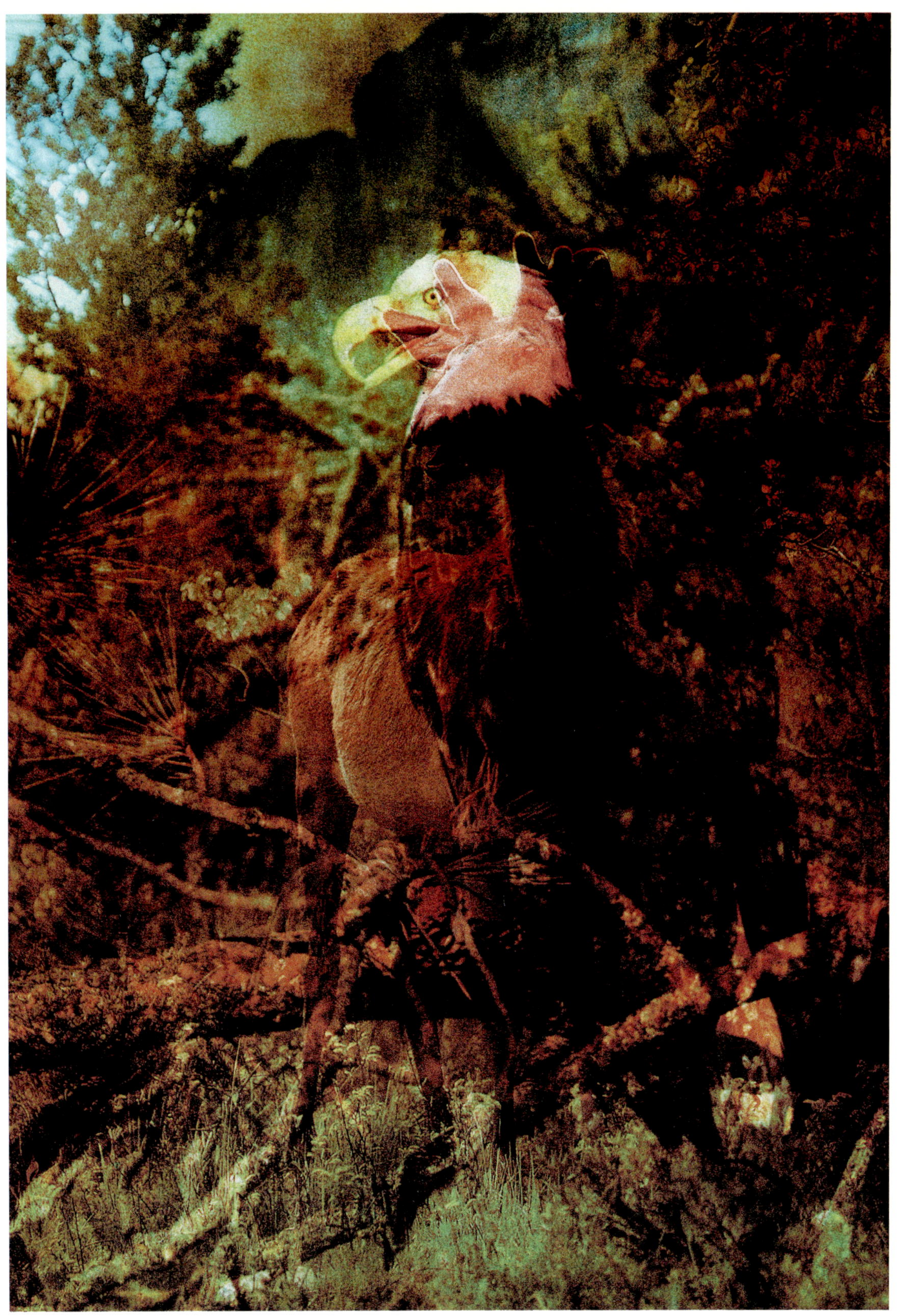

have once told you, that 'tis delicious! or delightful! (as the case happens) – that the soil was grateful, and that nature pours out all her abundance, etc. … they have then a large plain upon their hands, which they know not what to do with – and which is of little or no use to them but to carry them to some town; and that town, perhaps of little more, but a new place to start from to the next plain – and so on. *Laurence Sterne, Tristram Shandy*   There was a time when travelling brought the traveller into contact with civilizations which were radically different from his own and impressed him in the first place by their strangeness. During the last few centuries such instances have become increasingly rare. Whether he is visiting India or America, the modern

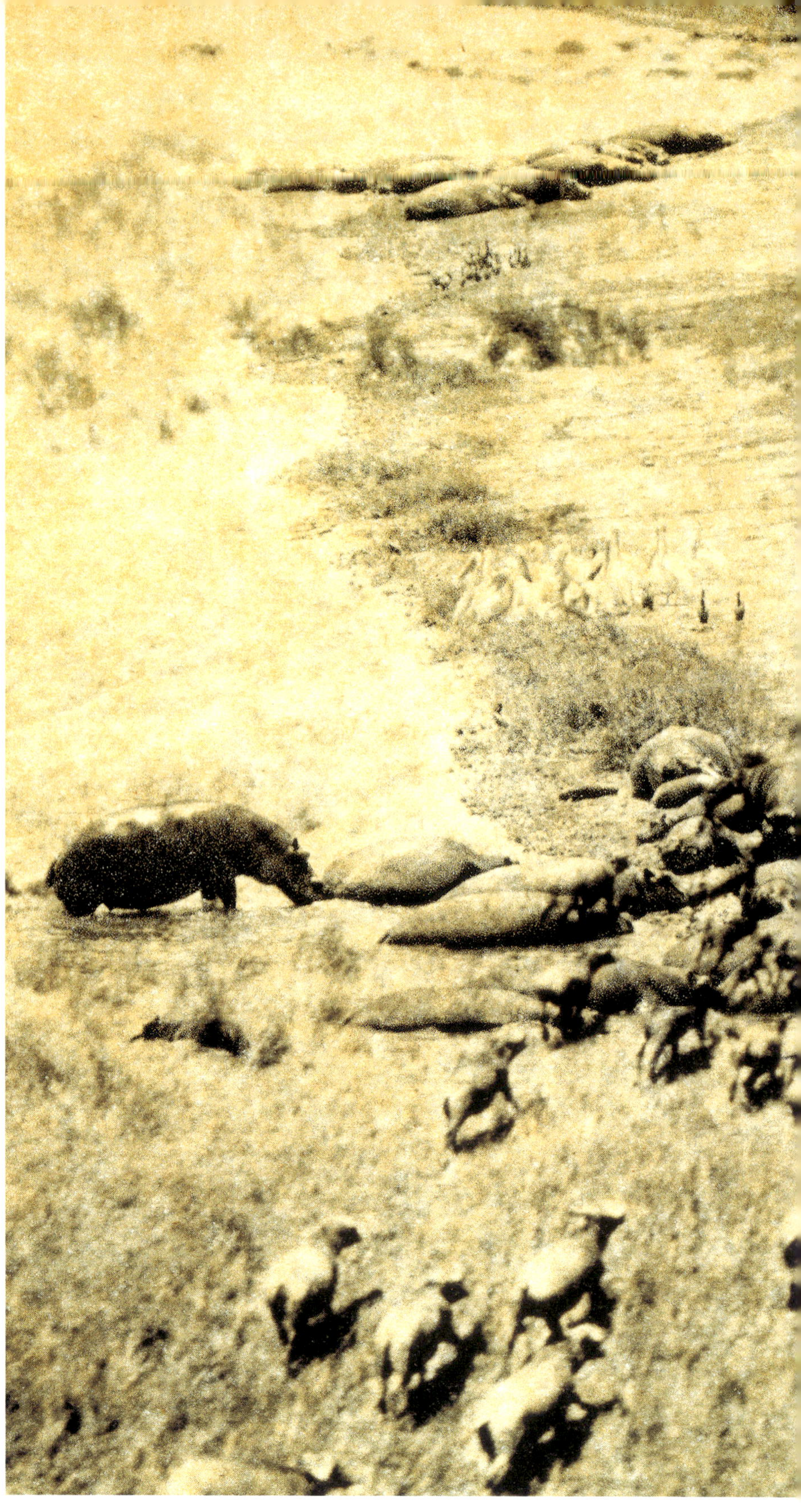

traveller is less surprised than he cares to admit. Claude Lévi-Strauss, *Tristes Tropiques* Perhaps some balance will be established whereby the constant intermingling of individuals will be redeemed by the small number of individuals who will retain the capacity to feel Diversity. Victor Segalen, *Essay on Exoticism* For what purpose does this race travel? To journey to the person within. One does not travel to distant lands with strange climates and astonishing experiences: if one did, one would be disappointed to encounter nothing but narrow-mindedness and disenchantment of which one has never been enraptured. Robert Müller, *Tropen* To travel: putting your head on the block a hundred times, picking it out of the bran tub a hundred times to find it almost

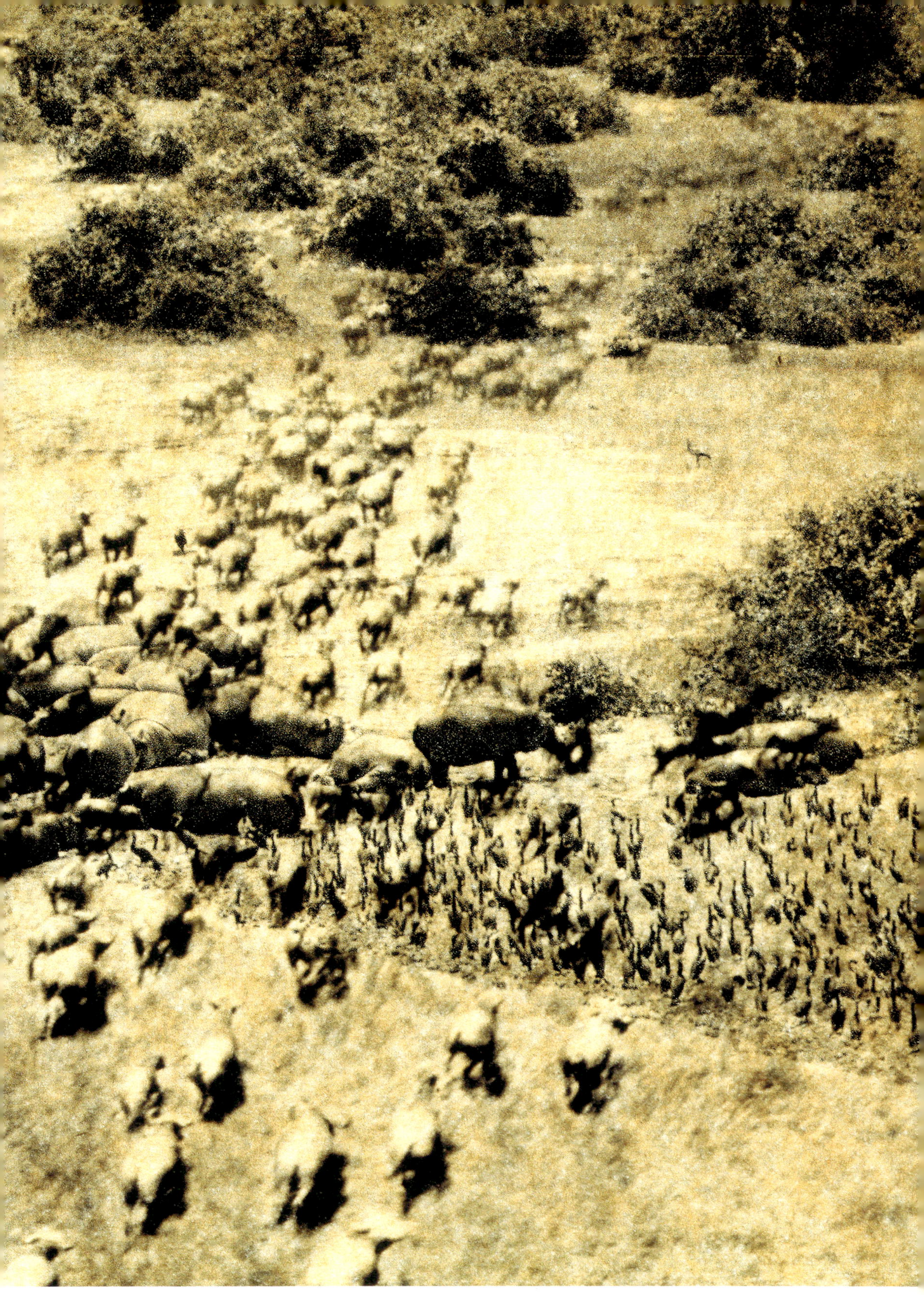

unchanged. You hope for a miracle, but you shouldn't expect one beyond the wear and tear of the life with which you have a rendezvous, against which you're wrong to kick. Nicolas Bouvier, *The Scorpion-Fish*   I closed my eyes in order to collect my thoughts. Then I heard curious nasal syllables being uttered nearby and looked up: two Chinamen, unmistakable in their Asiatic features (even if I were to doubt the authenticity of their costume) addressed me in what I imagine must have been the common local greeting. I got up and stepped back two paces. The Chinamen were gone, the landscape was altogether different: trees and forests stretched before me instead of rice fields. I studied the trees and other flora that blossomed around me: those I

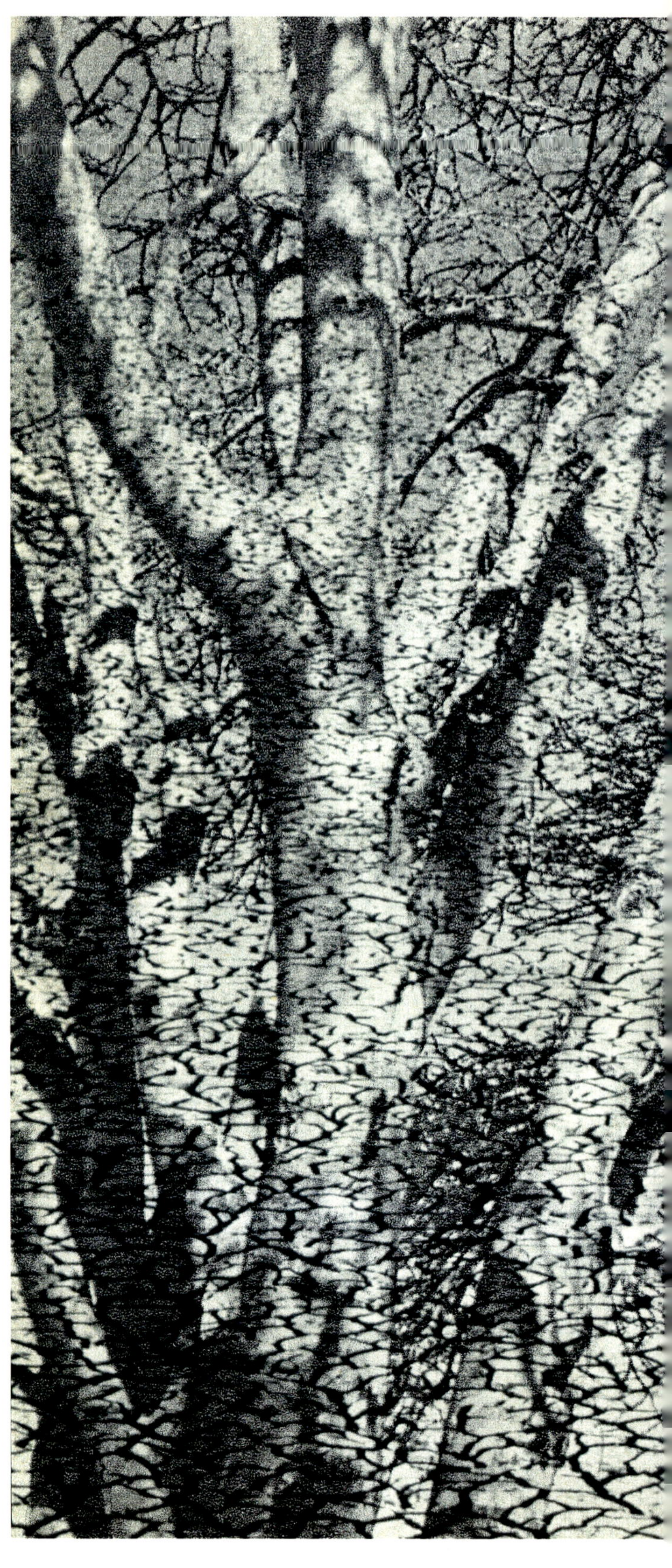

recognised were of a Southeast Asian species. Intending to approach one tree for a closer look,
I took a step forward – and once again, everything had changed. So I continued walking like a
recruit in training, proceeding slowly but with a dogged determination. Wondrously changing
vistas, flora, fields, mountains, tundras, and sandy deserts unfurled themselves before my
marveling gaze. There was no doubt about it: I had seven-league boots on my feet. Adelbert von
Chamisso, *Peter Schlemiel: The Man Who Sold His Shadow* About seventy yards from the pump a bridge crossed
the river. This bridge, built and owned by the oil company and made of crude heavy timber,
was wide enough so that trucks could pass over it, but it had no railings. The oil company had

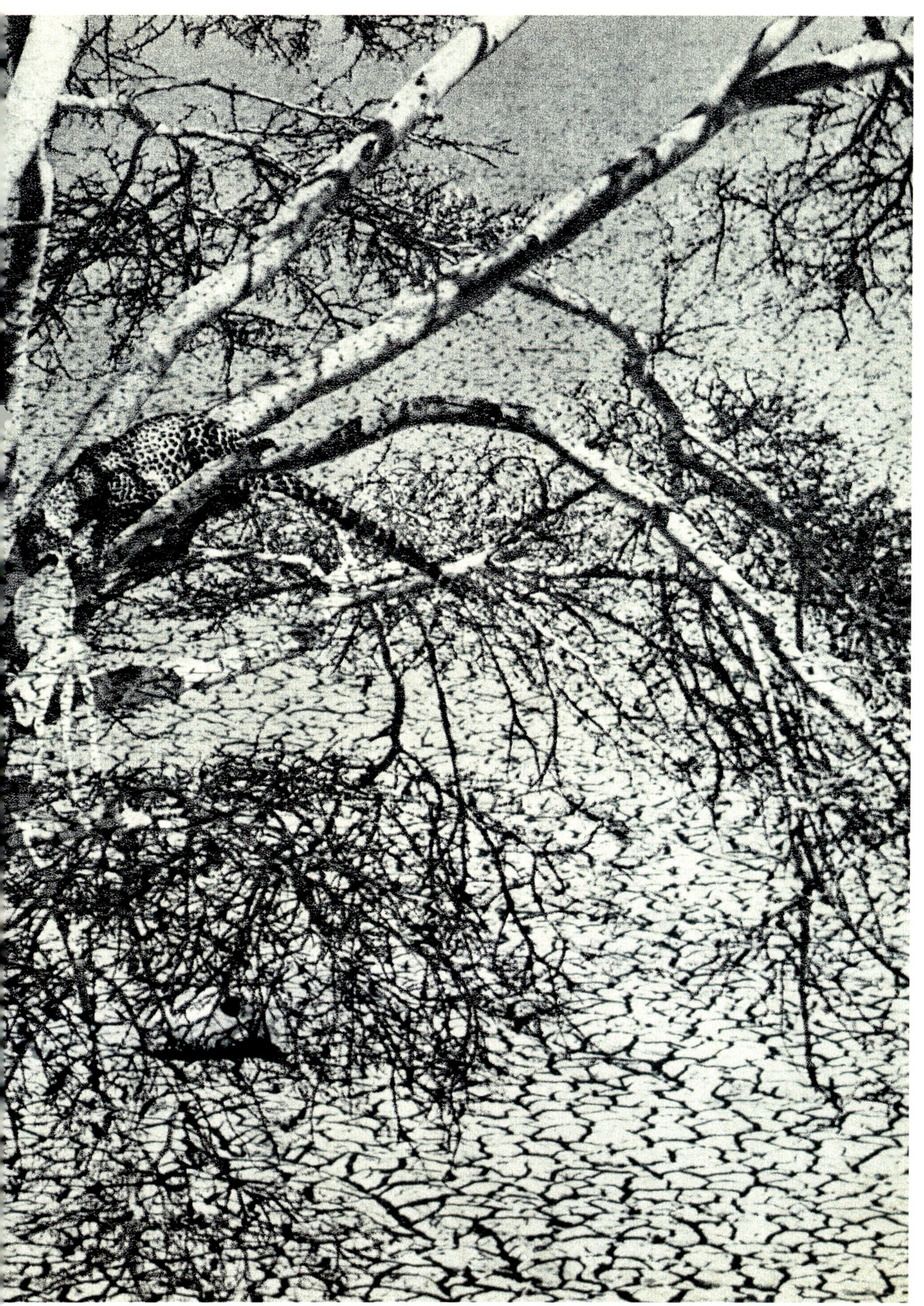

considered railings an unnecessary expense. B. Traven, *The Bridge in the Jungle*   The ceremony takes place outdoors (for the sake of the photographs), with Malkam Ayyahou sheltering under an umbrella held by one of the followers. In front of the door of the *wadadja* hut, the chickens are presented to those who are to receive them. Renewed discussions as to their allocation. Burning of incense for all the followers by Malkam Ayyahou, then *gourri* dance by each and every one. Collective dancing. Mutual embracing. Michel Leiris, *L'Afrique fantôme*   The sailors on shore whiled away the time, smoking opium day and night. Some of them bought quails, and set them fighting for amusement. Indeed, there was not the least anxiety manifested in regard to

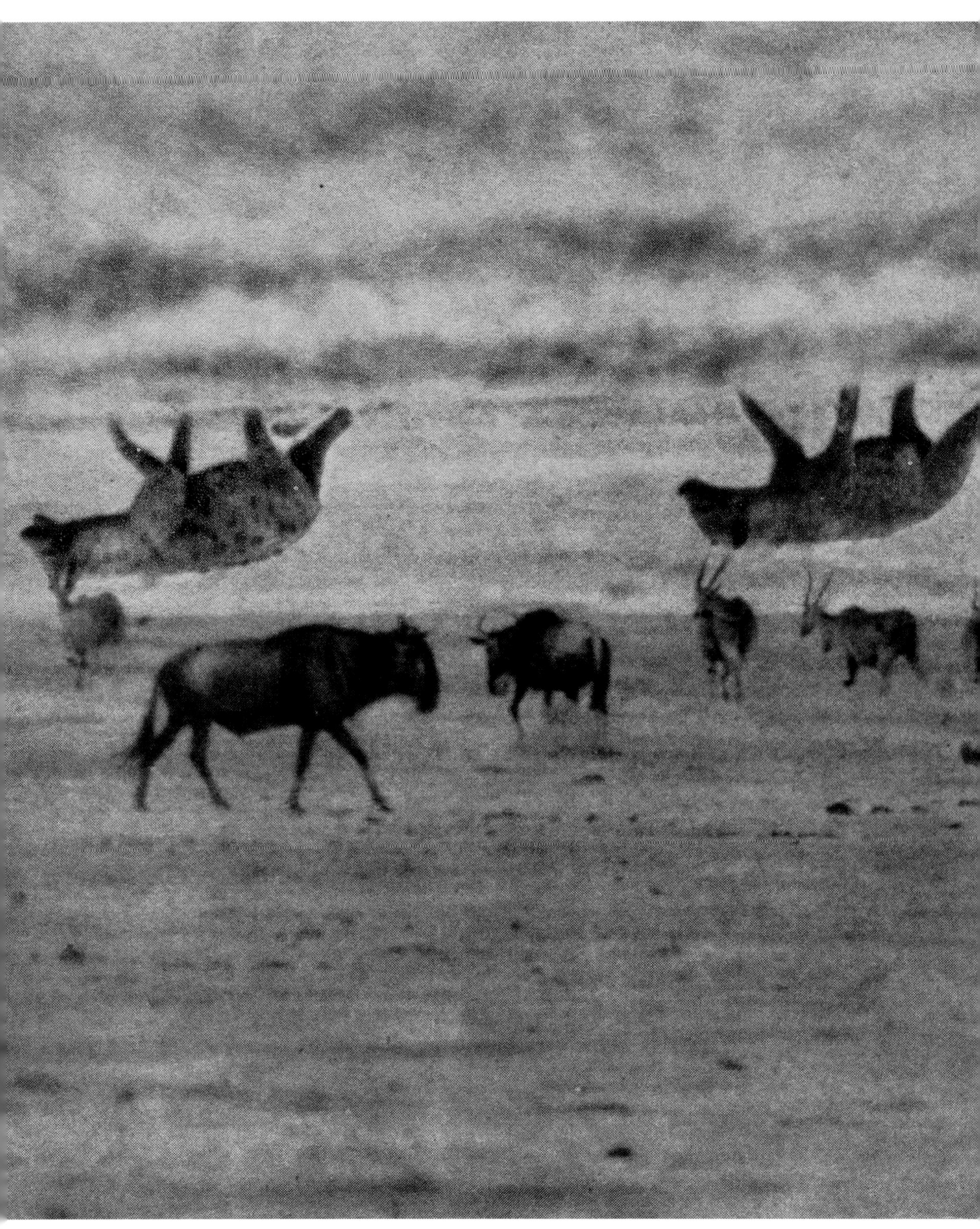

the vessel; and it was owing to the unremitting severity of the cold, that we were, at last, driven away from Kin-chow. Charles Gutzlaff, *Journal of Three Voyages along the Coast of China* There must indeed have been a continuous relationship between the French and the Indians to allow the frigate *La Pèlerine*, in 1531, to take back to France, along with three thousand leopard skins and three hundred monkeys of different species, six hundred parrots which "already knew a few words of French …" Claude Lévi-Strauss, *Tristes Tropiques* In Mexico alone there may have been 25 million people when the Europeans arrived in 1519. Fifty years later, the number had fallen to 2.7 million. Fifty more years later there were 1.5 million Indians left. Over 90 percent of the original population

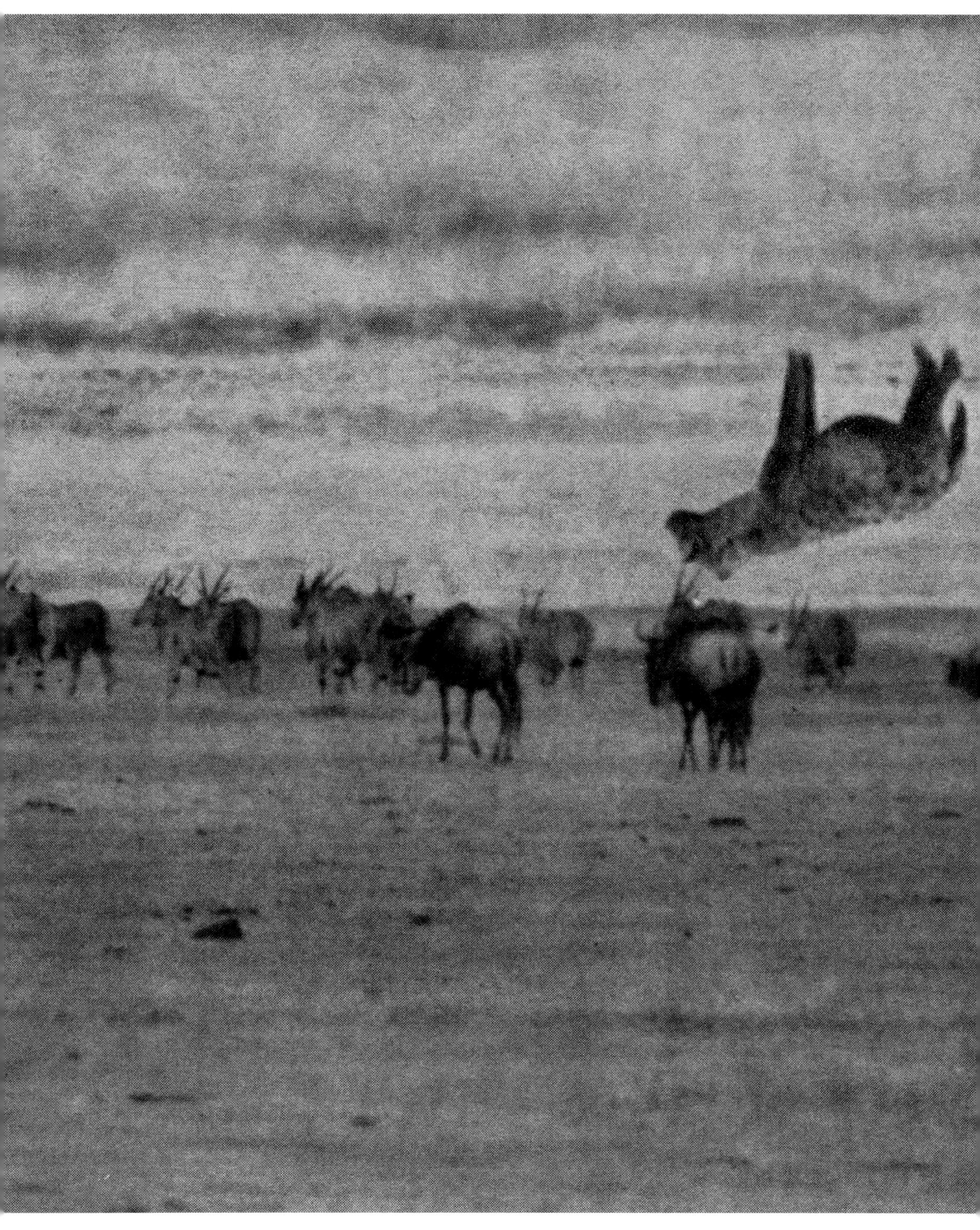

had been wiped out in a hundred years. Sven Lindqvist, *Exterminate All The Brutes*   When the behaviour of the civilised person is compared with that of the wolf, for those who know about animal societies, the insult is to the wolf, not the civilised person. Hubert Fichte, *Petersilie*   In the evening visitors to the Ashanti village knock on the wooden walls of the huts, for fun. Says the goldsmith Nôthëi: "Sir, were you to come to us at Accra as exhibits, we would not knock on your huts in the evening!" Peter Altenberg, *Ashantee*   Flaubert's lifelong relationship with Egypt seems like an invitation to deepen and respect our attraction to certain countries. From his adolescence onwards, Flaubert insisted that he was not French. His hatred of his country and his people was

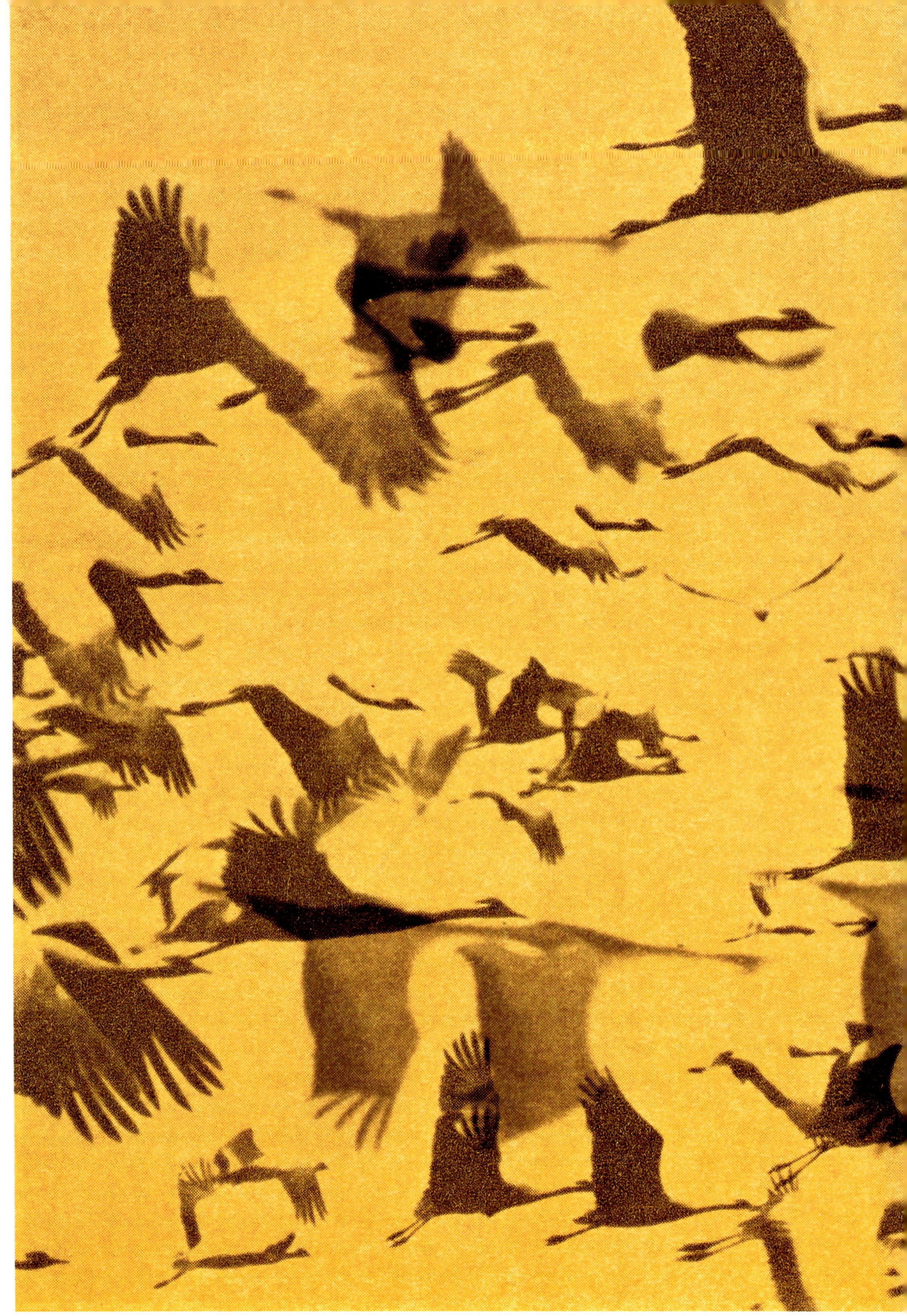

so profound, it made a mockery of his civil status. And hence he proposed a new way of ascribing nationality: not according to the country one was born in or to which one's family belonged, but according to the places to which one was attracted. Alain de Botton, *The Art of Travel* The otherness – within oneself – becomes a privilege, not to say the basic prerequisite for any creative action. This also explains the diversity of symptoms with which 19th century artists and writers discover and celebrate their femininity, i.e. that which is different about one's own self. Flaubert refers to himself as a "fat hysterical girl". Baudelaire, Mallarmé and Proust express similar sentiments about their own femininity. It is a time when one cultivates migraines and

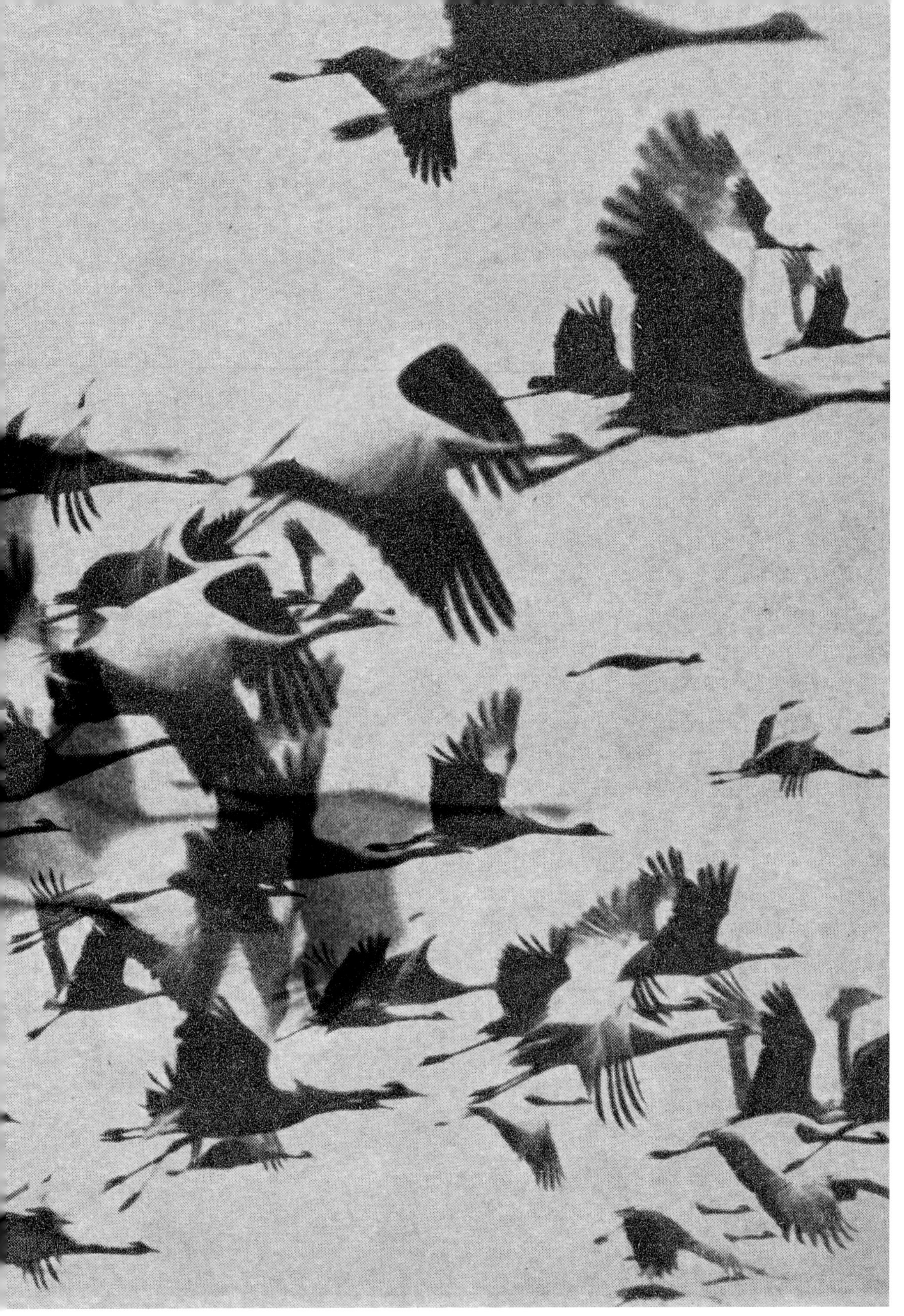

consumptive physical states. Christina von Braun, *Der Einbruch der Wohnstube in die Fremde*   Maxime killed a small green bird this morning, and has just thrown it into the water – it drifted like a flower borne by the waters – causing him wittily to remark: "Are birds not the flowers of the air?" Gustave Flaubert, *Voyage en Égypte*   I drank too much absinthe last night because the sunset was so lovely, and the fever is the result. It is such a pity, because I love absinthe and I love the additional powers of appreciation of colour that it gives. Robert James Fletcher, *Isles of Illusion*   The coconut trees, with their frivolous elegance, grew thickly on the banks, all clad with trailing plants, and they were reflected in the green water. It was just such a scene as you might see in Devonshire among

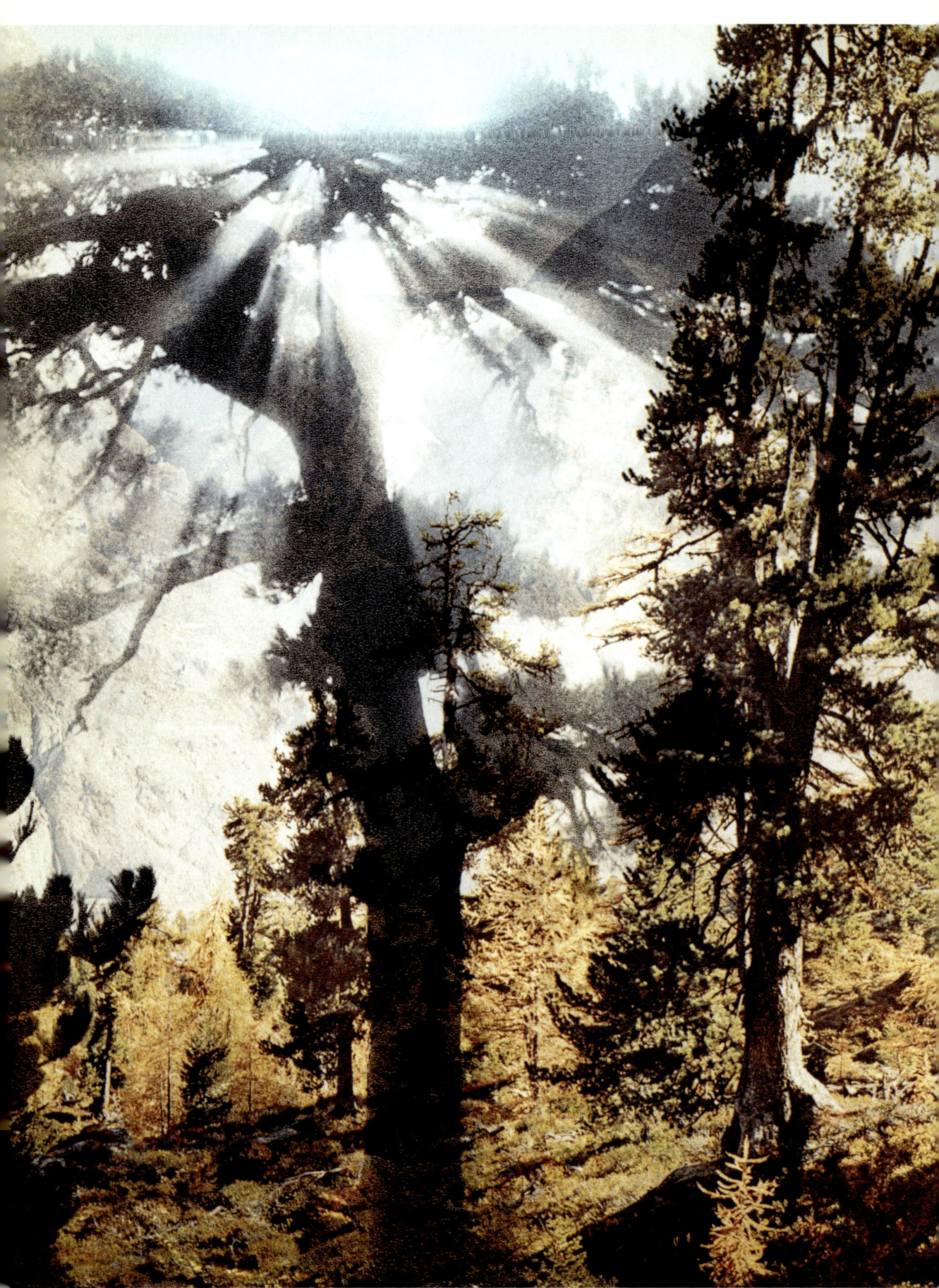

the hills, and yet with a difference, for it had a tropical richness, a passion, a scented languor which seemed to melt the heart. The water was fresh, but not cold; and it was delicious after the heat of the day. To bathe there refreshed not only the body but the soul. W. Somerset Maugham, *The Trembling of a Leaf* "Whatever you want." "Everything I want?" "Everything." "Really everything?" "Everything! Everything!" and her passion was so brilliantly and passionately acted, that the theatrical quality of it, up here, nearly 5,000 feet above sea-level, left him quite bewildered. After this he could not rid himself of the feeling that this life, which was brighter and more highly spiced than any life he had led before, was no longer part of reality, but a

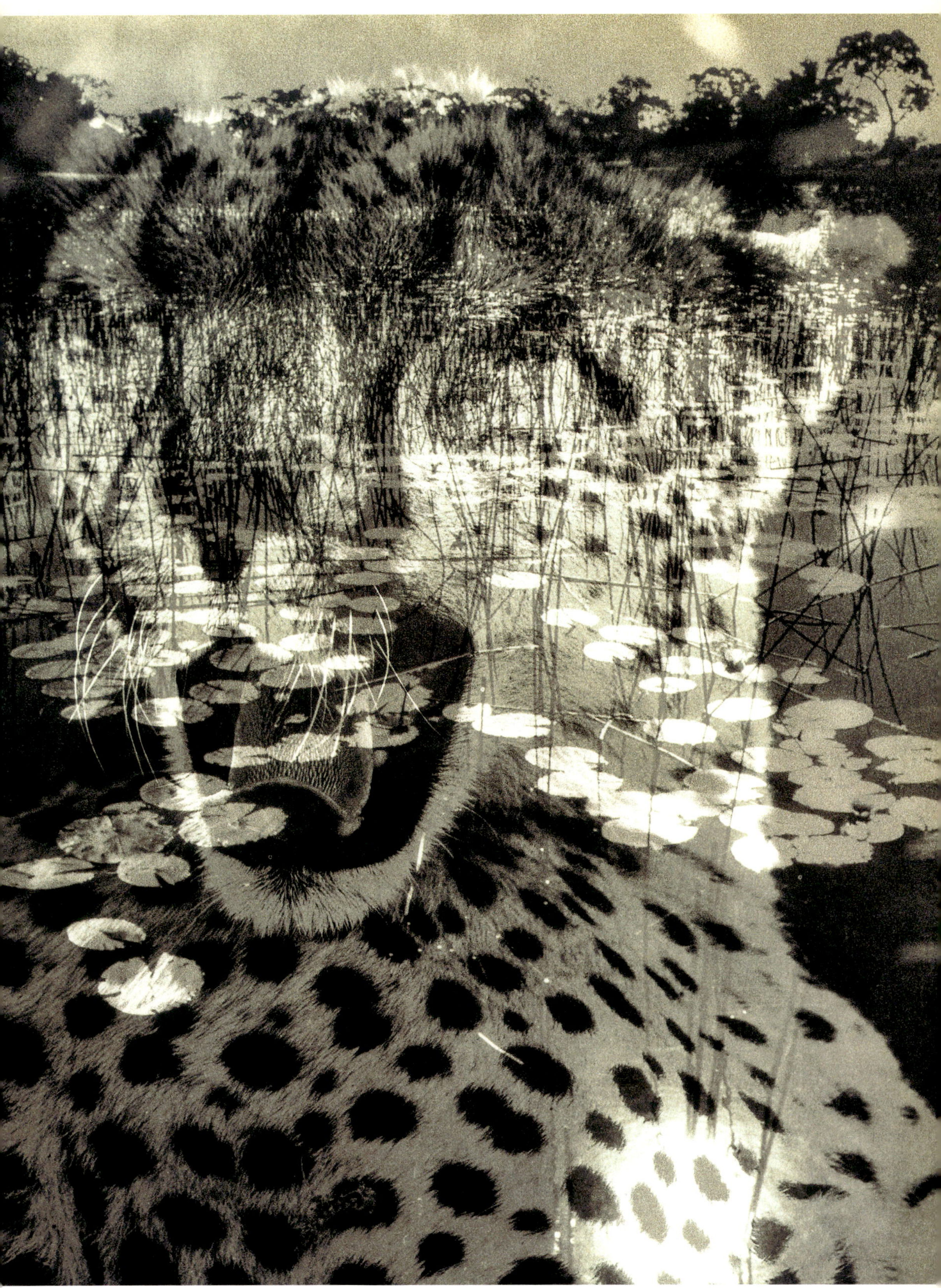

play floating in the air. Slim began by claiming that the savages' existence had one more source of happiness: desire. They were experienced in it; they had more culture in it than in the world's most cultivated centre, Paris. I do not mean to insist here on the disadvantage of hiring compared with owning, but it is evident that the savage owns his shelter because it costs so little, while the civilized man hires his commonly because he cannot afford to own it; nor can he, in the long run, any better afford to hire. You can be certain that a traveller who comes back with a rich harvest of information and ethnographic studies (*études des moeurs*) owes these for the most part to the women

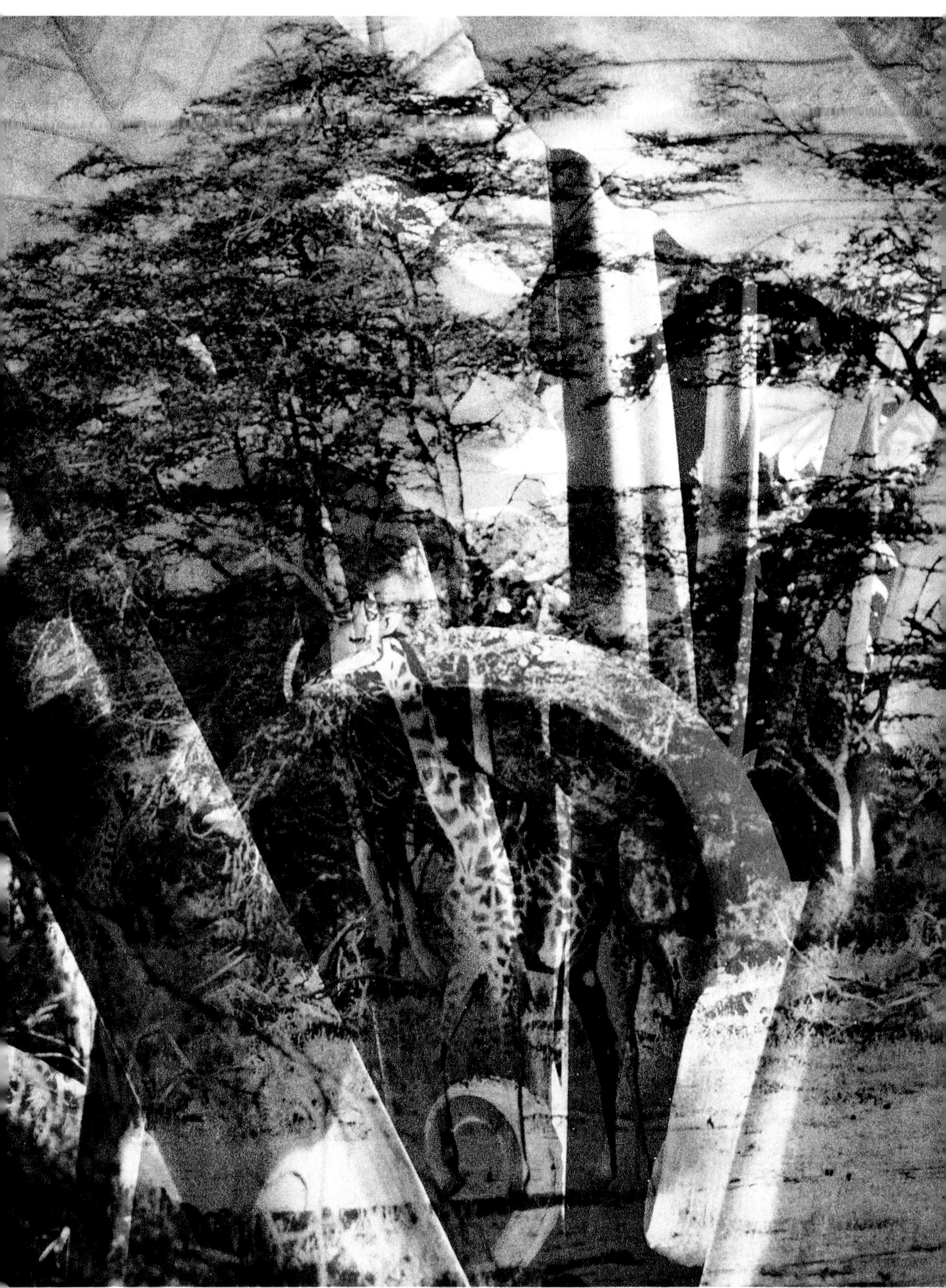

in his escort. Jérôme Becker, in: Johannes Fabian, *Out of Our Minds*   Abba Jérôme is a precious informer albeit a somewhat fanciful one. If he is not kept on a tight rein, he is wont to wander off into the landscape. And so I took the decision not to let him out of my sight and to follow him on his constitutionals to be sure to bring him back to the fold. Michel Leiris, *L'Afrique fantôme*   The painter ventures among the savages, they threaten him with bamboo daggers and cleavers, but he continues to draw "as if nothing had happened". What is also significant is how Nolde made clear to his models what it was that he wanted from them: He would show them a picture of the emperor and say: "This big fellow emperor wants to see what you look like and that is

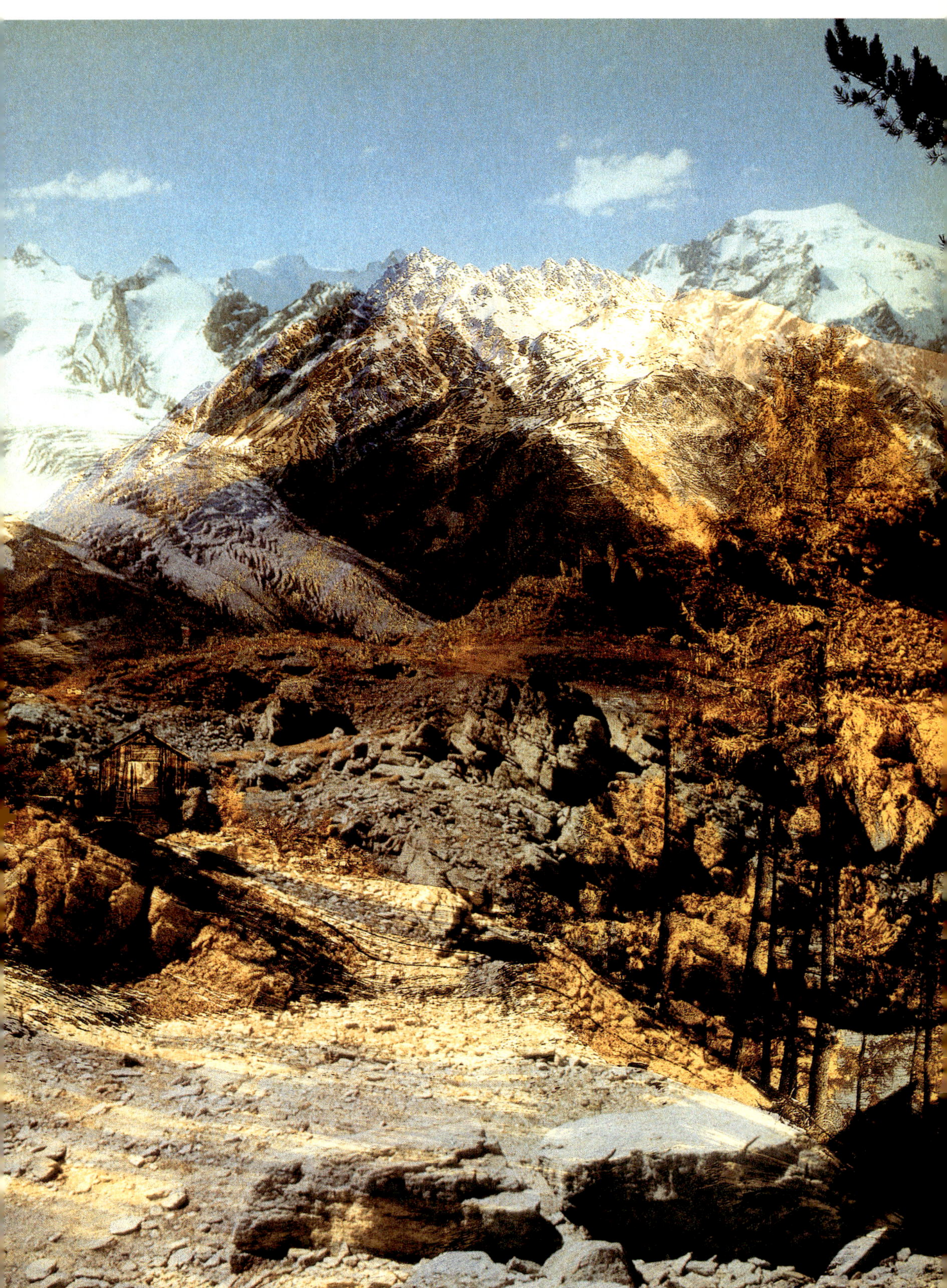

why you are being painted." Strickland made no particular impression on the people who came in contact with him on Tahiti. To them he was no more than a beach-comber in constant need of money, remarkable only for the peculiarity that he painted pictures which seemed to them absurd; and it was not till he had been dead for some years and agents came from the dealers in Paris and Berlin to look for any pictures which might still remain on the island, that they had an idea that among them had dwelt a man of consequence. W. Somerset Maugham, *The Moon and Sixpence* "Land in a swamp, march through the woods, and in some inland post feel the savagery, the utter savagery, had closed round him, – all that mysterious

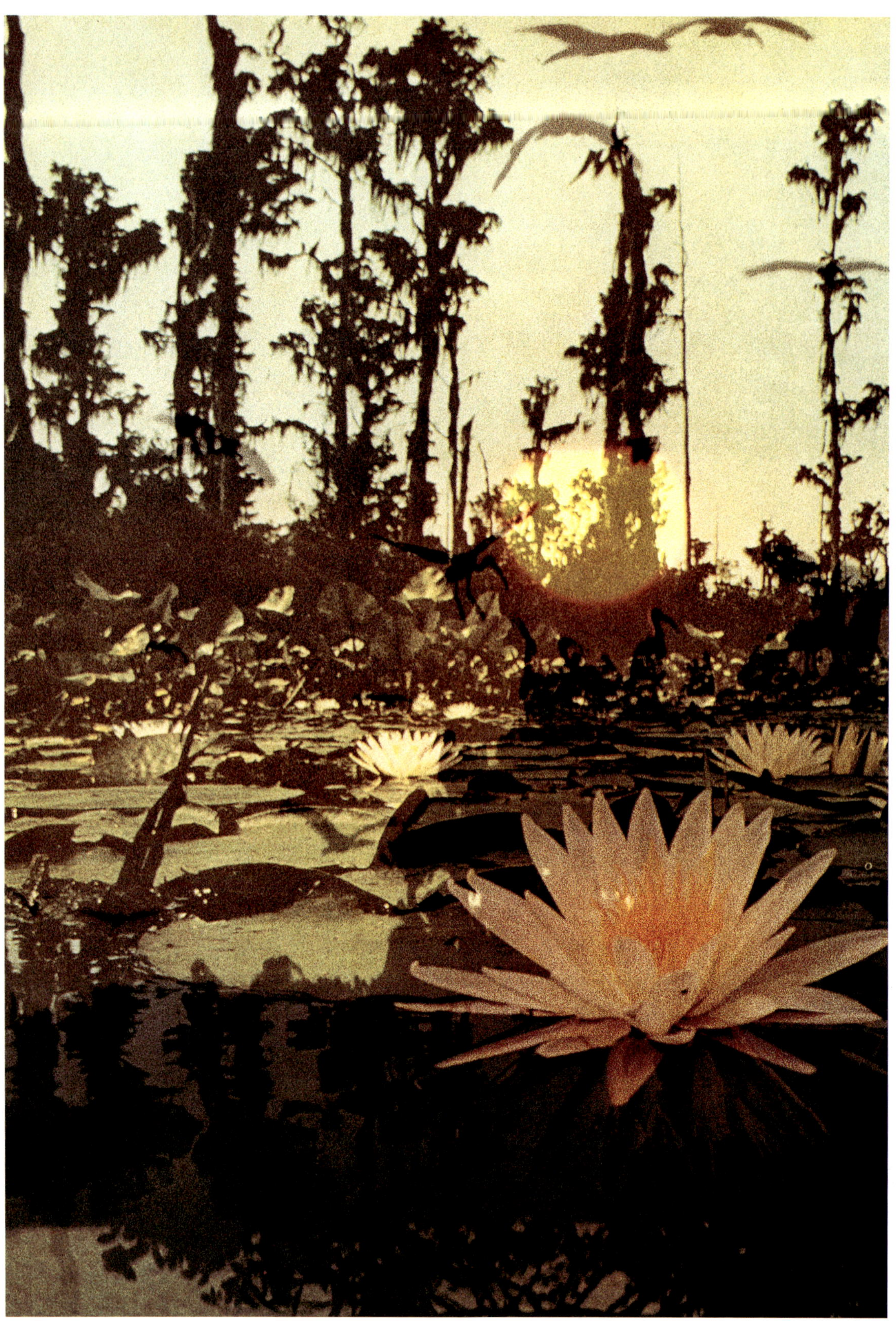

life of the wilderness that stirs in the forest, in the jungles, in the hearts of wild men. There's no initiation either into such mysteries. He has to live in the midst of the incomprehensible, which is also detestable. And it has a fascination, too, that goes to work upon him. The fascination of the abomination – you know, imagine the growing regrets, the longing to escape, the powerless disgust, the surrender, the hate." Joseph Conrad, *Heart of Darkness* Everywhere there were bones. In the distance women came out of the woods with bundles of grass and firewood on their heads. It was a glimpse of normality. Famine or no famine, in Africa it is women who do the work. John Ryle, *The Road to Abyei* Just press onwards, he tells himself, regardless

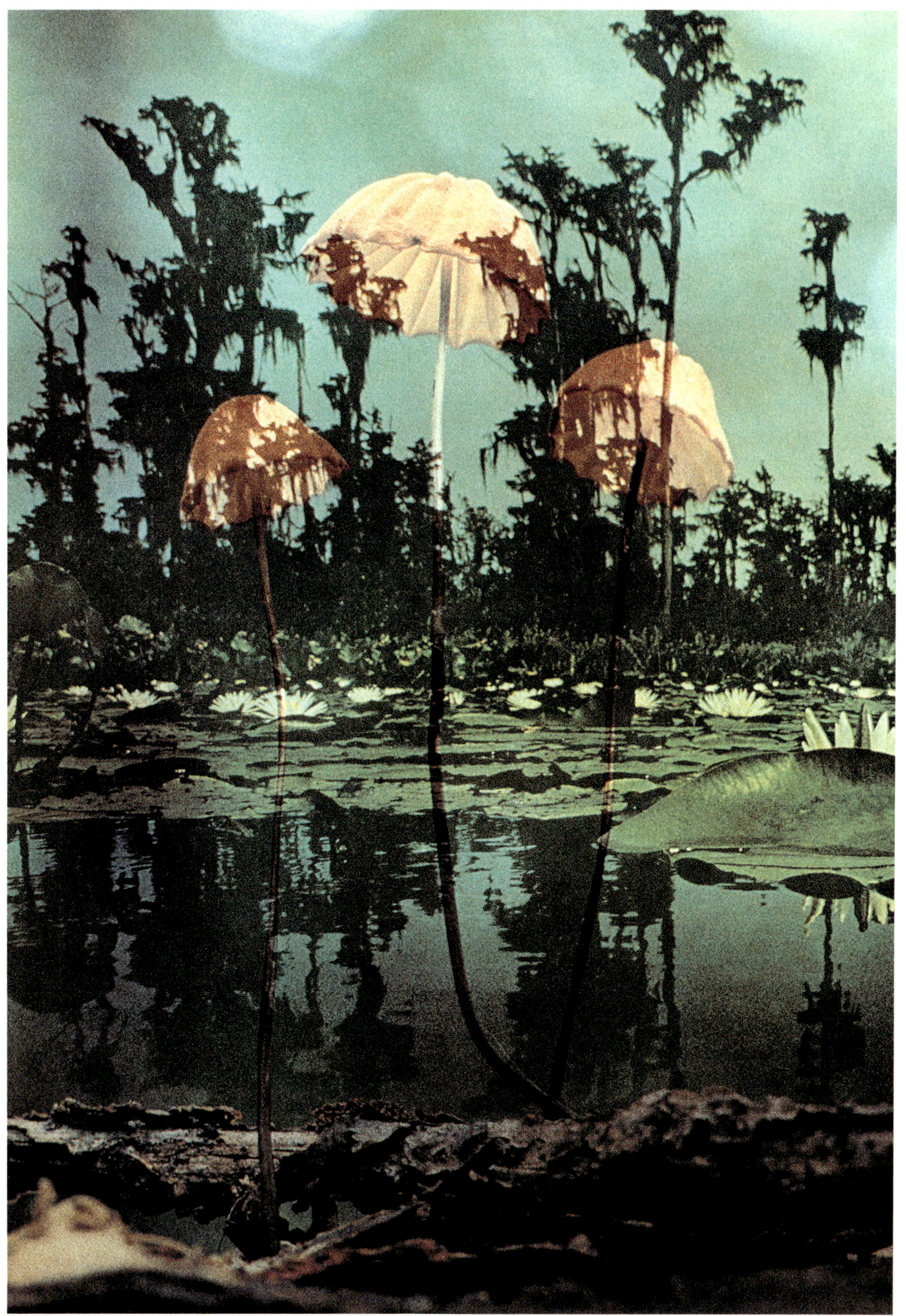

of the uncertainty as to whether there is an "onwards" to press on to. A compass would be good now, one that showed illusion and reality. One ought to be able to agree on a reality in extremis, and any reality would do. Up ahead in this hollow lined with ground fog he sees a brightly lit tavern steaming in the mist, caterwauling with awful music. There's no other hamlet in this meadowed valley, with forests to the left and forests to the right. Hermann Burger, *Schilten* It was unearthly, and the men were – No, they were not inhuman. Well, you know, that was the worst of it – this suspicion of their not being inhuman. It would come slowly to one. Joseph Conrad, *Heart of Darkness* "These uniforms are too heavy for the tropics, surely," said the

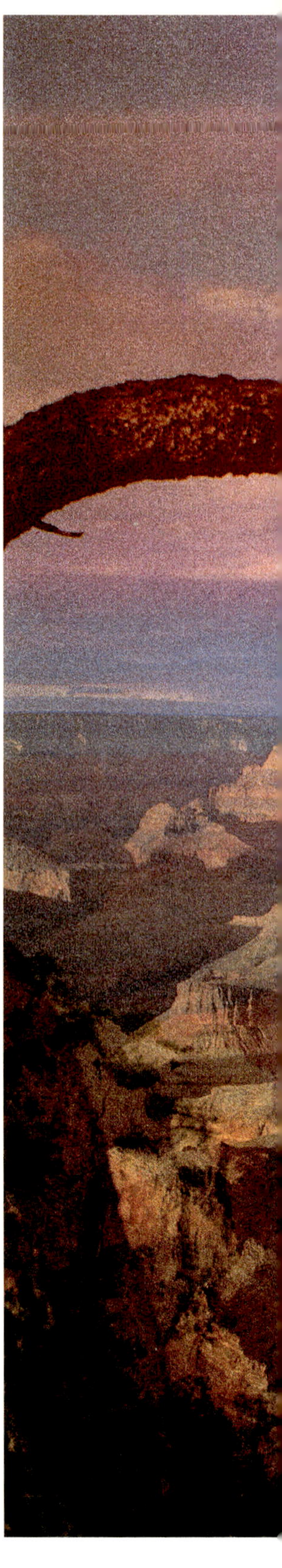

explorer, instead of making some inquiry about the apparatus, as the officer had expected. "Of course," said the officer, washing his oily and greasy hands in a bucket of water that stood ready, "but they mean home to us; we don't want to forget about home. Now just have a look at this machine," he added at once, simultaneously drying his hands on a towel and indicating the apparatus. Franz Kafka, *The Penal Colony* God and gunboats, liquor and holy water. For several centuries the Christian West has been the centre, the rest of the planet a suburb of Europe. Nicolas Bouvier, *The Scorpion-Fish* The character of the nation has appeared mild and beneficent to us. Though the isle is divided into many little districts, each of which has its own master, yet

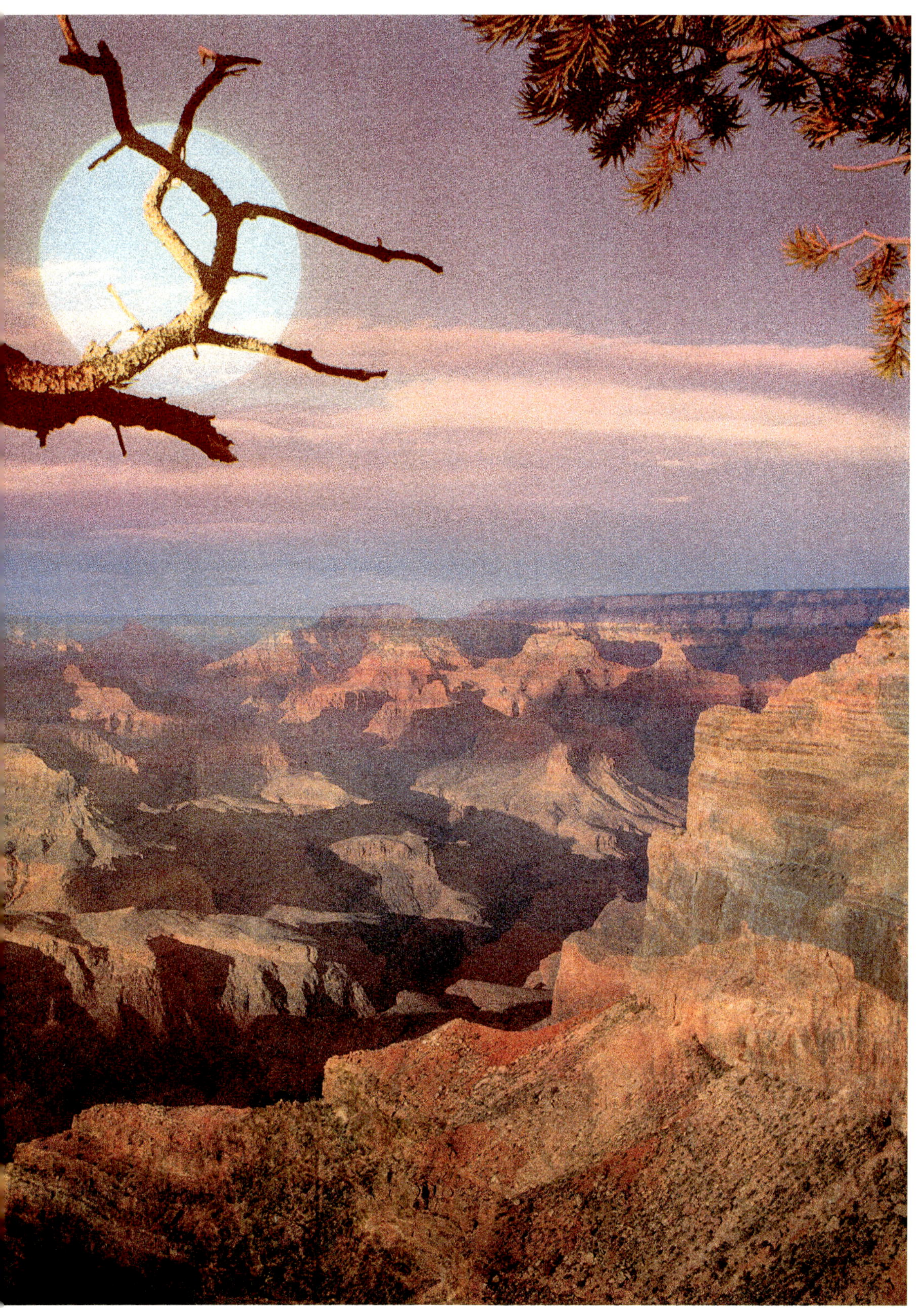

there does not seem to be any civil war, or any private hatred in the isle. It is probable, that the people of Taiti deal amongst each other with unquestioned sincerity. Whether they be at home or no, by day or by night, their houses are always open. Every one gathers fruits from the first tree he meets with, or takes some in any house into which he enters. It should seem as if, in regard to things absolutely necessary for the maintainance of life, there was no personal property amongst them, and that they all had an equal right to those articles. *Lewis de Bougainville, A Voyage Round the World* In order to grasp the absolute, total and intransigent nature of the dilemmas by which the men of the sixteenth century felt themselves to be faced, one

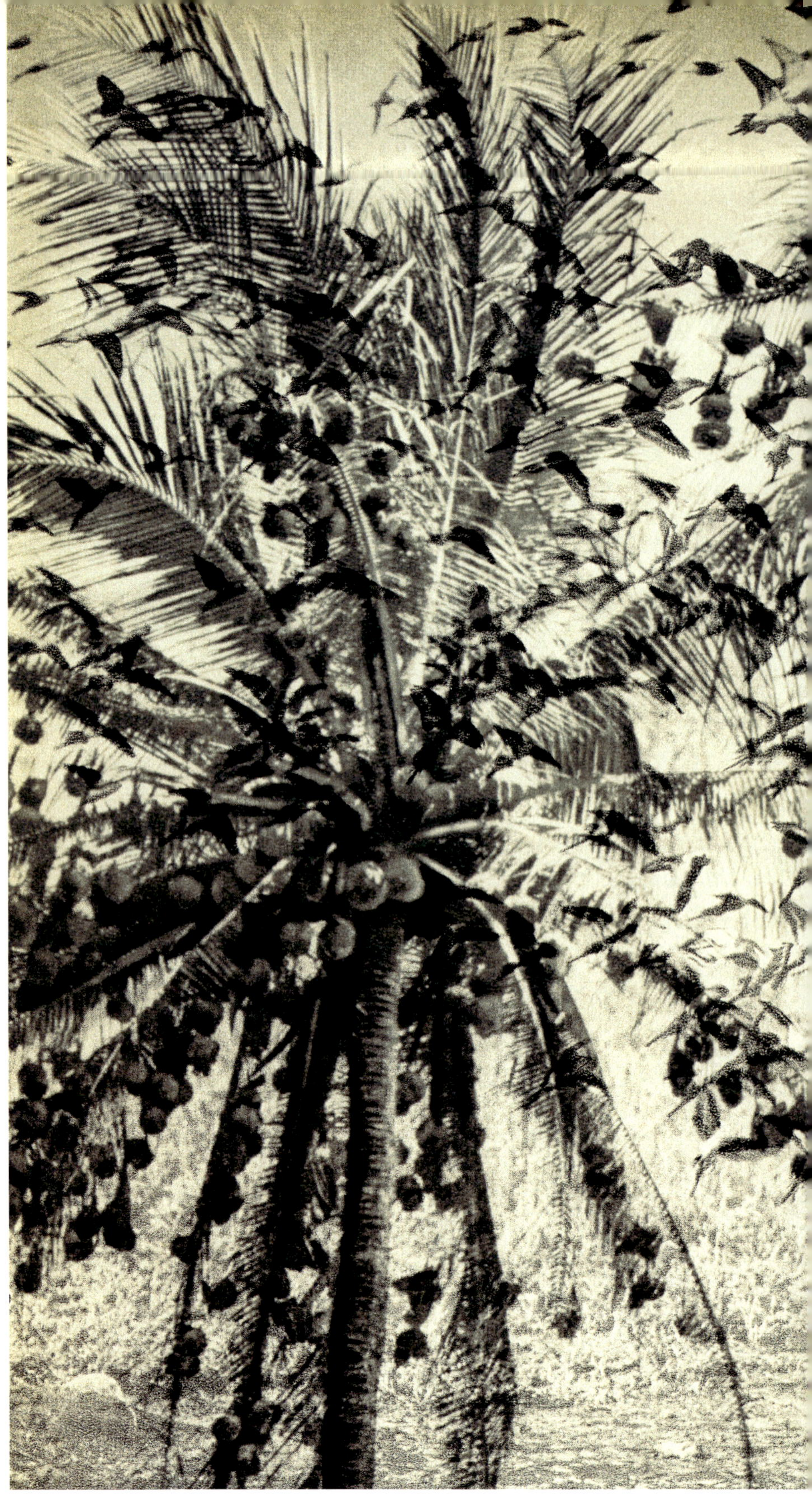

must remember certain incidents. In what used to be called Hispaniola (today Haiti and Santo Domingo) the native population numbered about one hundred thousand in 1492, but had dropped to two hundred a century later, since people died of horror and disgust at European civilization even more than of smallpox and physical ill-treatment. Commission after commission was sent out to determine the nature of the inhabitants. Claude Lévi-Strauss, *Tristes Tropiques*   There are those who say that the savage, like a child, has to be kept under strict control, yet the comparison is incorrect. There is something childlike about the Indians on the Orinoco, the way in which they express their joy, and their rapid change of moods. And yet they are by no

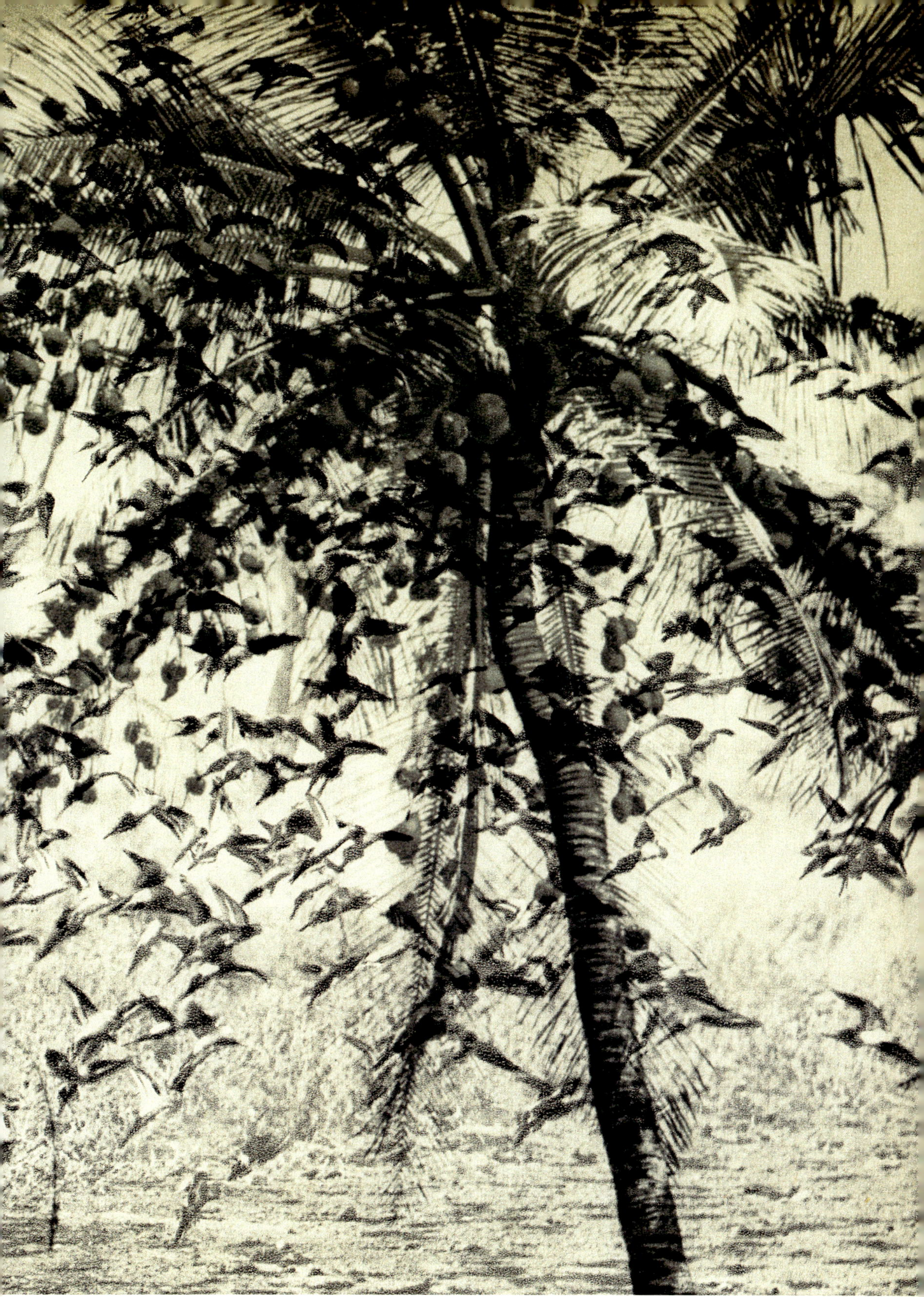

means children, no more than the peasants of eastern Europe who in the barbarity of the feudal system cannot break away from their deepest debasement. Alexander von Humboldt, *Auf Steppen und Strömen Südamerikas* Yet to give the impression of protecting Negroes of Dominican nationality, Trujillo gave orders to herd the Blacks together, the men, women, children, voodoo priests and minstrels now awaiting their beheading as they were forced to say the word "parsley" – *perejil*. If they pronounced it *pelejil*, they were hacked to pieces with machetes as Haitians. They all said *pelejil*, the way they had been taught to say it as children or immigrants. Trujillo later paid the Haitian government a compensation fee of 40 dollars per head. Hubert Fichte, *Petersilie*

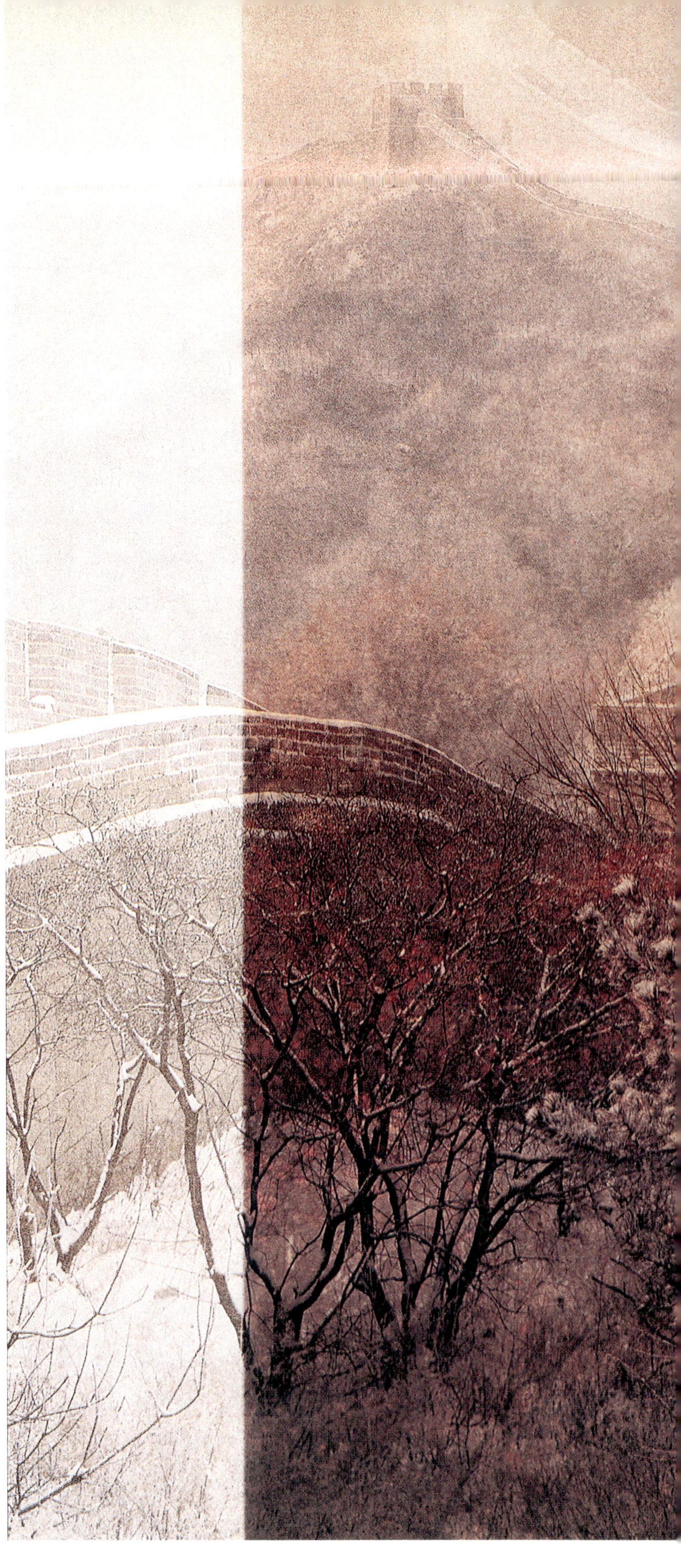

So it was that the tune played (as befitted the sailor suit) was *Taintgonnarainnomo*, which was the latest around here. It was a long time since I had heard that tune. And since the time that tune was the rage back home, we Americans, tough guys that we are, have happily survived weddings of painted dolls, sonnyboys, and mammies crooned by poor devils suffering from St. Vitus's dance; we had also had to swallow the strange news that only God can make a tree, a fact which none of us ever knew until we were told so by night-club entertainers. Then there was the coming (two hundred times every day and night) of the moon over the mountains with my mem'ries of you. Then we took our sugar to tea, asked for just one more chance, and

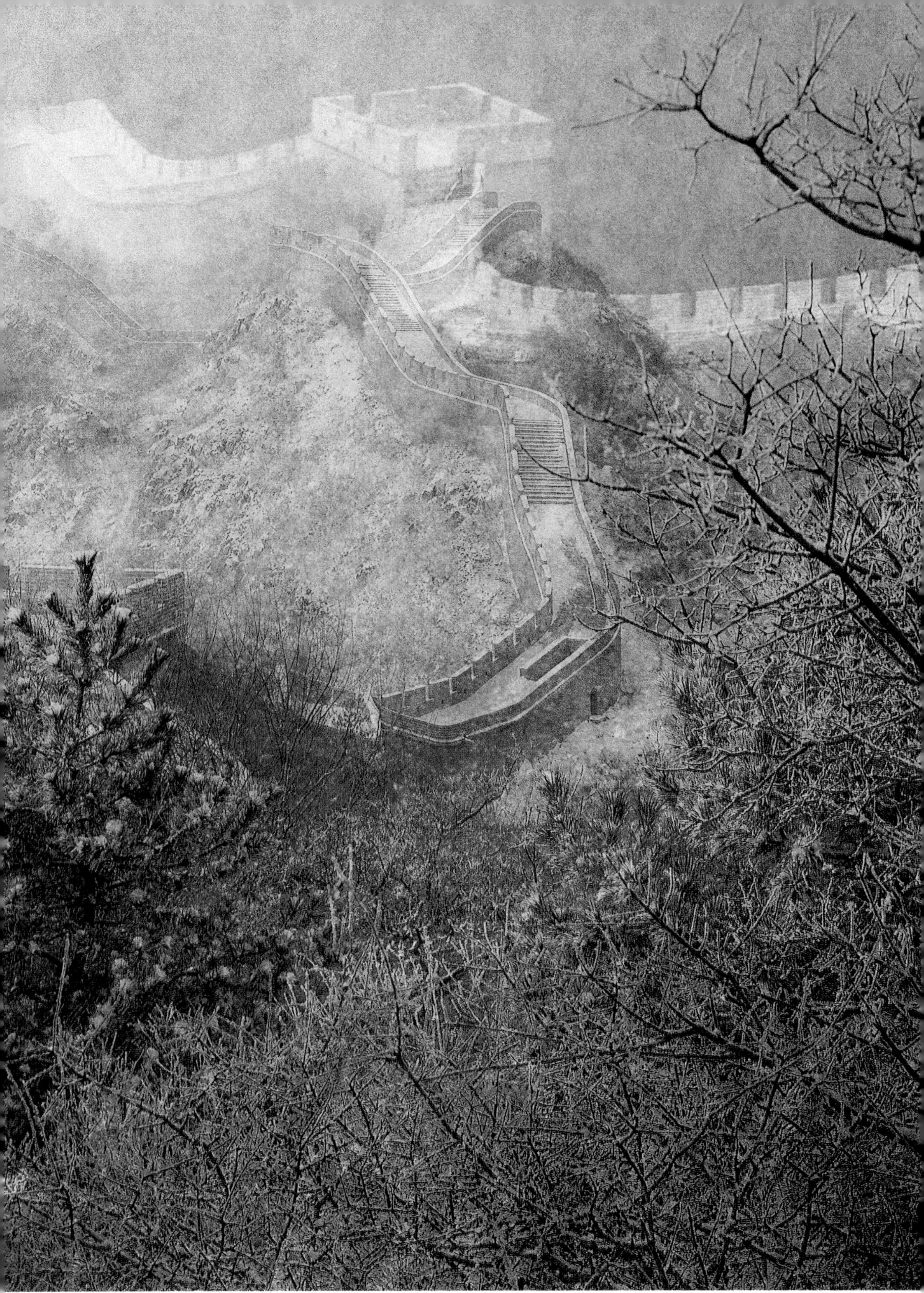

incorporated the little innocent cucaracha, which used to be sung by Mexican revolutionists under the fire of machine-guns, but was sung by us under the fire of booze. B. Traven, *The Bridge in the Jungle*   This much I can say: I am toying with a most laudable proposition; my task: to record the gradual effect of tropical conditions on the northerner's nervous system; or to put it as a question: what is the distinguished way of going mad? Robert Müller, *Tropen*   Cecil Jones performs *Red Roses for a Blue Lady* for himself, or his audience of one, or his wife and her three poodles, and outside, beyond the windows, in a late summer's night in Africa, the snow fell ever thicker, onto the bougainvillea blossoms, swirling down from the tops of the yellowwood trees, onto

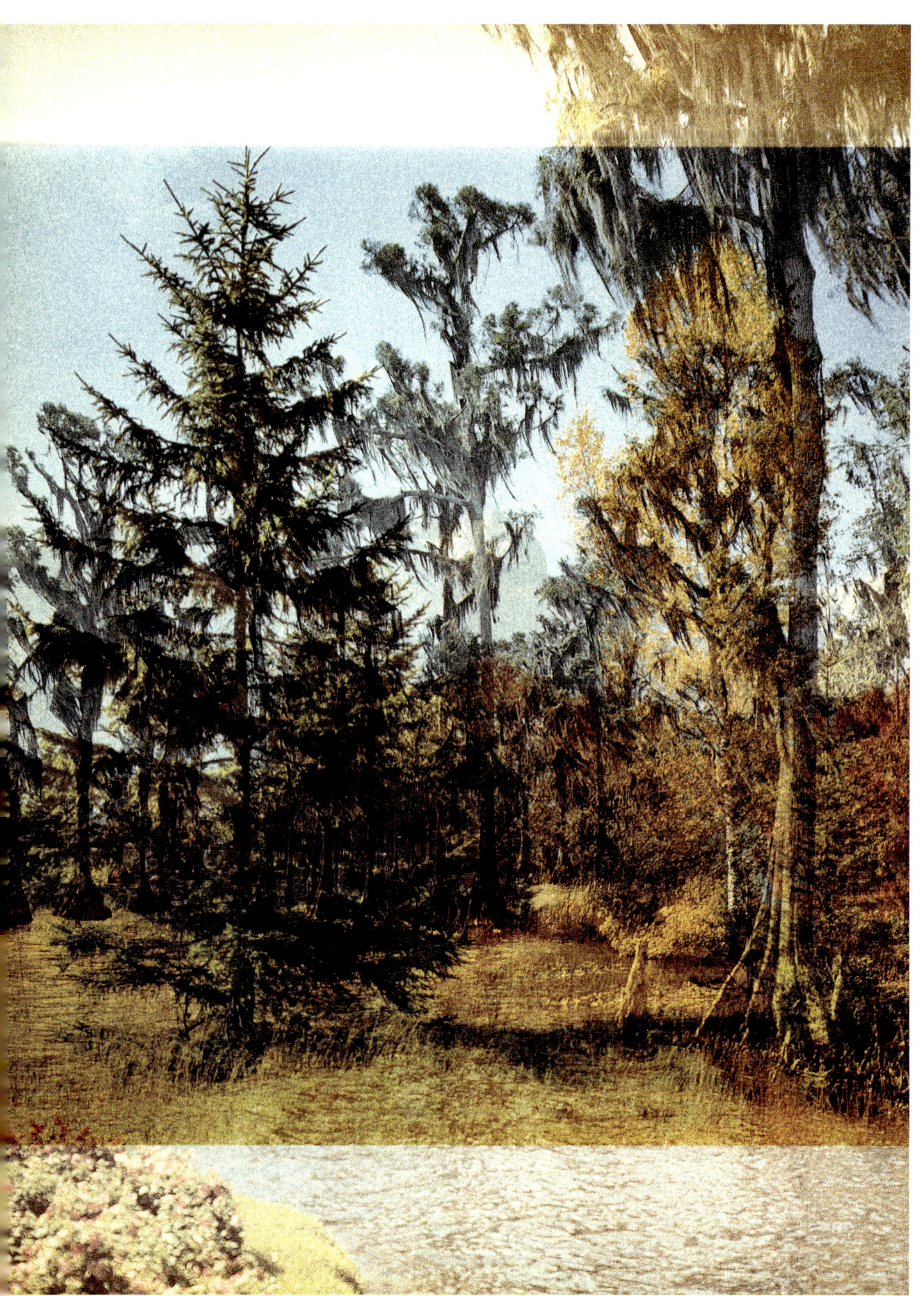

the grass roofs out in the darkness, onto the backs of the elephants huddled together sleepily deep down in the Addo valley, covering the mountain zebras standing anxiously still so as not to disturb this camouflage that made them as white as the rest of the wilderness. Africa was disappearing beneath the snow, and I was back where I had come from, somewhere between the coastline of the Indian Ocean and the night-time highlands of southern Africa; I was home again on the head of the Zuurberg pass. Christoph Ransmayr, *Der Weg nach Surabaya*   Ere long, the Bongo as a people will be quite forgotten, superseded by a rising race. Georg Schweinfurth, *The Heart of Africa* All expeditions to central Africa had among their supplies varying quantities and qualities of

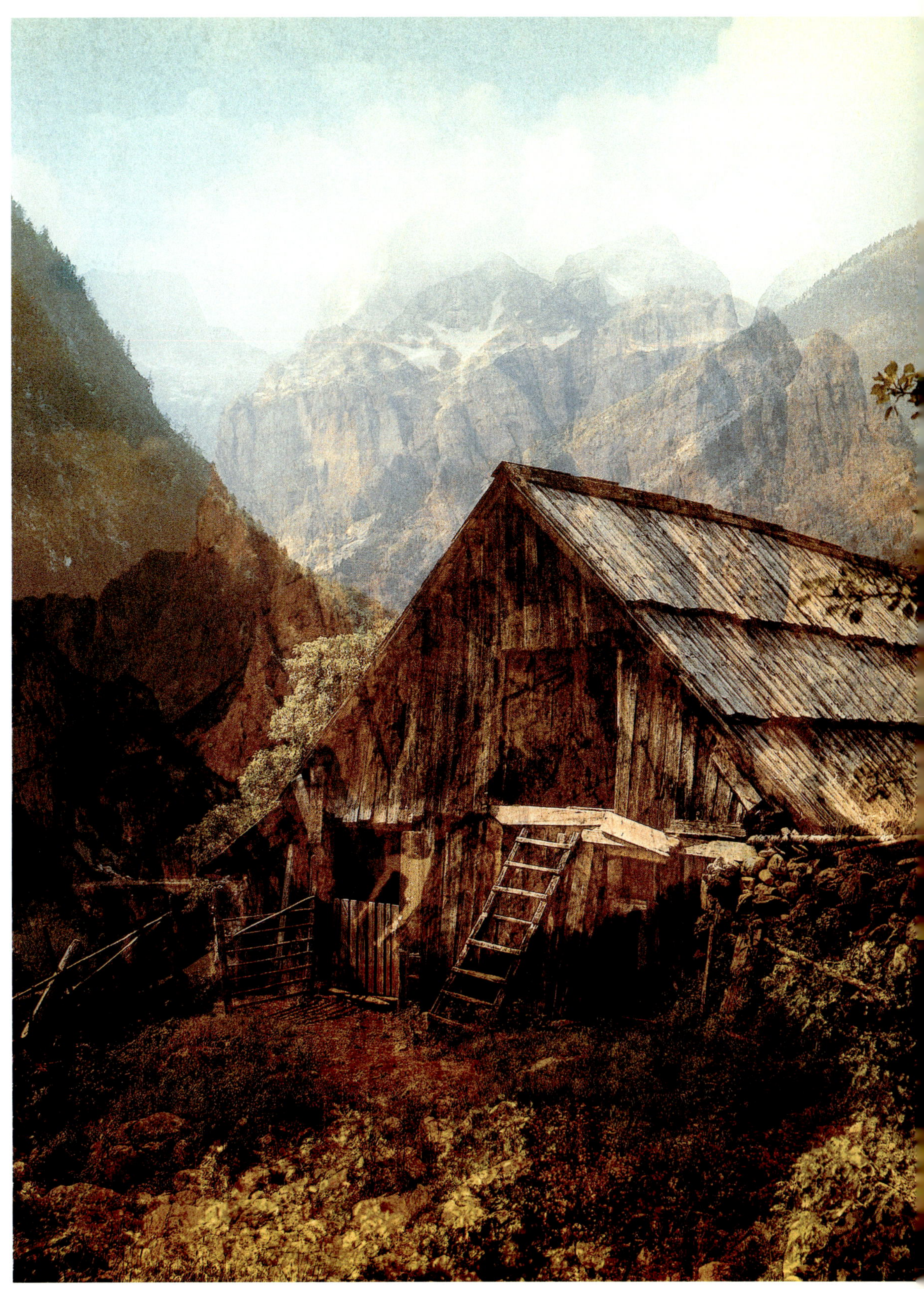

alcohol. Its uses for medication or celebration or gift exchange were sometimes hard to tell apart. Travelers appreciated cognac and rum, Bordeaux and champagne for their alleged or real medicinal properties, as relief in situations of physical or mental stress, as obligatory ingredients of festive meals, and, of course, as sources of pleasure and as rewards they accorded themselves when they had overcome hardship. Johannes Fabian, *Out of Our Minds* He was an Irishman, bankrupt, fifty-two years of age. He knew nothing of Africa whatever, but he came cheap. I'll do it for three hunnert pund, he said. And a case o' Scots whisky. Houghton sallied up the Gambia in a dugout canoe, drank from fetid puddles and ate monkey meat, and

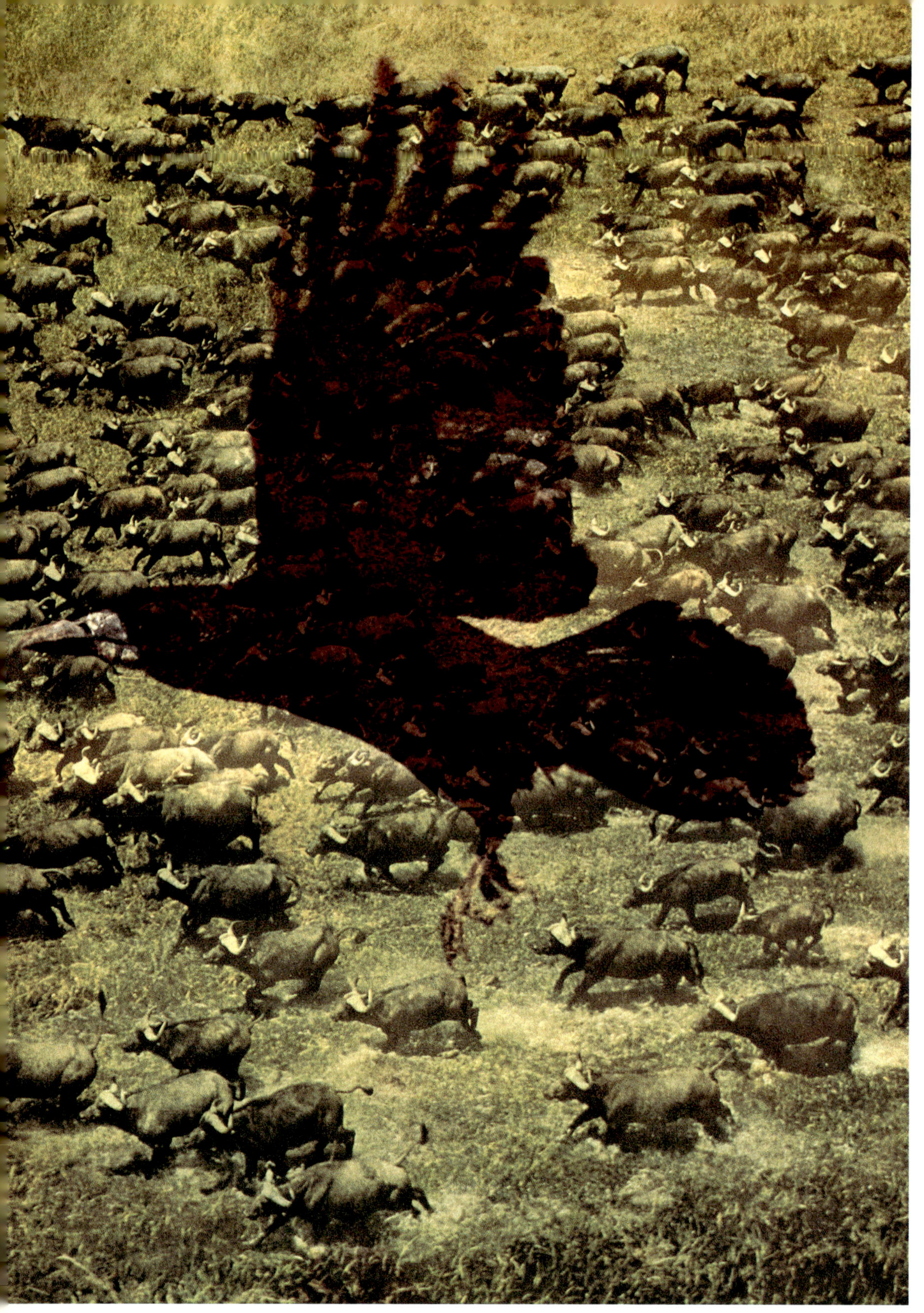

through sheer grit and force of intoxication survived typhus, malaria, loiasis, leprosy and yellow fever. Unfortunately, the Moors of Ludamar stripped him naked and staked him out on the crest of a dune. Where he died. T. Coraghessan Boyle, *Water Music*   The "gunboat" became a symbol of imperialism on all the major African rivers – the Nile, the Niger, and the Congo – making it possible for Europeans to control huge, hitherto inaccessible areas by force of arms. Sven Lindqvist, *Exterminate All The Brutes*   The only Martian military success was the capture of a meat market in Basel, Switzerland, by seventeen Parachute Ski Marines. Everywhere else the Martians were butchered promptly, before they could even dig in. As much butchering was done by amateurs as by

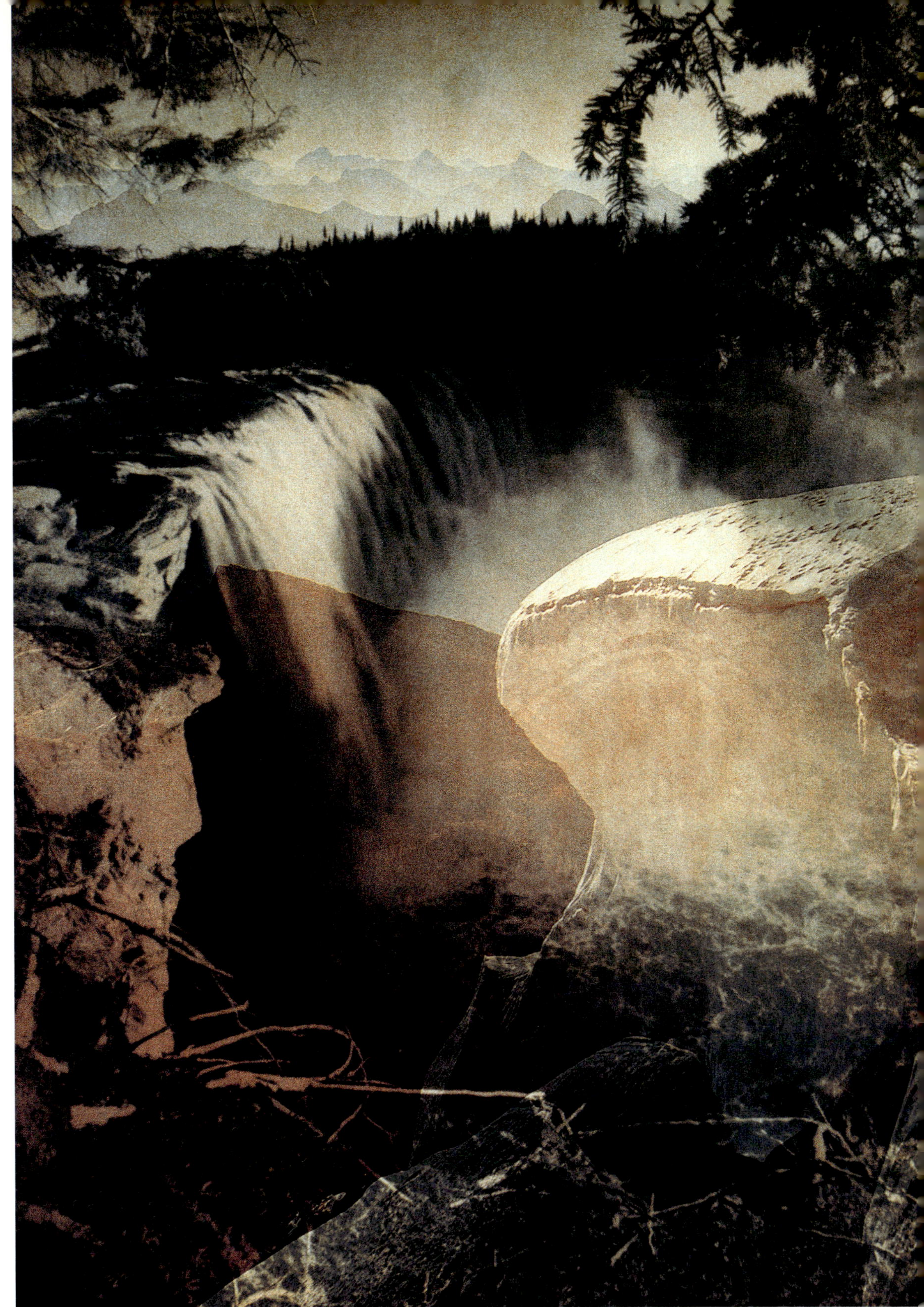

professionals. Kurt Vonnegut, *The Sirens of the Titan* Only a few individuals (in fact those who considered themselves the wisest and most enlightened) believed it was not politically shrewd to punish a white man at a time when the Blacks on S. Domingo were on the point of open revolt. When institutions that have become hated are suddenly under threat, there is never a shortage of people who, to preserve those institutions, advise that they should be upheld, no matter how blatantly they contradict the notions of justice and reason. Alexander von Humboldt, *Auf Steppen und Strömen Südamerikas* The book on torture in Algeria was called *La Question*. It is a question looked down upon in any civilisation. Civilisation and its discontents brings forth confessions, show trials,

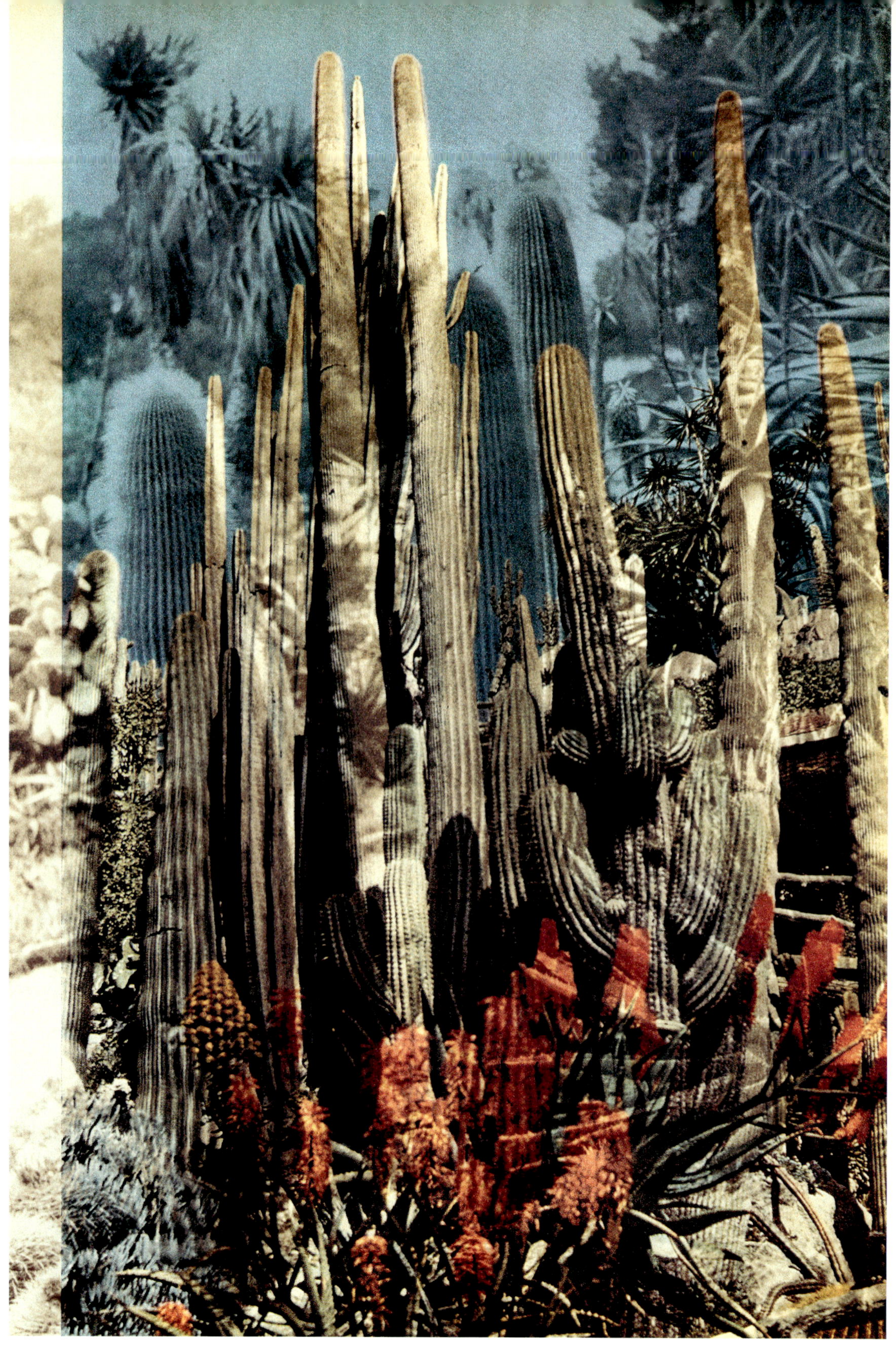

psychoanalysis, interviews and ethnological research. Hubert Fichte, *Das Haus der Mina in São Luiz de Maranhão*
You already know that. So do I. It is not knowledge we lack. What is missing is the courage to
understand what we know and draw conclusions. Sven Lindqvist, *Exterminate All The Brutes*   In its inaugural
year the Association commissioned an exhibition headed by John Ledyard. He was to begin
in Egypt, traverse the Sahara, and discover the course of the Niger. Ledyard was an American.
He played the violin and suffered from strabismus. He'd been across the pacific with Cook,
into the Andes, through Siberia to Yakutsk on foot. I've tramped the world under my feet, he
said, laughed at fear, derided danger. Through hordes of savages, over parching deserts, the

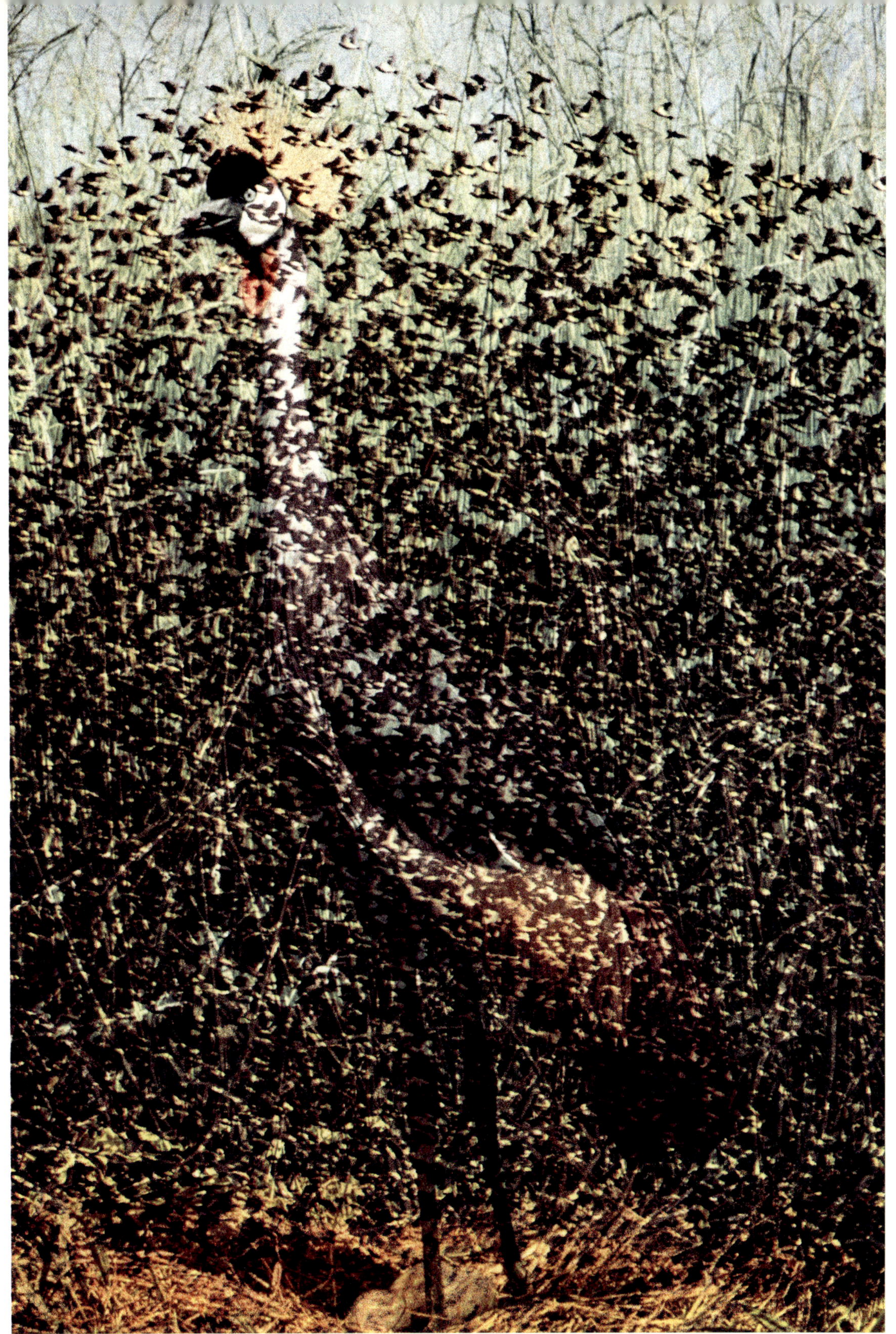

freezing north, the everlasting ice and stormy seas have I passed without harm. How good is my God! Two weeks after landing at Cairo he died of dysentery. T. Coraghessan Boyle, *Water Music*   The conquest of the earth, which mostly means the taking it away from those who have a different complexion or slightly flatter noses than ourselves, is not a pretty thing when you look into it too much. Joseph Conrad, *Heart of Darkness*   At the same time I was surprised by a strange sensation. In the change from chill to heat I suddenly felt a strange illusion of my senses. I definitely felt that my body was growing, the head enlarged more and more till it reached nearly to the ceiling, the hands became enormous, the fingers became as thick and as big as my arms. Nikolai Mikloucho-

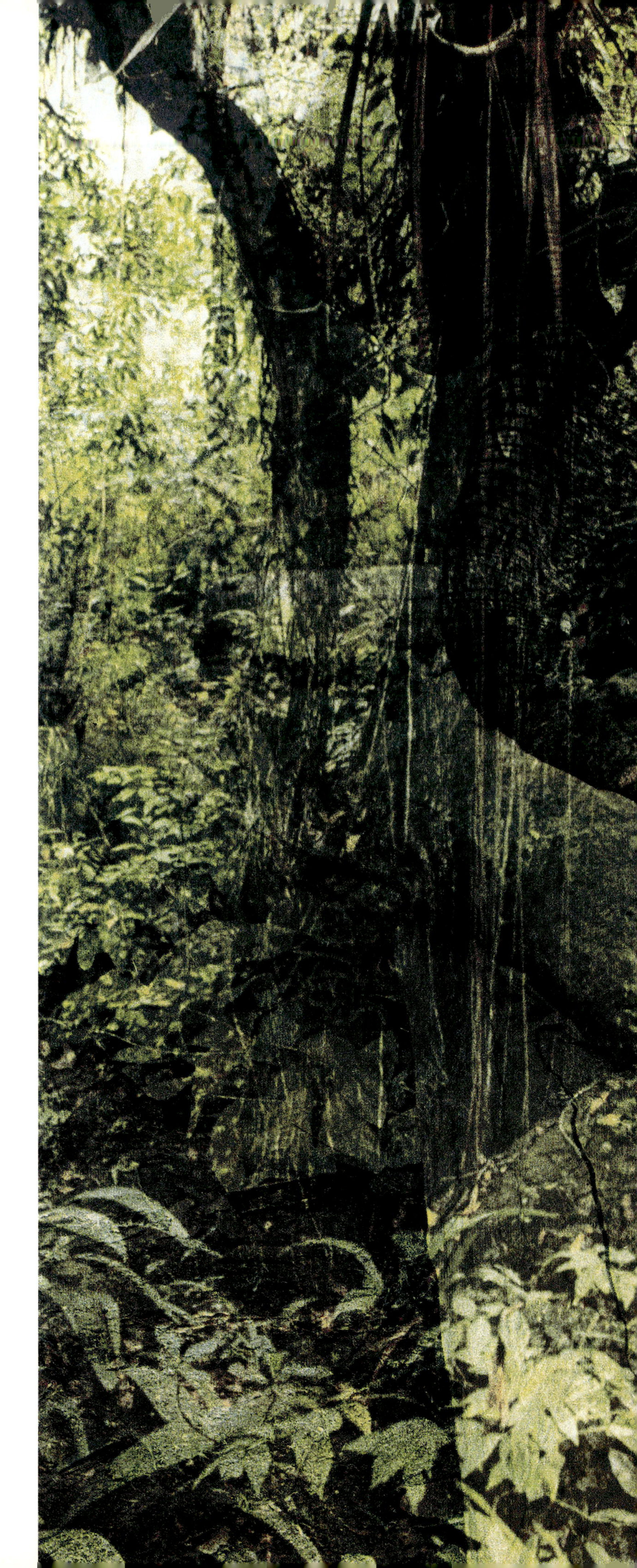

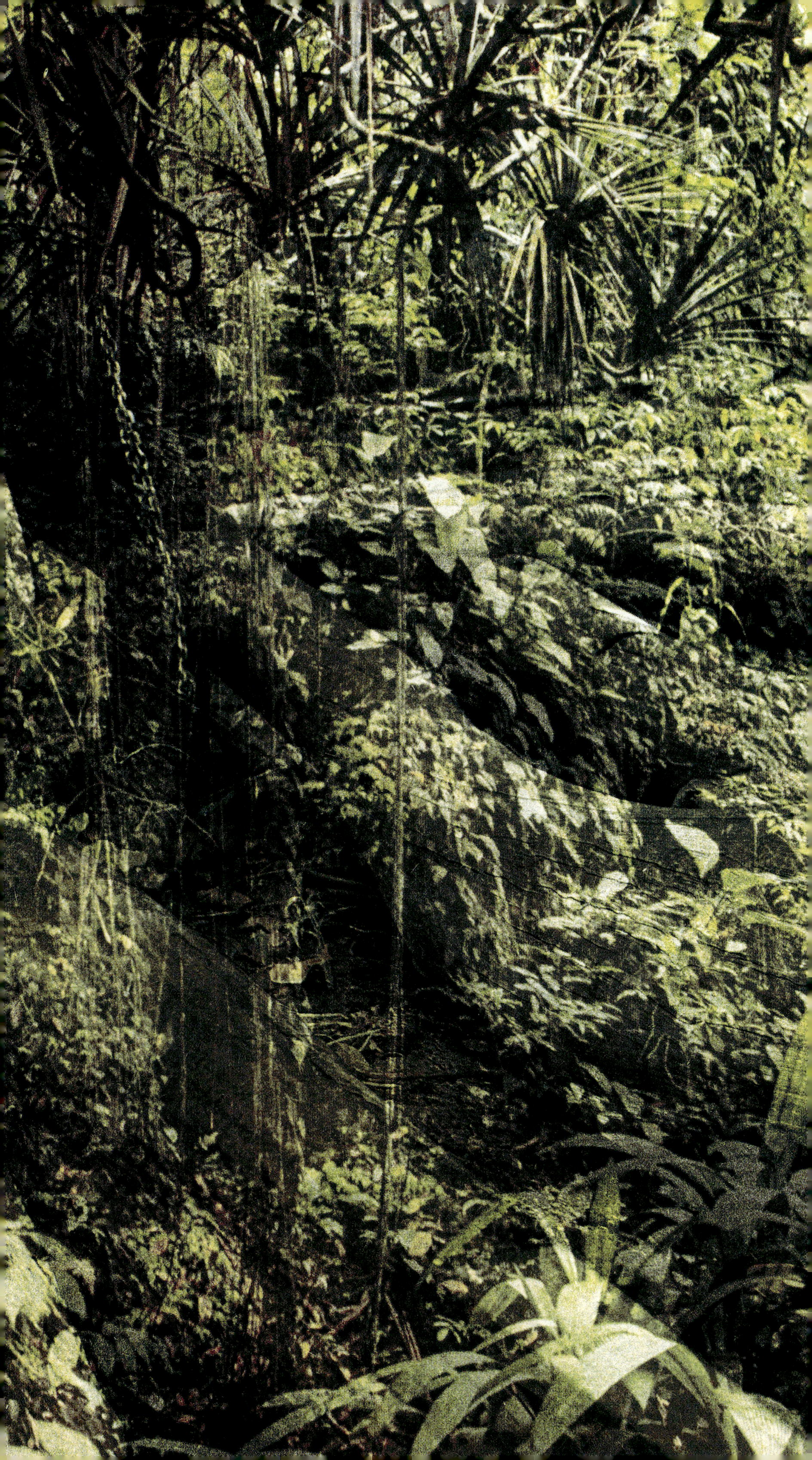

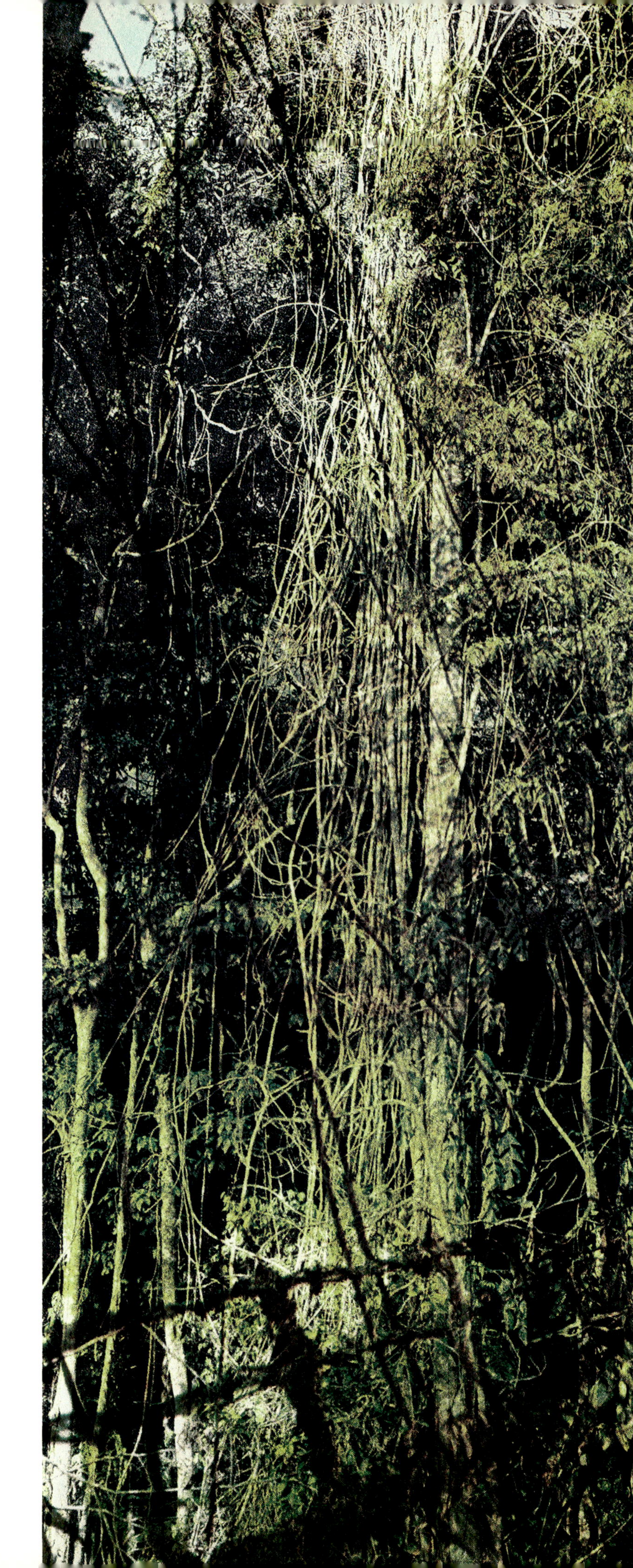

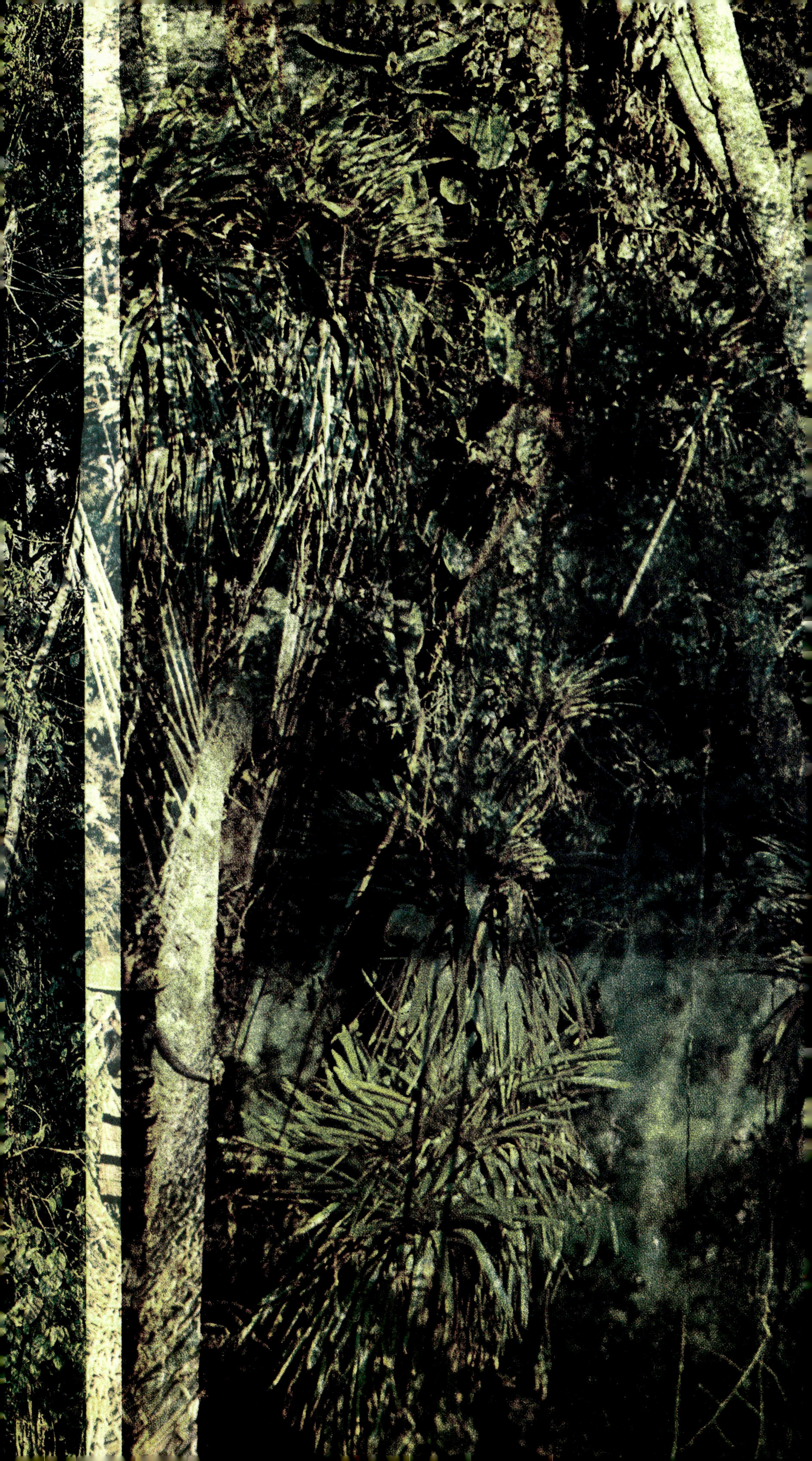

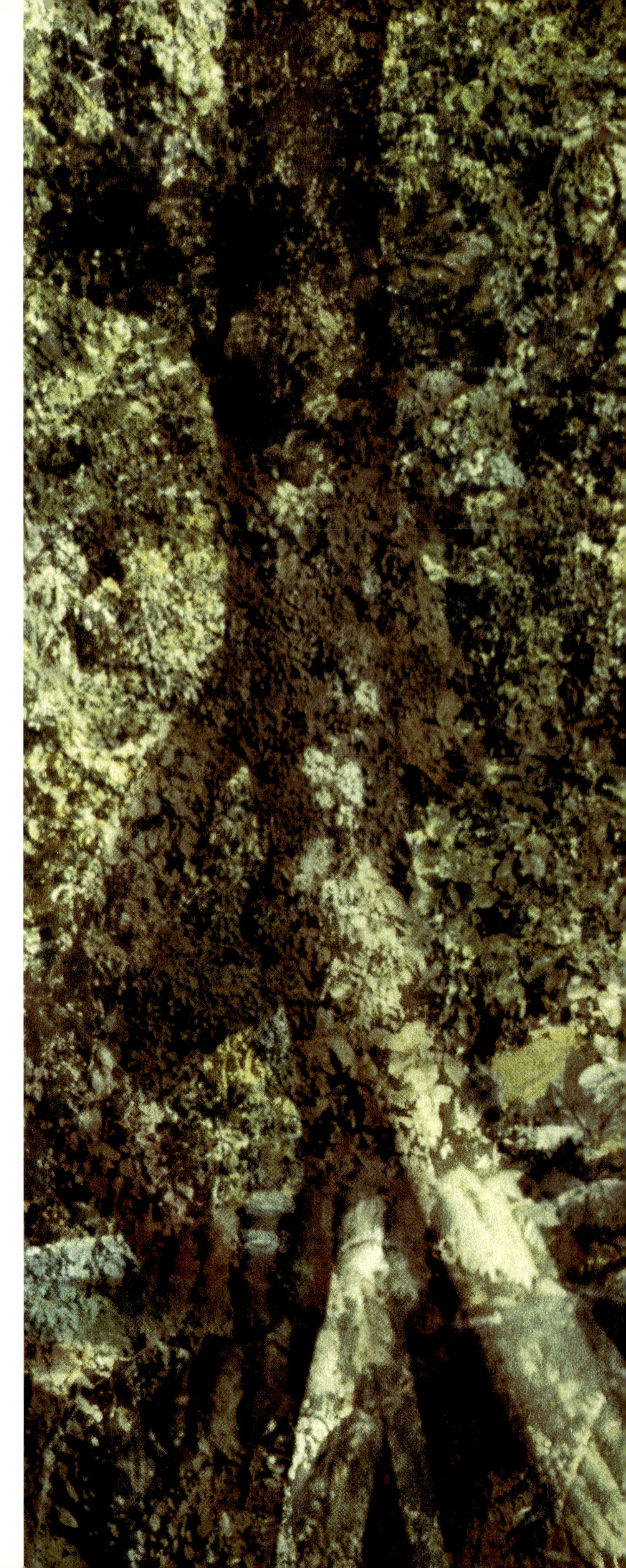

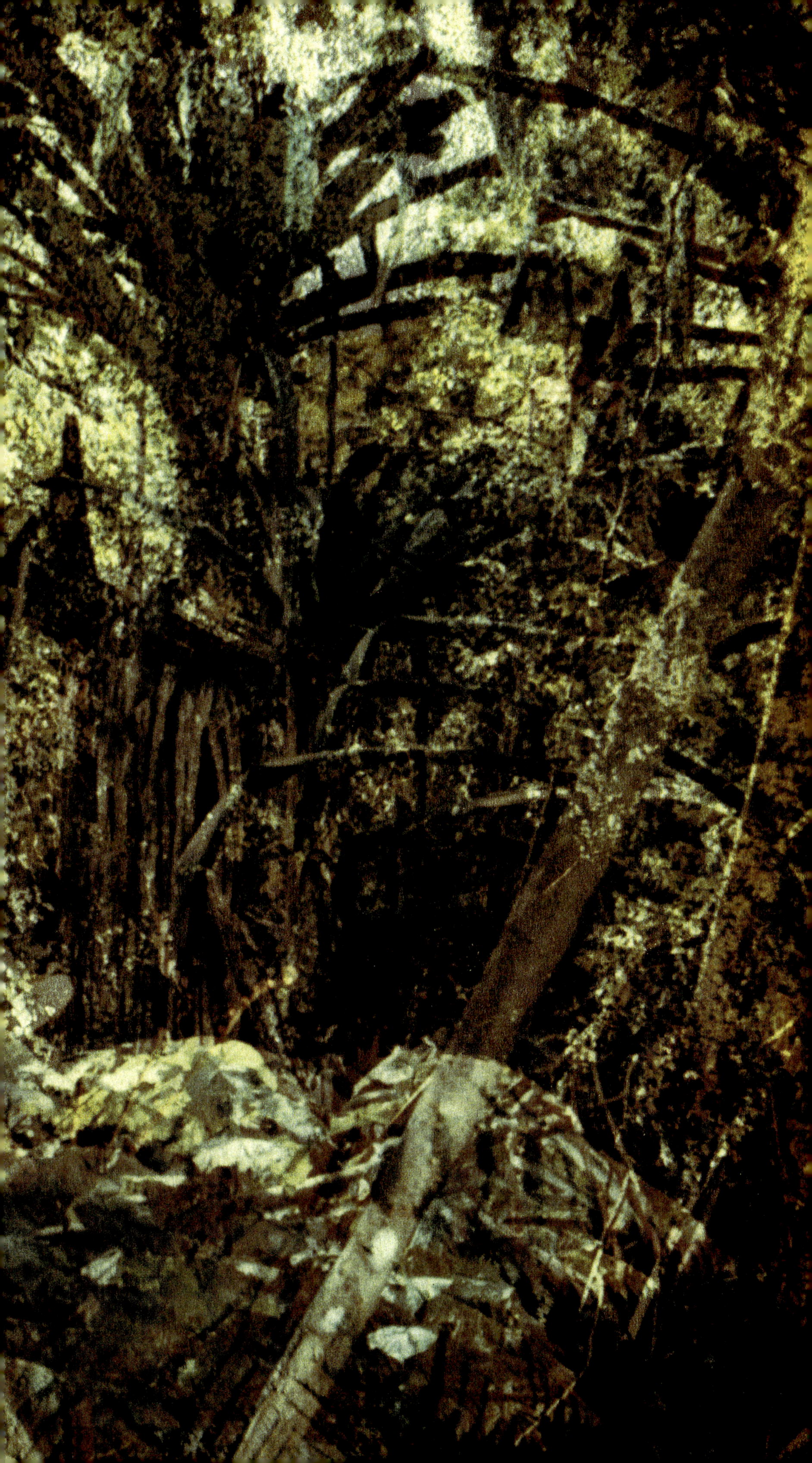

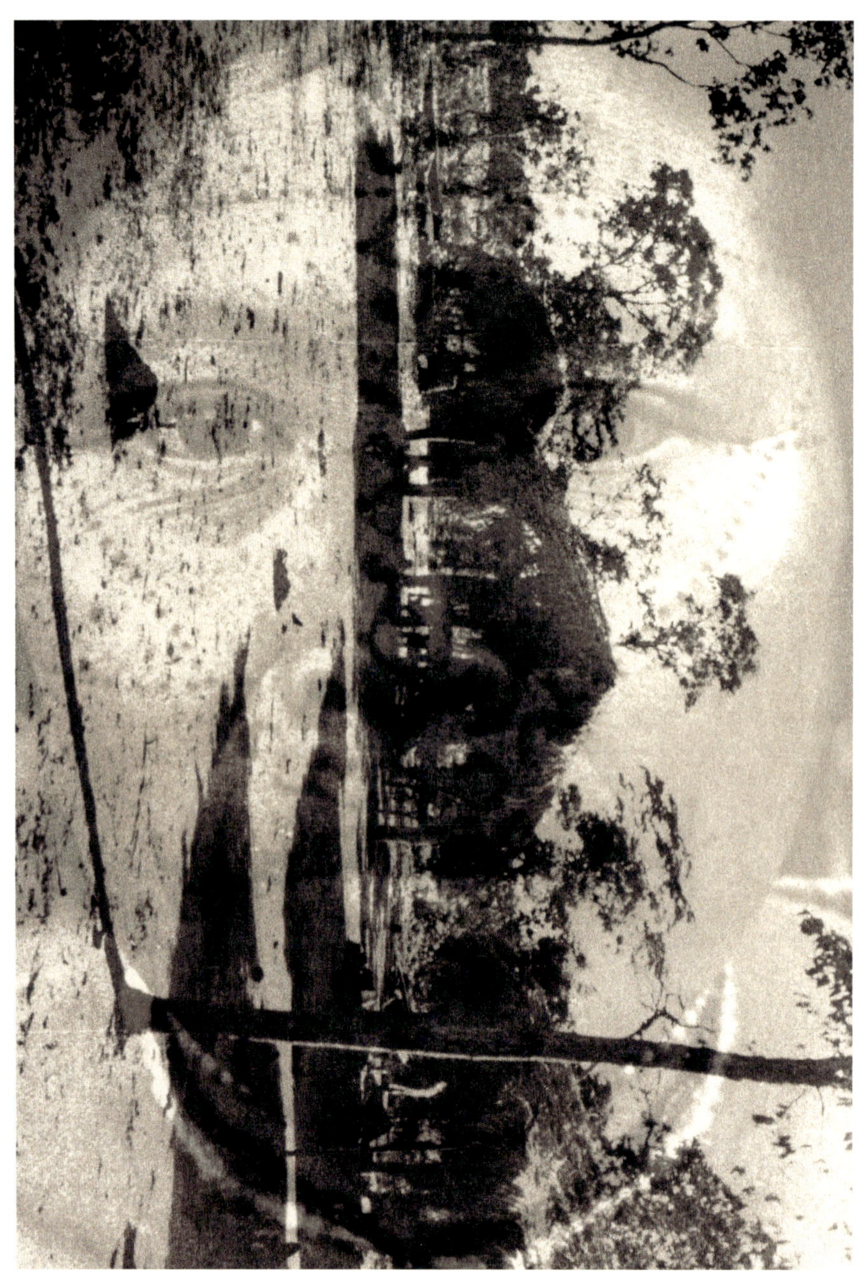

 European animals and plants adapted without difficulty to the climate and soil of America and Australia, but only a few American and Australian plants, among them the potato, gained distribution in Europe. These parallels from the worlds of plants and animals provided apparent confirmation of the belief in the biological superiority of Europeans and the inevitable decline of the other races. But the parallels could also bring about doubts. Why did the weed spread more quickly and effectively in the colonies than any other European plants?

 For all that, many of the illustrators would certainly have been capable of painting the portraits of Europeans, yet for all the ethnographic accuracy their

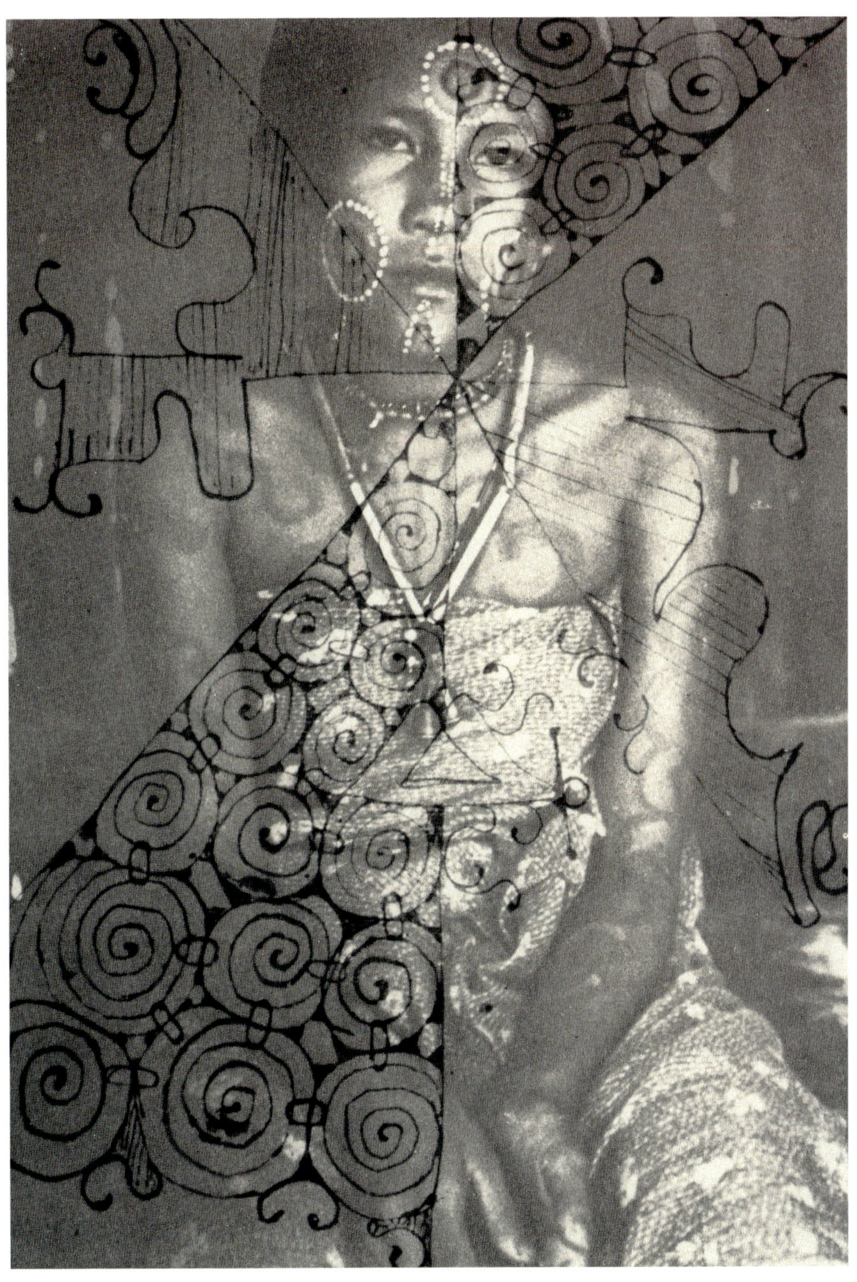

"savages" remain costumed Europeans, their expression rooted in the clichés of youth and travel literature. "Lots of kisses from Lake Chad (large lake in Central Africa that's slowly drying out; crocodiles. Negro women carrying baskets on their head; elephant hunting, antelopes and warthogs, too. Cultural influences: none). The natives here recommend the fat of cassava roots for rheumatism. Tell your dear Mother that." When I saw it crossing the road, I thought it was a mouse. It turned out to be a dung-beetle of the tropical variety, horned, five times as big as the ones La Fontaine used to see at Versailles. Snuff-box size. He was pushing a ball of dung, afraid that the sea-wind

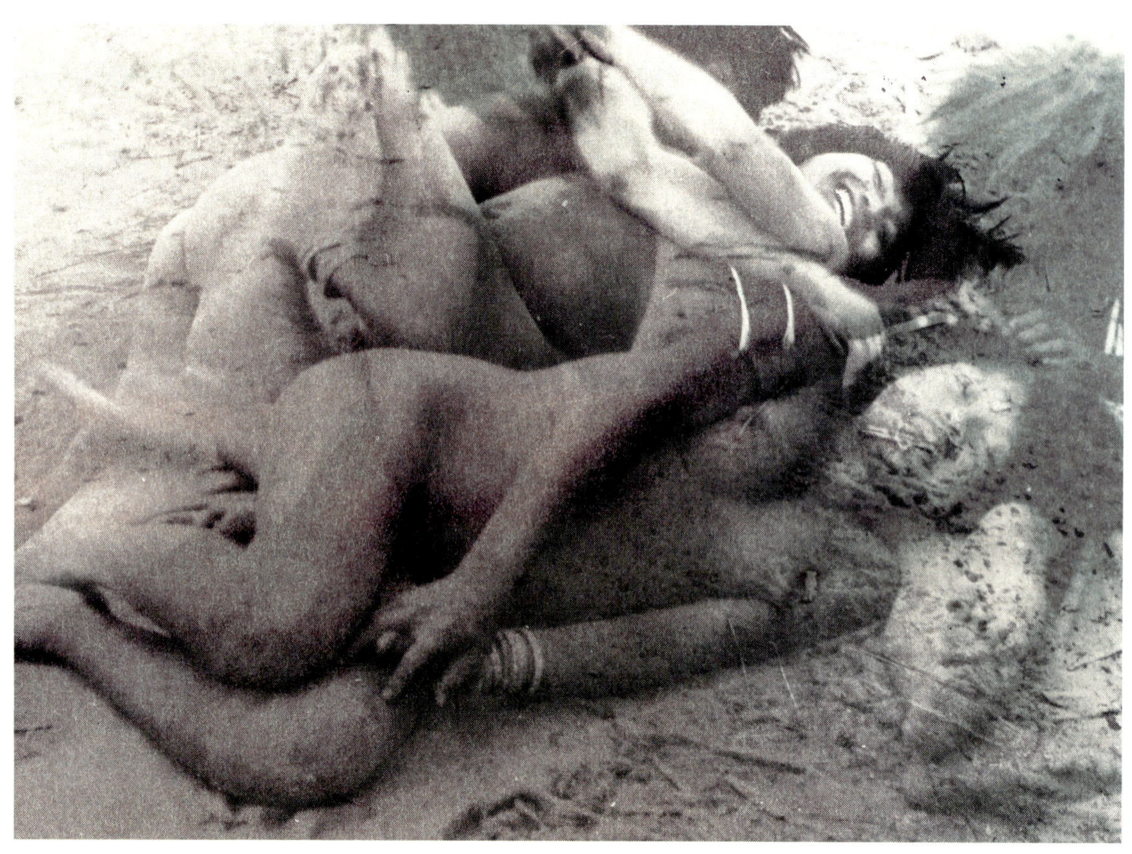

would wrest it from him. I was in the barber's chair, covered in soap. I pushed aside the razor at my throat and rushed into the street to catch him. He didn't like this idea at all, and by way of greeting split my thumb open. Nicolas Bouvier, *The Scorpion-Fish* 'I have read for the last time.' 'I hope not,' said Mr Todd politely. That evening at supper only one plate of dried meat and farine was brought in and Mr Todd ate alone. Tony lay without speaking, staring at the thatch. Next day at noon a single plate was put before Mr Todd but with it lay his gun, cocked, on his knee, as he ate. Tony resumed the reading of *Martin Chuzzlewit* where it had been interrupted. Evelyn Waugh, *A Handful of Dust* Yes, here he is, the mover of Mummah, the champion, the Sungo. Here

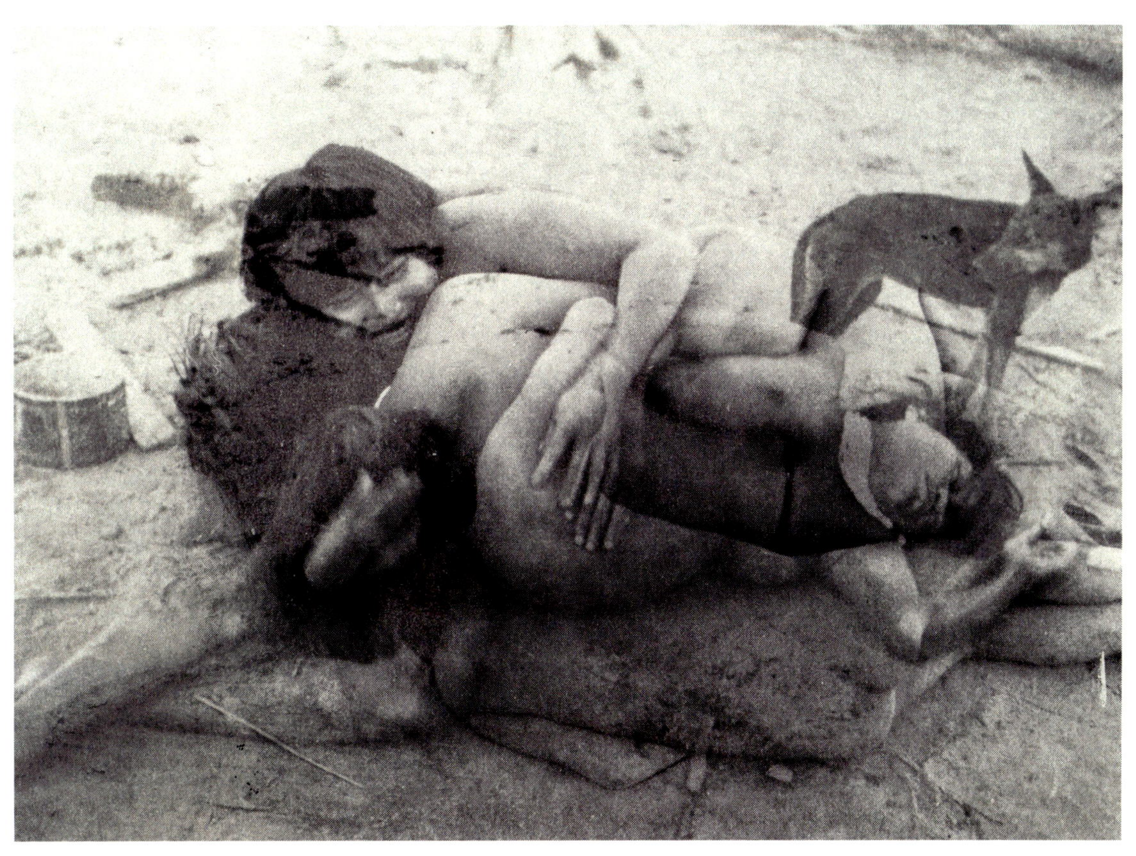

comes Henderson of the U.S.A. – Captain Henderson, Purple Heart, veteran of North Africa, Sicily, Monte Cassino, etc., a giant shadow, a man of flesh and blood, a restless seeker, pitiful and rude, a stubborn old lush with broken bridgewood, threatening death and suicide. Saul Bellow, *Henderson the Rain King* Rousseau, who has been so maligned, who is more misunderstood now than ever before and is preposterously accused of having glorified the state of nature – an error that can be attributed to Diderot but not to him – when in fact he said exactly the opposite and is the only thinker who can show us how to escape from the contradictions in which we are still floundering in the wake of his opponents; Rousseau, the most anthropological of the

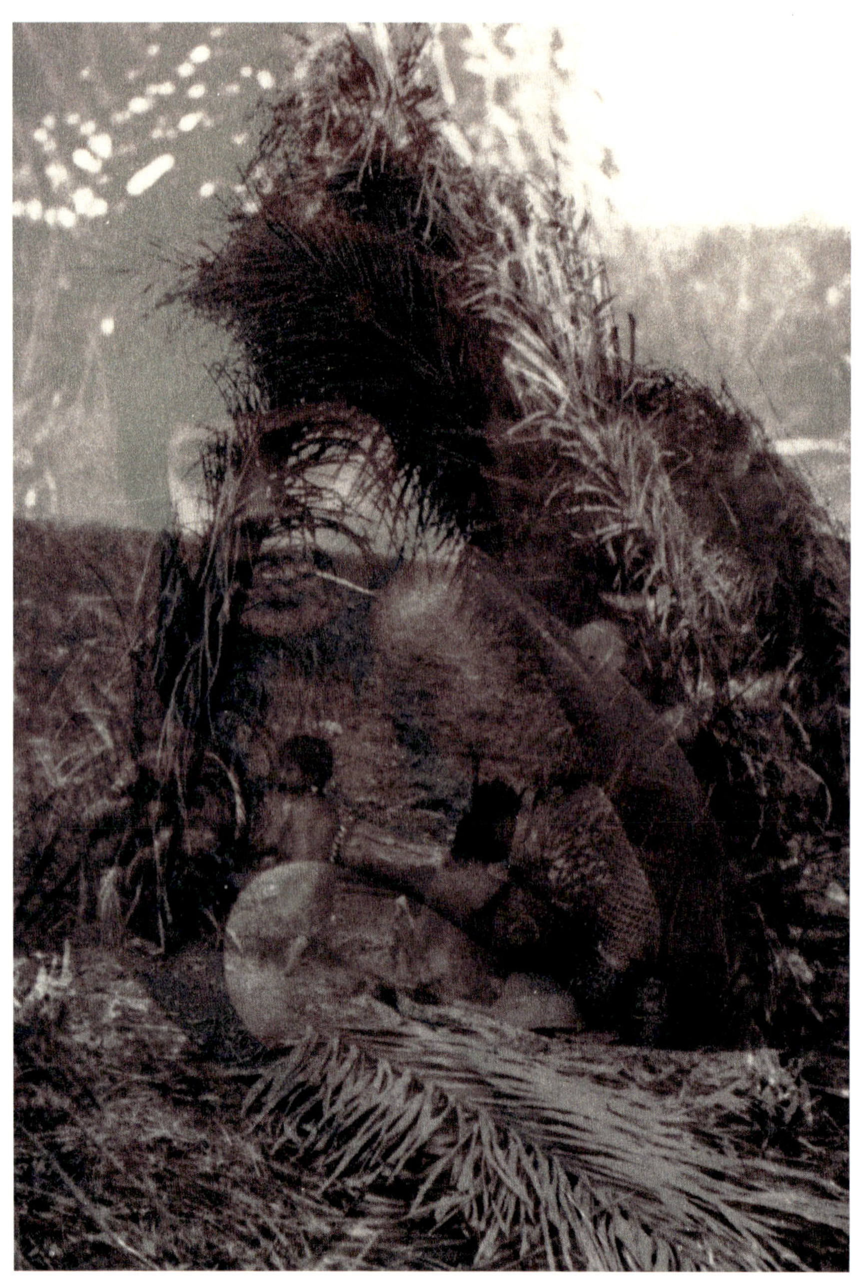

philosophes: although he never travelled to distant lands, his documentation was as complete as it could be for a man of his time and, unlike Voltaire, he infused life into it by his warm-hearted curiosity about peasant customs and popular thought; Rousseau, our master and brother, to whom we have behaved with such ingratitude but to whom every page of this book could have been dedicated, had the homage been worthy of his great memory. The cries, they now perceived, came from two young women, who were running nimbly along the edge of the meadow, pursued by two monkeys, which were biting their buttocks. Candide had learnt musketry with the Bulgarians, and could hit a filbert in a

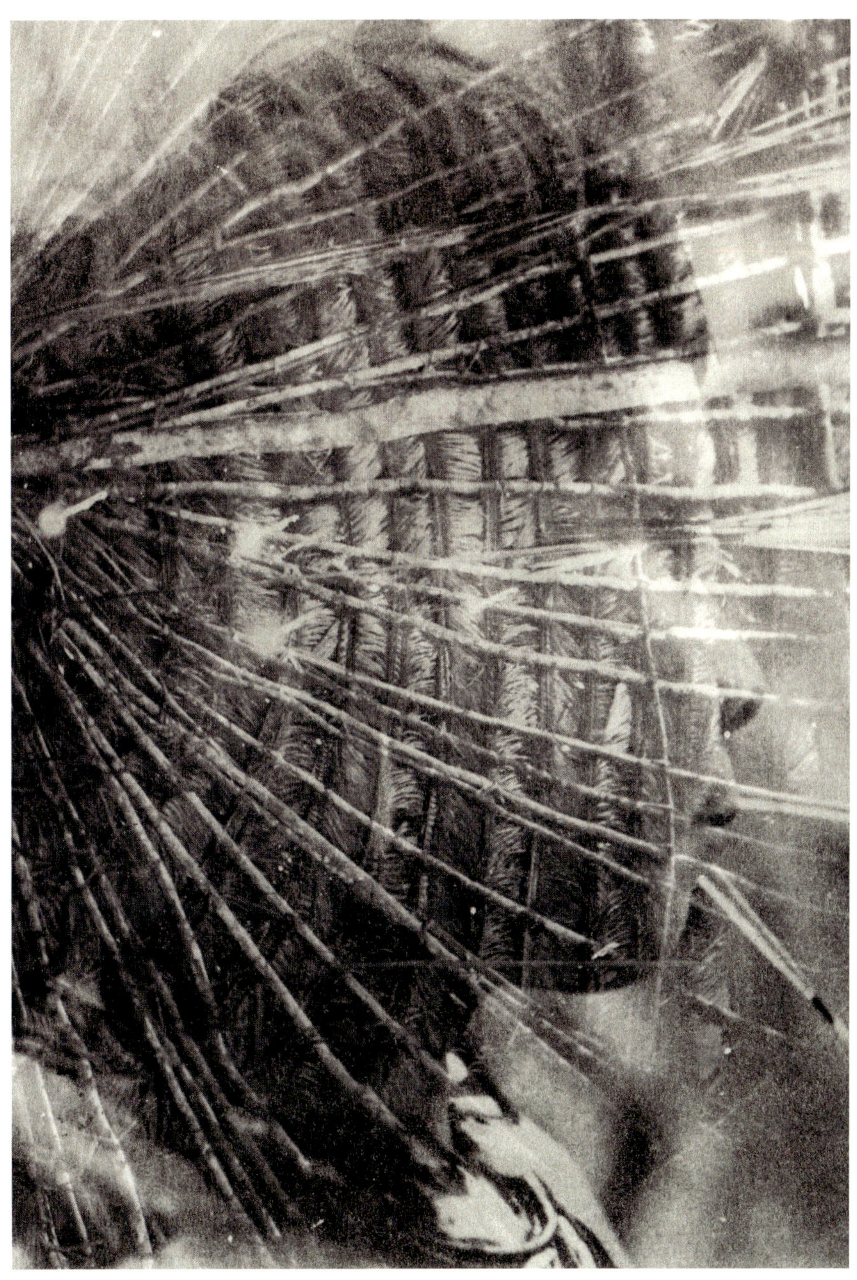

hedge without touching a leaf. He picked up his double-barrelled Spanish musket and killed both monkeys. 'God be prised, my dear Cacambo,' he said, 'I have rescued these two poor creatures from a grave peril. If it was a sin to kill an Inquisitor and a Jesuit, I have atoned for it by saving two girls' lives. Perhaps they are young ladies of good family, and this adventure may be of great service to us in this country.' Voltaire, *Candide or Optimism*   Whilst I was reposing beneath an awning that had been put up as a shelter from the sun, the natives bestowed upon me such a prolonged and decided stare that I had ample opportunity for transferring a few of their portraits to my sketch-book. Georg Schweinfurth, *The Heart of Africa*   Their faces, and sometimes even

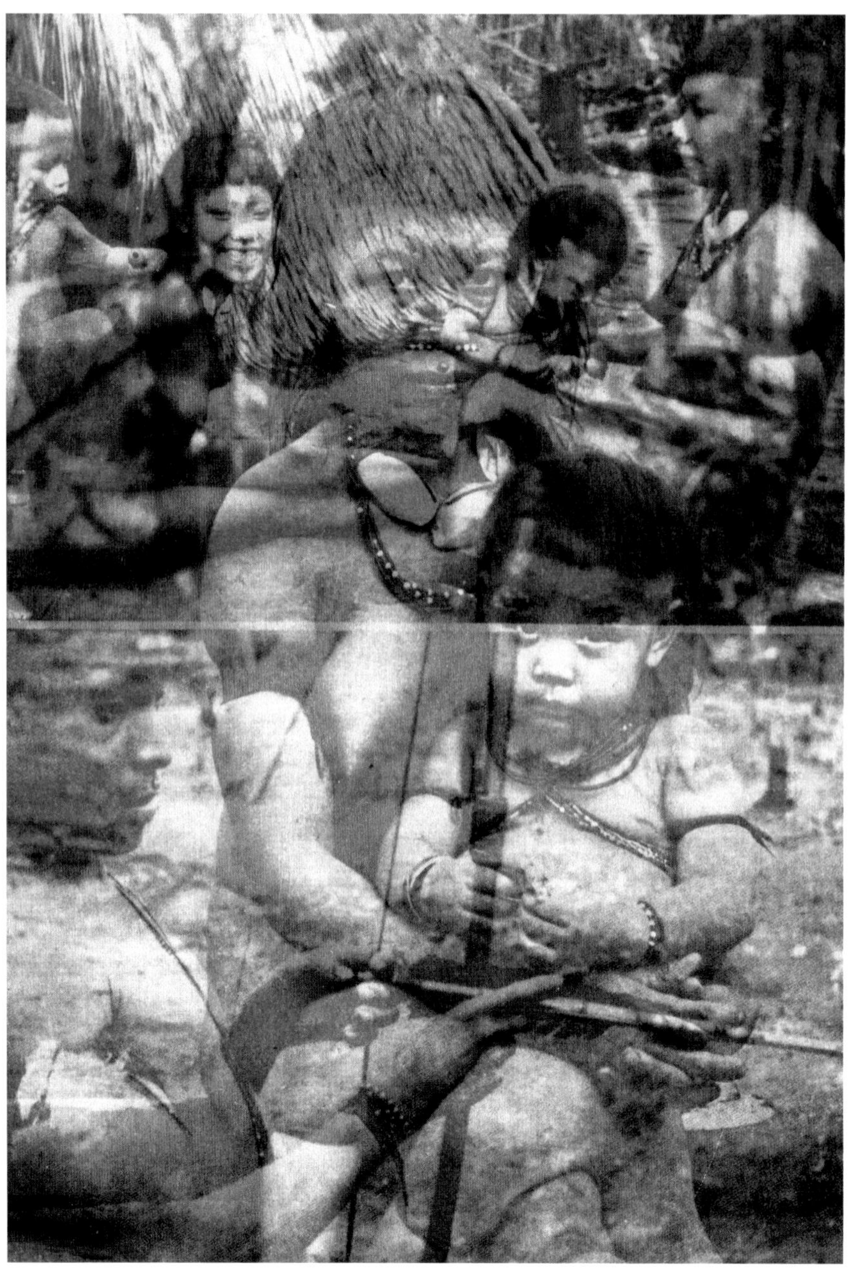

their whole bodies, were covered with a network of asymmetrical arabesques, alternating with delicate geometrical patterns. The first person to describe this feature was the Jesuit missionary, Sanchez Labrador, who lived among them from 1760 to 1770, but exact reproductions were only made a century later by Boggiani. In 1935, I myself collected several hundred designs in the following manner. My first intention was to photograph the faces, but the financial demands of the ladies of the tribe would soon have exhausted my resources. I next tried to draw faces on sheets of paper and suggested to the women that they should paint them, as they would have painted their own countenances; the result was so successful that I

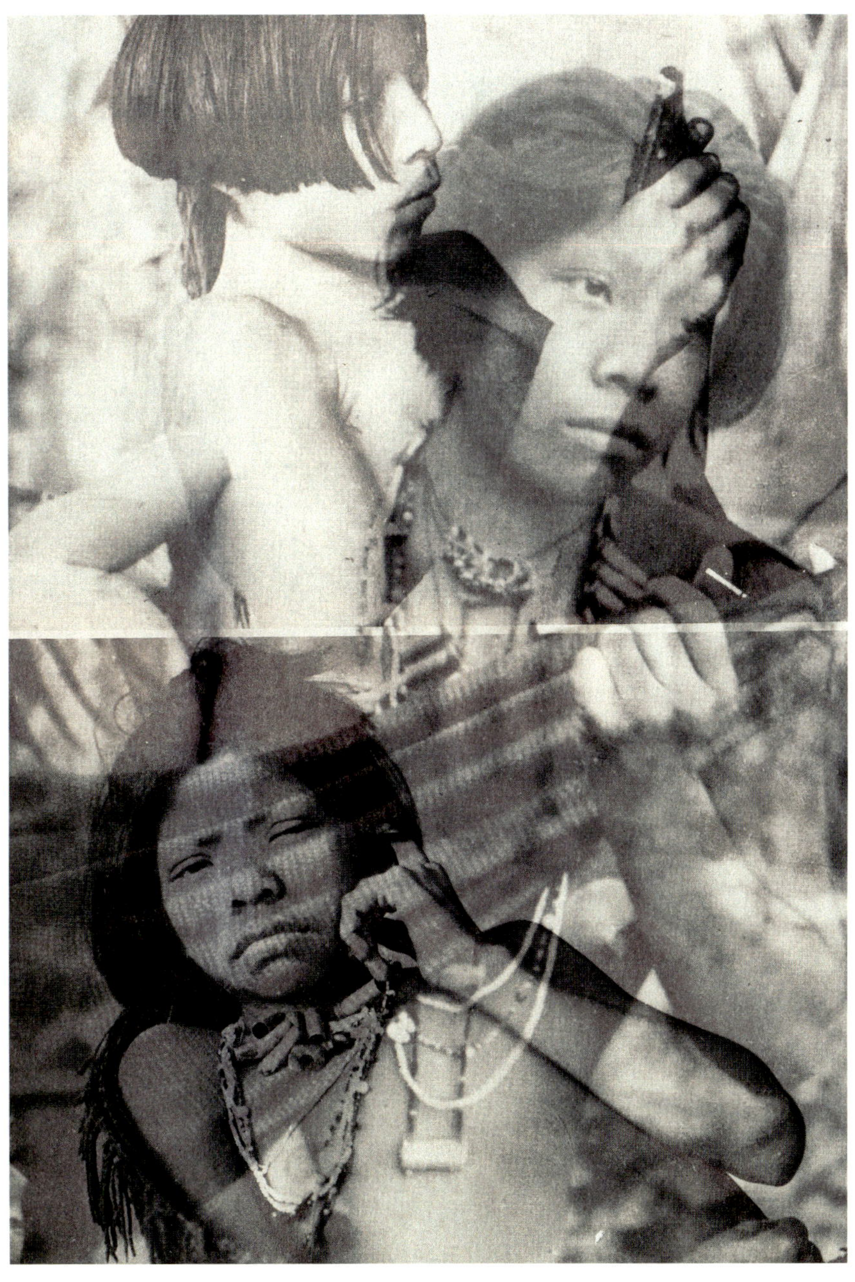

abandoned my clumsy sketches. The women were not put off by the blank sheets, and this showed that their art in no way depended on the natural contours of the human face. Claude Lévi-Strauss, *Tristes Tropiques* They may make a design on their faces to go have lunch at a friend's, then rub it out on the way home. Everyone has mentioned how attractive this is. There are certain colors, however, that smudge badly. For us they would be an inconvenience. The Turks were quite right to have pointed out how unseemly a face is. There it is on top of your clothing, sticking out, with glances escaping from it like madmen. Everything unhealthy and bestial that your skin has about it vanishes with the application of a line, a spot of rouge. Henri Michaux, *Ecuador*

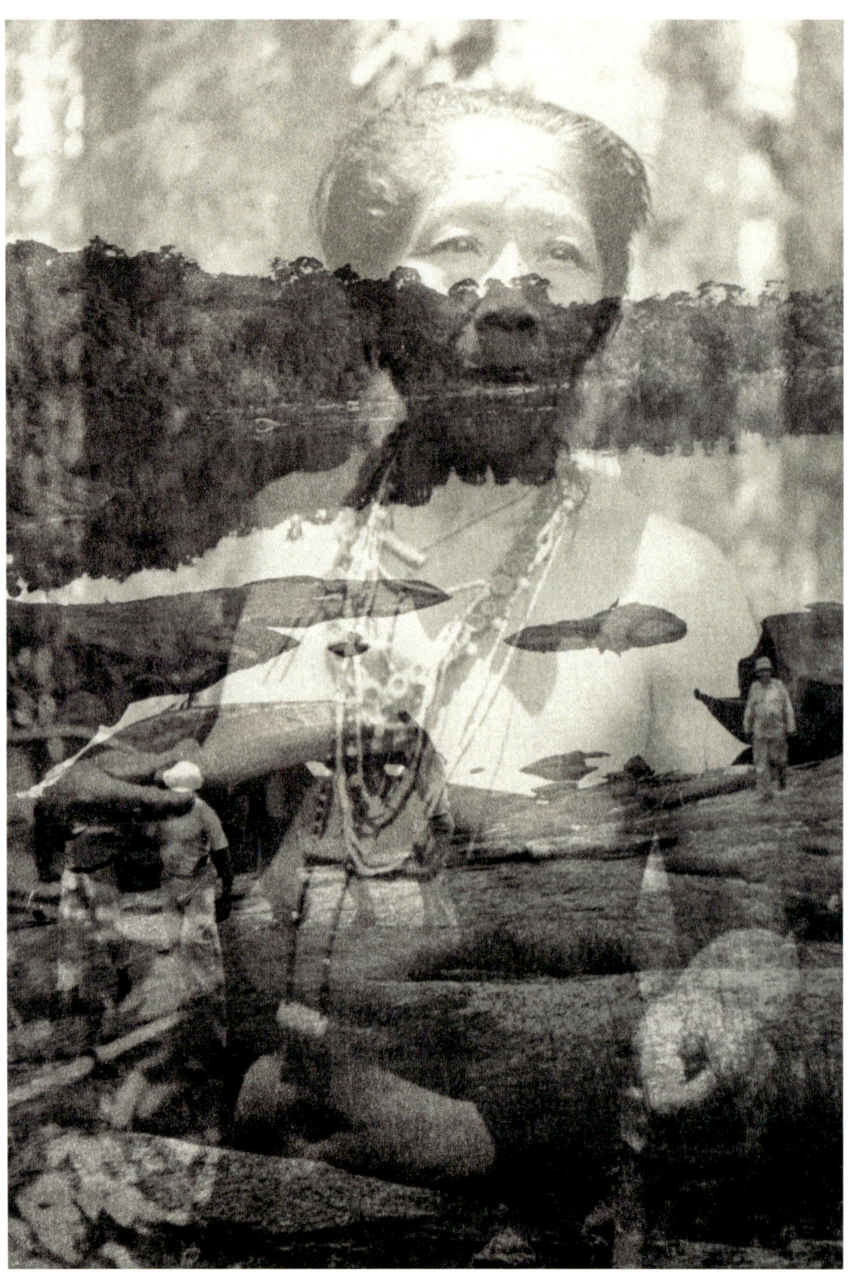

Often enough one may recognise the painter's nationality in the physiognomy of the supposed Polynesians and Indians. Lafiteau's Iroquois are Frenchmen as clearly as the Easter Islanders of La Pérouse, while Cook's Tahitians are undoubtedly Englishmen. Likewise the gestures and mimics of 18th century life at court remain determining. Fritz Kramer, *Verkehrte Welten* It does not take much of a prophet to predict that before long the white race will on its own take up tattooing. I am told that current opinion is flatly opposed to this – and much else. Prophets say, 'You'll see'; that suffices for both them and me. Henri Michaux, *Ecuador* Whilst the women in Europe paint their cheeks red, those of Taiti dye their loins and buttocks of a deep blue. This is an ornament,

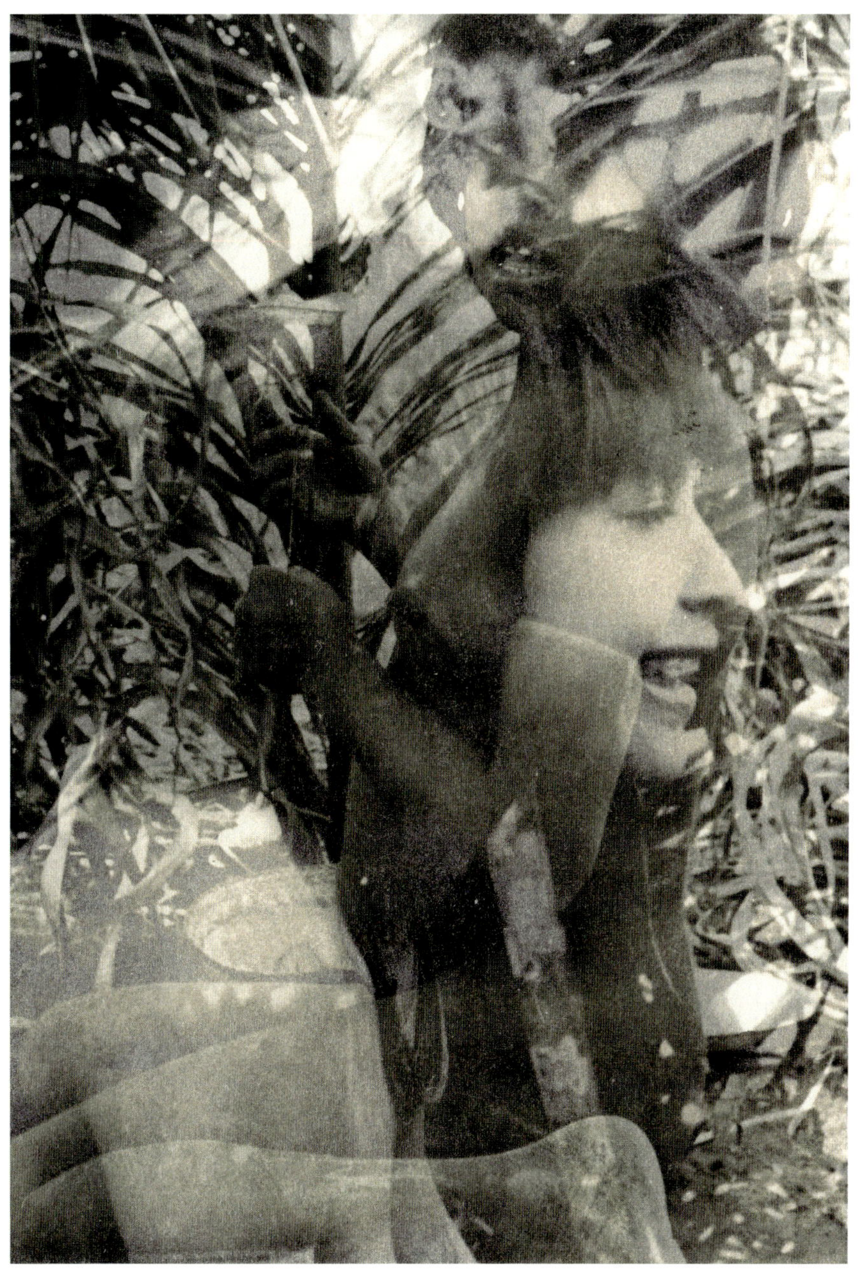

and at the same time a mark of distinction. The men are subject to the same fashion. I cannot say how they do to impress these indelible marks, unless it is by puncturing the skin, and pouring the juice of certain herbs upon it, as I have seen it practised by the natives of Canada. Lewis de Bougainville, *A Voyage Round the World* It is very difficult to get those Moumou natives to do any- thing. They are spoiled by the French for one thing, and have very little use for money for another. The only temptation is alcohol. With the promise of alcohol I had managed to get a carpenter to make and fit mosquito-doors to the house. Robert James Fletcher, *Isles of Illusion* To some- one not acquainted with the South Sea landscape it is difficult to convey the permanent

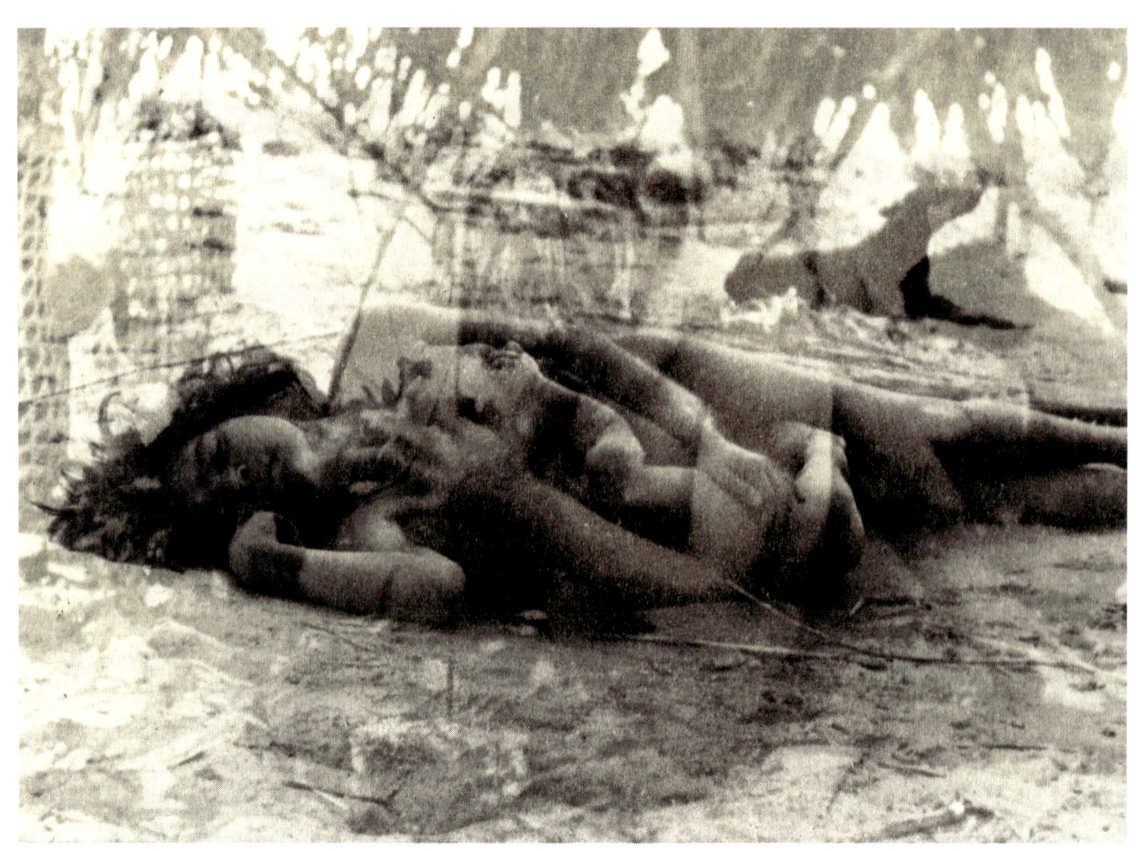

impression of smiling festiveness, the alluring clearness of the beach, fringed by jungle trees and palms, skirted by white foam and blue sea, above it the slopes ascending in rich, stiff folds of dark and light green, piebald and shaded over towards the summit by steamy, tropical mists. Bronislaw Malinowski, *Argonauts of the Western Pacific* Eritrea is two altitudes, two climates, two religions. In the highlands, where Asmara lies and where it is cooler, lives the Tigrinya ethnic group. The majority of the country's inhabitants belong to it. The Tigrinya are Coptic Christians. The other part of Eritrea is the hot, semidesert lowlands – the shores of the Red Sea, between Sudan and Djibouti. Various pastoral people live there, professing Islam (Christianity seems to tolerate the

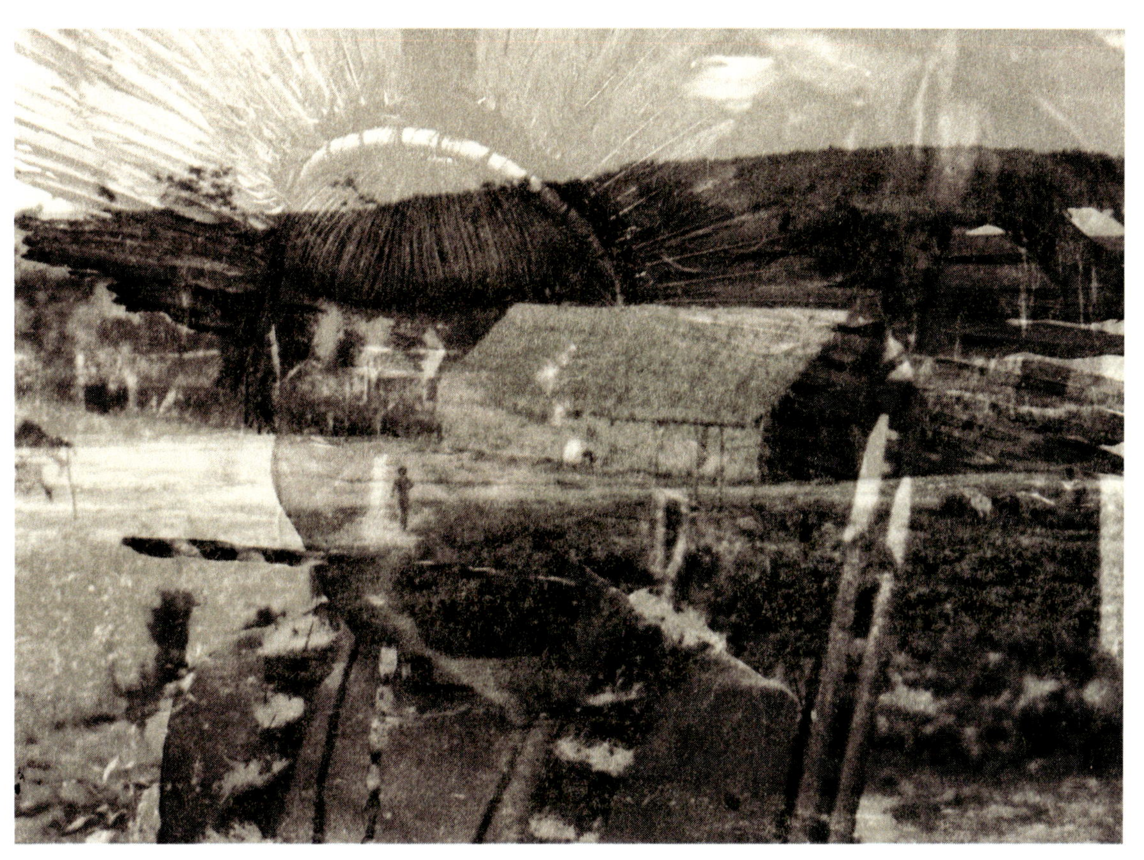

tropics less well, while Islam takes to them). Ryszard Kapuściński, *The Shadow of the Sun* I am only too well aware of the reasons for the uneasiness I felt on coming into contact with Islam: I rediscovered in Islam the world I myself had come from; Islam is the West of the East. Or, to be more precise, I had to have experience of Islam in order to appreciate the danger which today threatens French thought. I cannot easily forgive Islam for showing me our own image, and for forcing me to realize to what extent France is beginning to resemble a Moslem country. Claude Lévi-Strauss, *Tristes Tropiques* "We found a great number of these books in Indian characters, and because they contained nothing but superstition and the Devil's falsehoods, we burned them all; and this

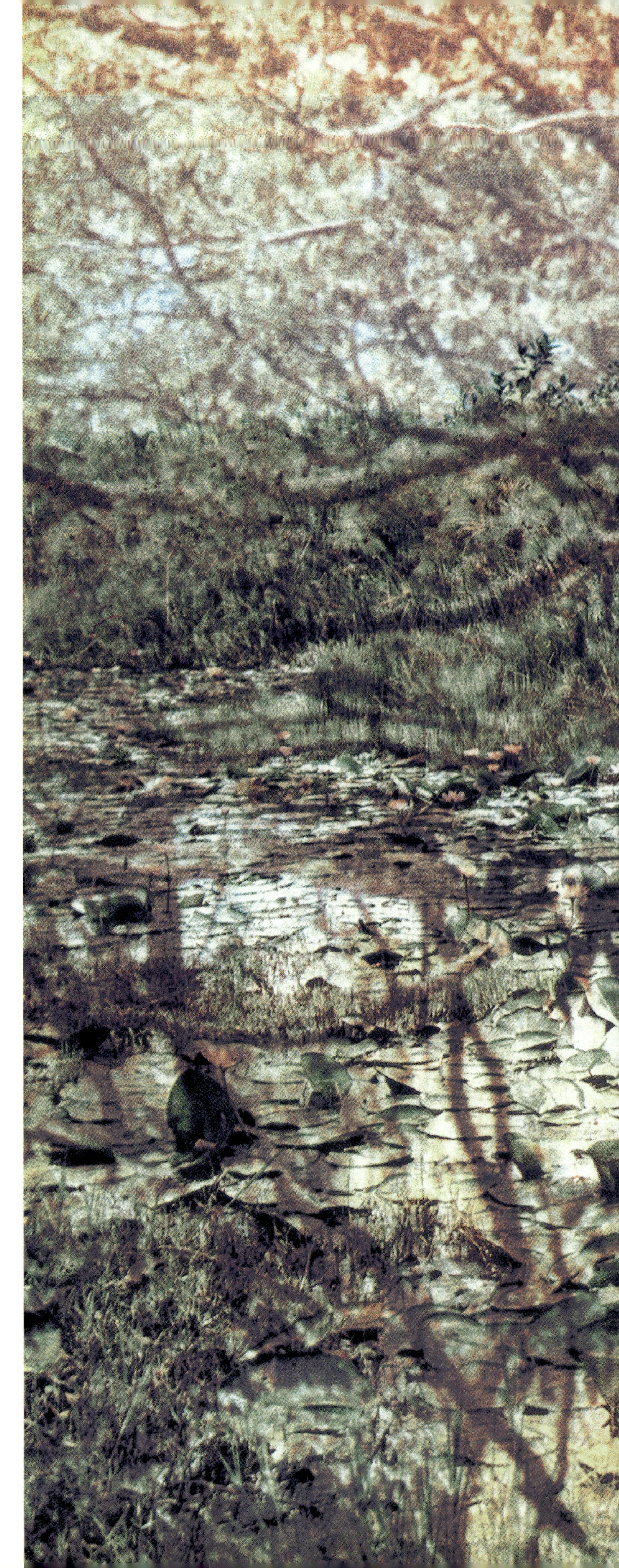

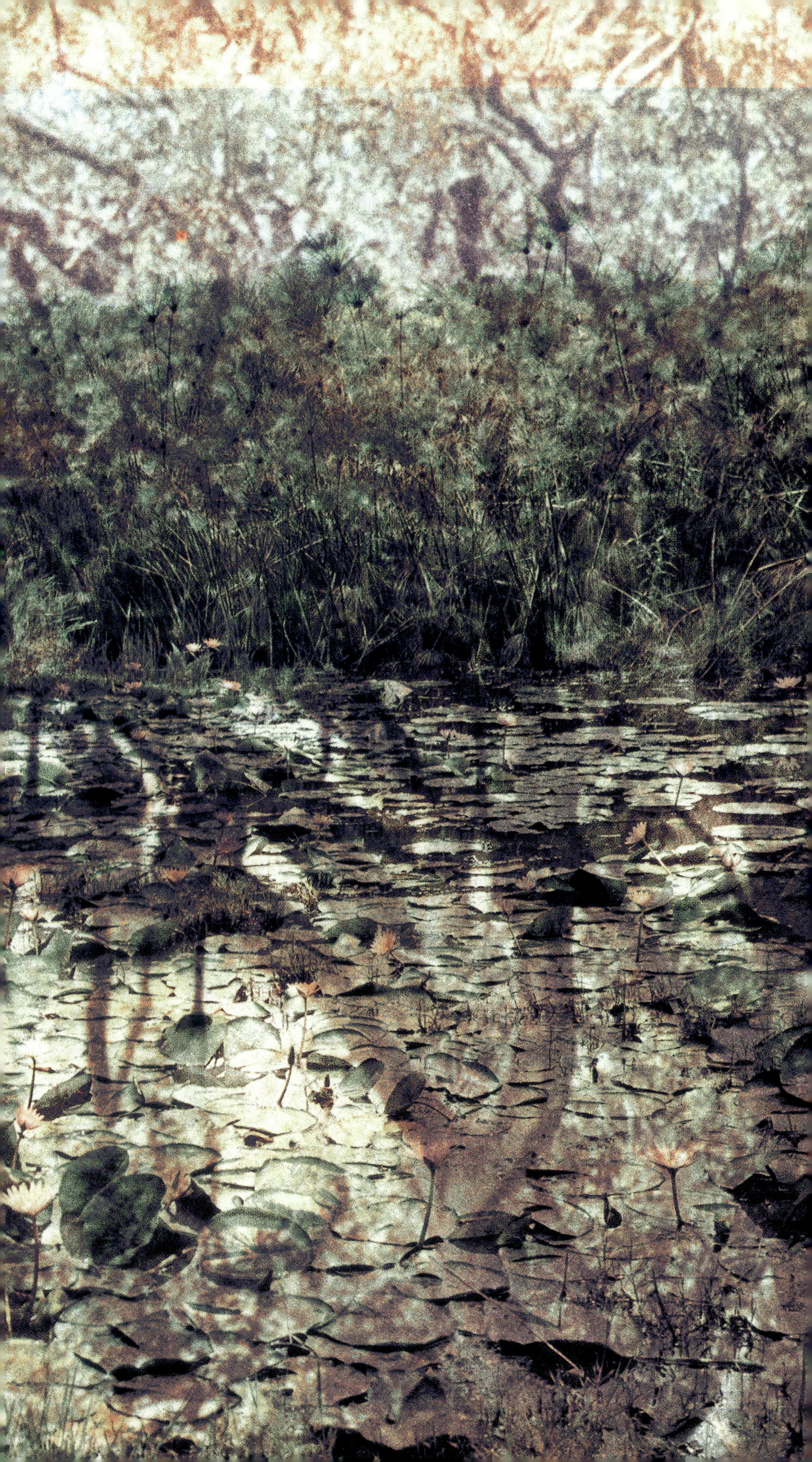

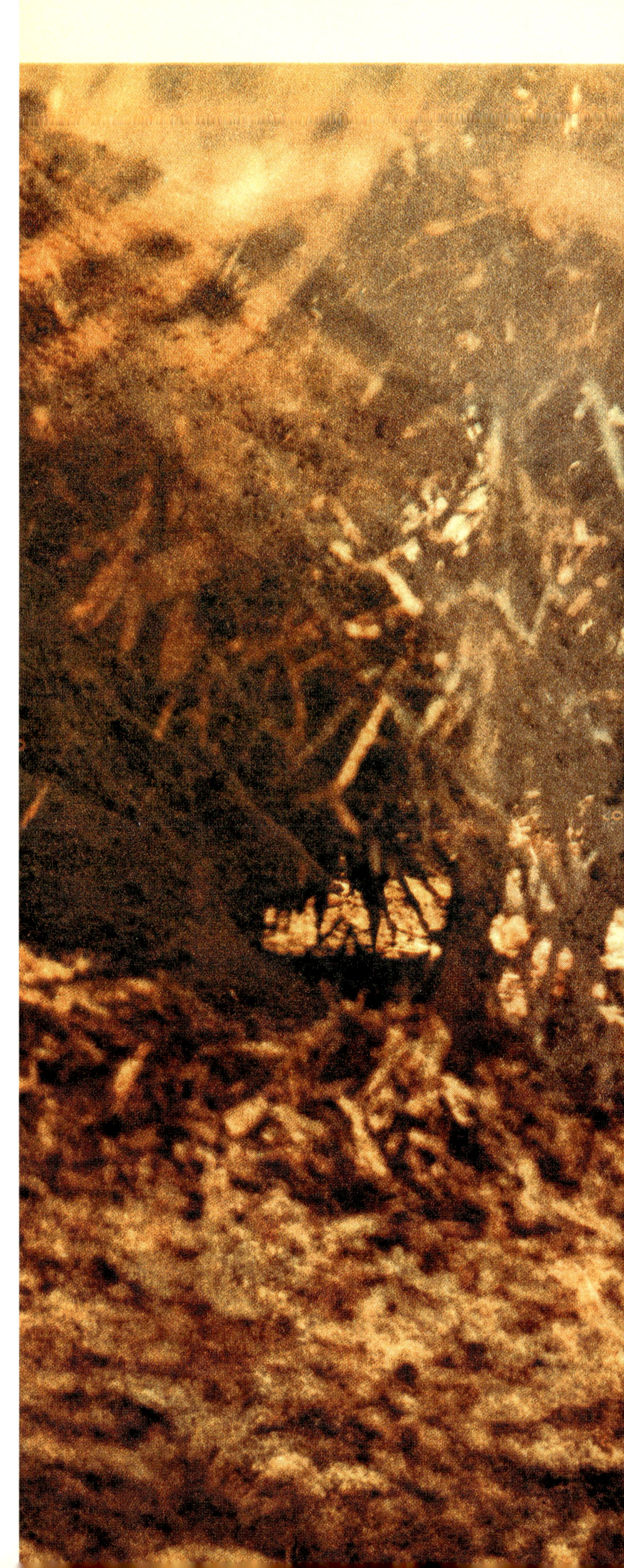

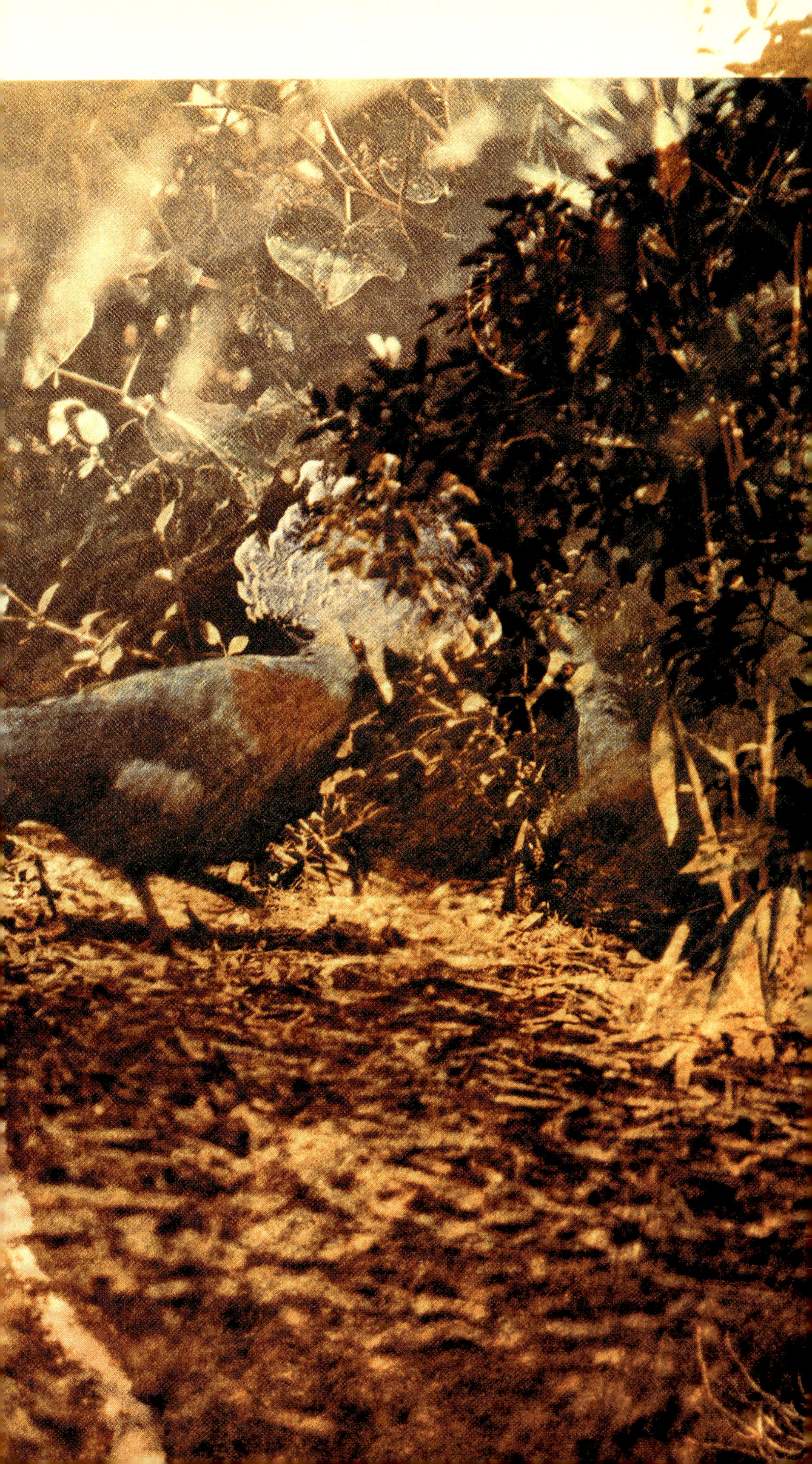

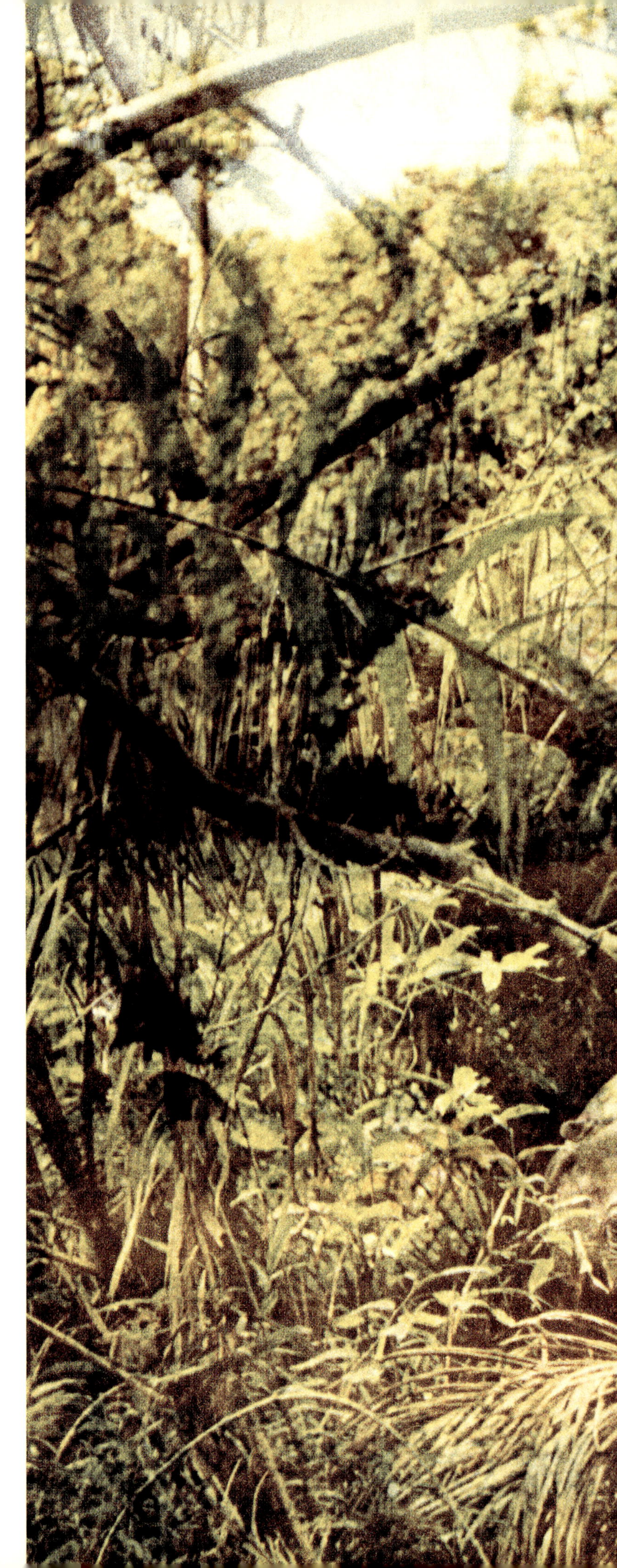

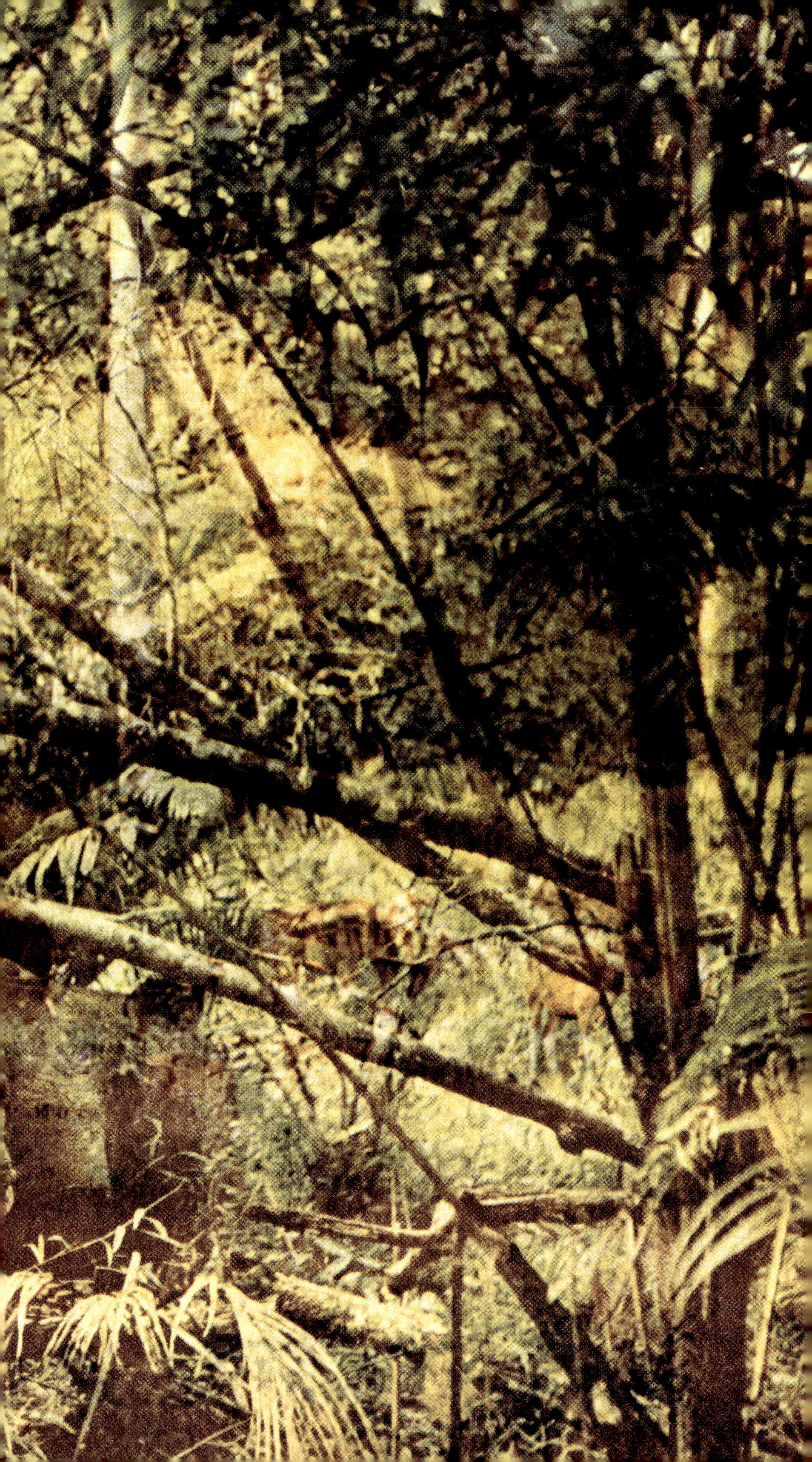

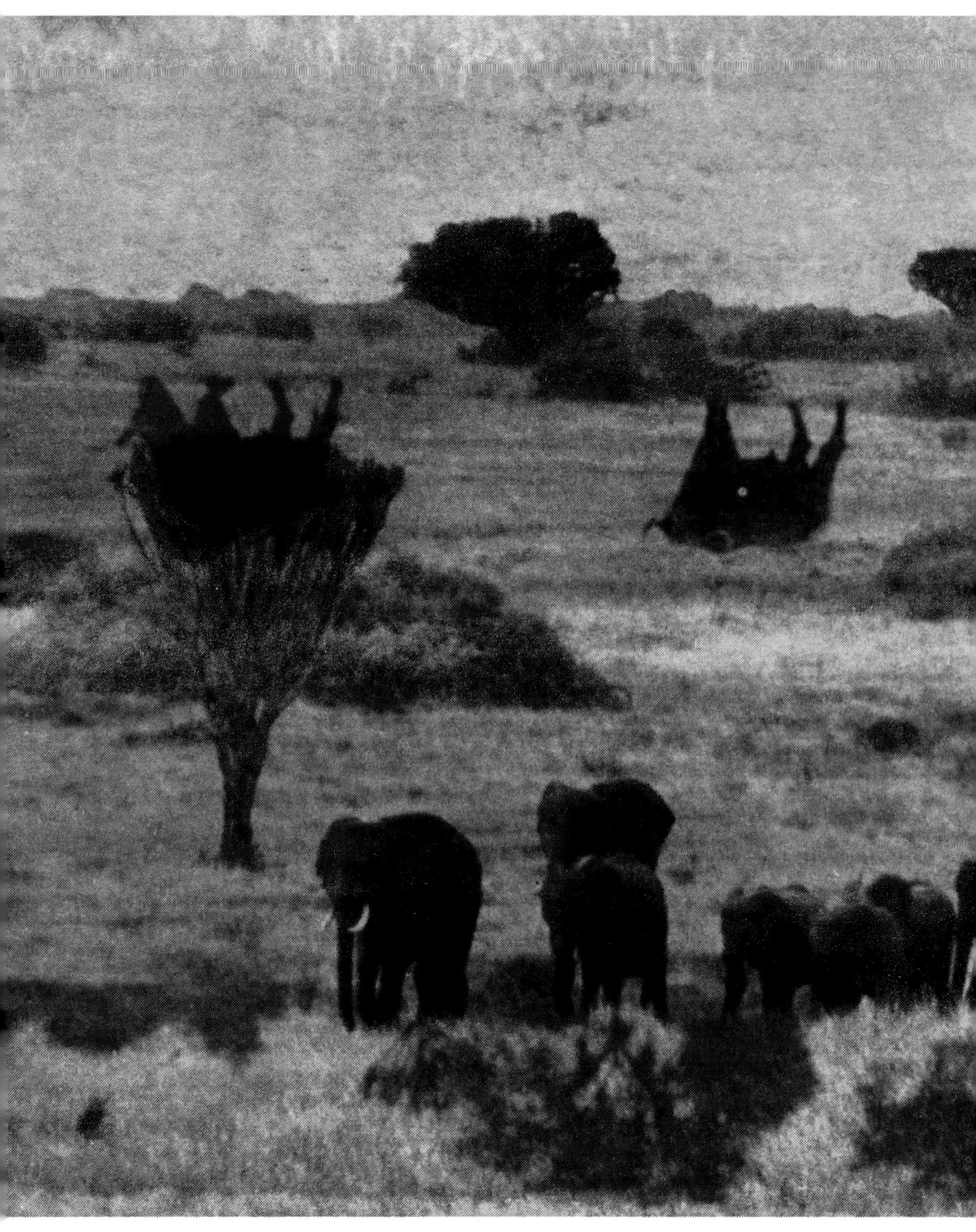

they felt most bitterly and it caused them great grief." D. de Landa, in: Tzvetan Todorov, *The Conquest of America* Here we began to distribute christian books. They had never been seen before, and their contents excited wonder. To see this poor friendly people, anxious for the word of eternal life, but unable to obtain it, is truly distressing. Charles Gutzlaff, *Journal of Three Voyages along the Coast of China* The natives round here are in the half-way stage. Usually they are nude and picturesque. On Sundays they put on Christianity in the form of a lava-lava for the men and a smock for the women, but once outside the school off come the signs of grace, to be hidden carefully in the bush against the 'time of the evening sacrifice'. Robert James Fletcher, *Isles of Illusion* "... Do you

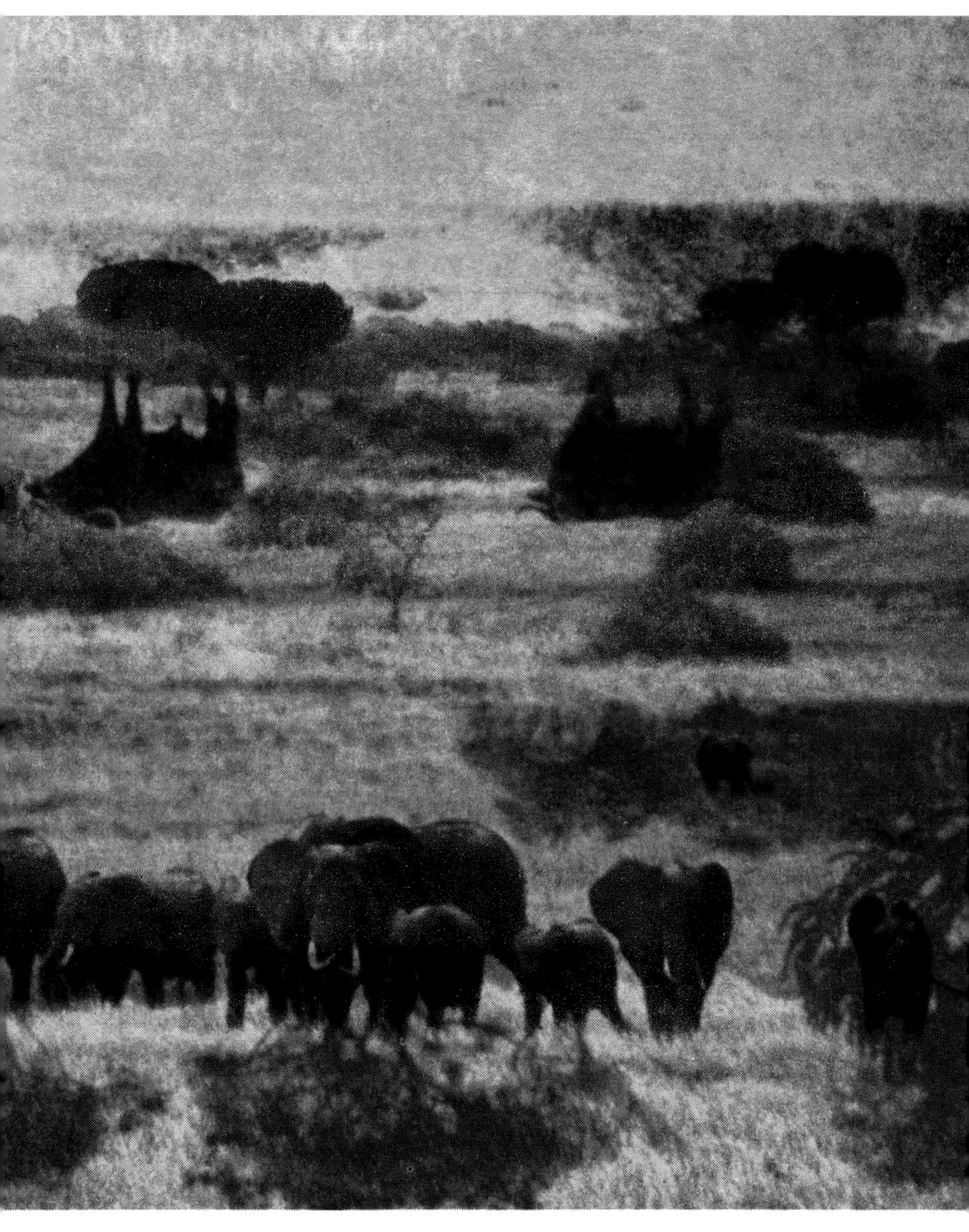

know what the missionary woman said to me, the one I gave the wall hanging to? '*If your children don't obey you, you must punish them. You must carefully consider how much of a beating they have deserved, and you must beat them accordingly. Then you must sit down with your children and pray with them.*' That's what she told me." Florence Weiss, *Vor dem Vulkanausbruch*   In this thankful Frame I continu'd all the Remainder of my Time, and the Conversation which employ'd the Hours between *Friday* and I, was such, as made the three Years which we liv'd there together perfectly and compleatly happy, *if any such Thing as compleat Happiness can be form'd in a sublunary State*. The Savage was now a good Christian, a much better than I; though I have

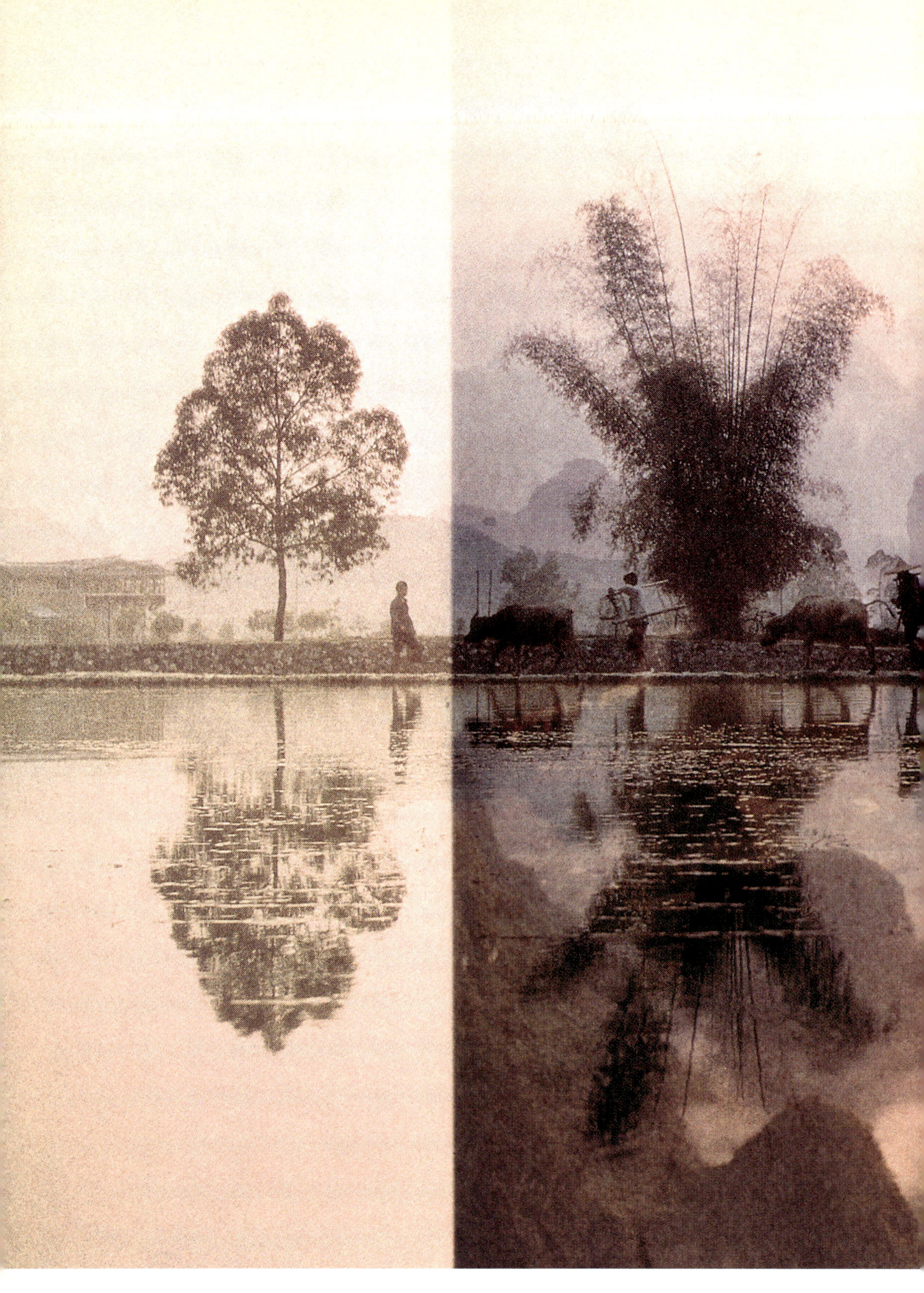

reason to hope, and bless God for it, that we were equally penitent, and comforted restor'd Penitents; we had here the Word of God to read, and no farther off from his Spirit to instruct, than if we had been in *England*. Daniel Defoe, *Robinson Crusoe*   I pulled myself together, and without a moment's hesitation took a quick look around, laying instant claim to the field I would hence-forth be harvesting. I stood on the mountain tops of Tibet, and the sun that had just risen before my eyes a few hours ago was already sinking into the firmament of the night sky; I strode through Asia from east to west, keeping a step ahead of the sun in its rapid descent, and crossed over into Africa. I looked around eagerly, scanning the entire continent in all

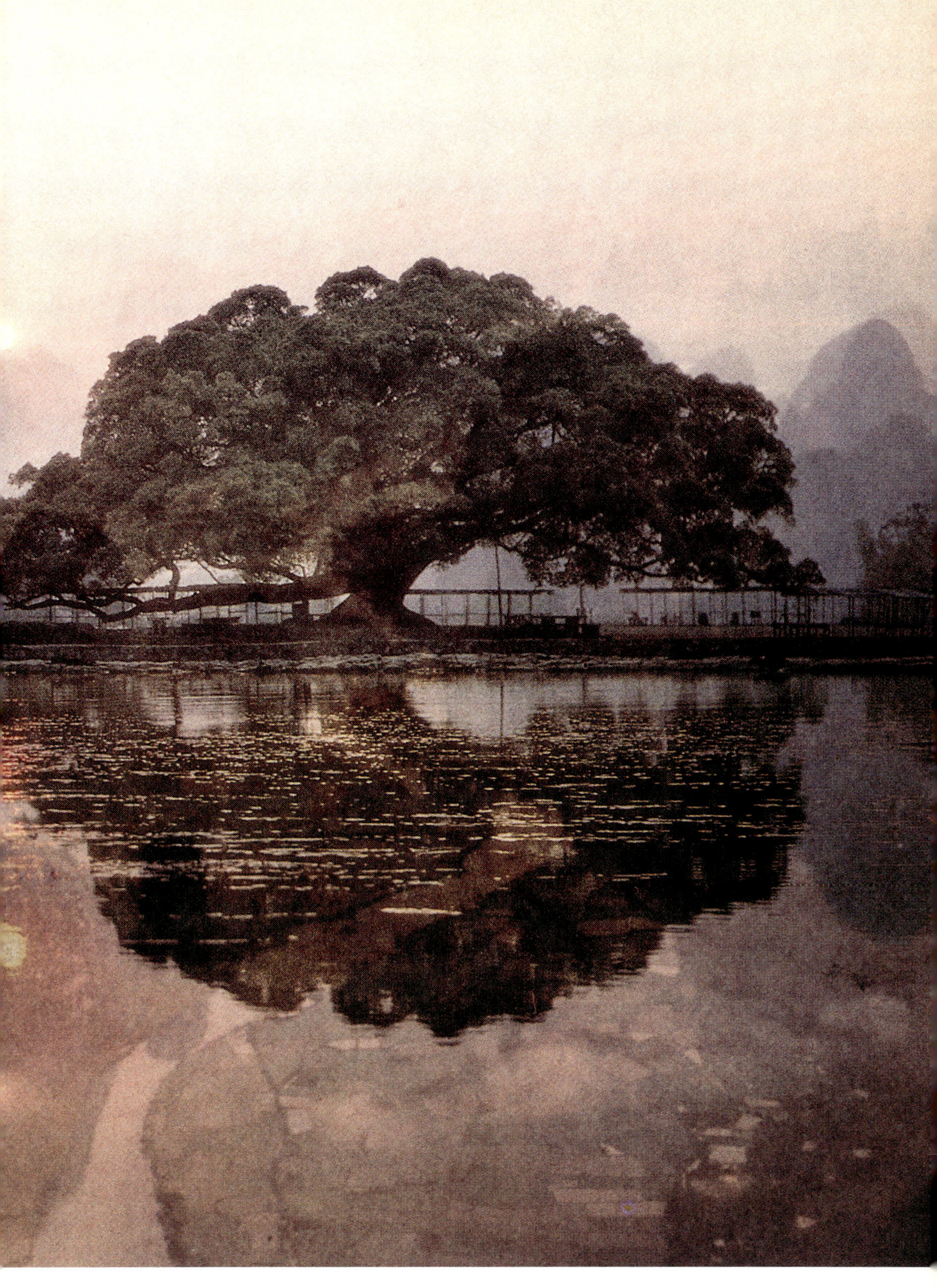

directions. Adelbert von Chamisso, *Peter Schlemiel: The Man Who Sold His Shadow*   We want genocide to have begun and ended with Nazism. That is what is most comforting. Sven Lindqvist, *Exterminate All The Brutes*   As I have had three severe fever attacks in the space of thirty-four hours I took 4 grains of quinine (0.5 per dose). In reality New Guinea's true guardians are not the natives, not the tropical heat and not the dense forest; the indigenous population's most powerful ally in its defence against outside invaders is the pale, cold shudder and then the raging fever. Nikolai Mikloucho-Maclay, *Bei den Papuas*   Before the British H-Bomb test at Maralinga, the Army posted 'Keep Out!' signs, in English, for Aboriginals to read. Not everyone saw them or could read English. Bruce Chatwin,

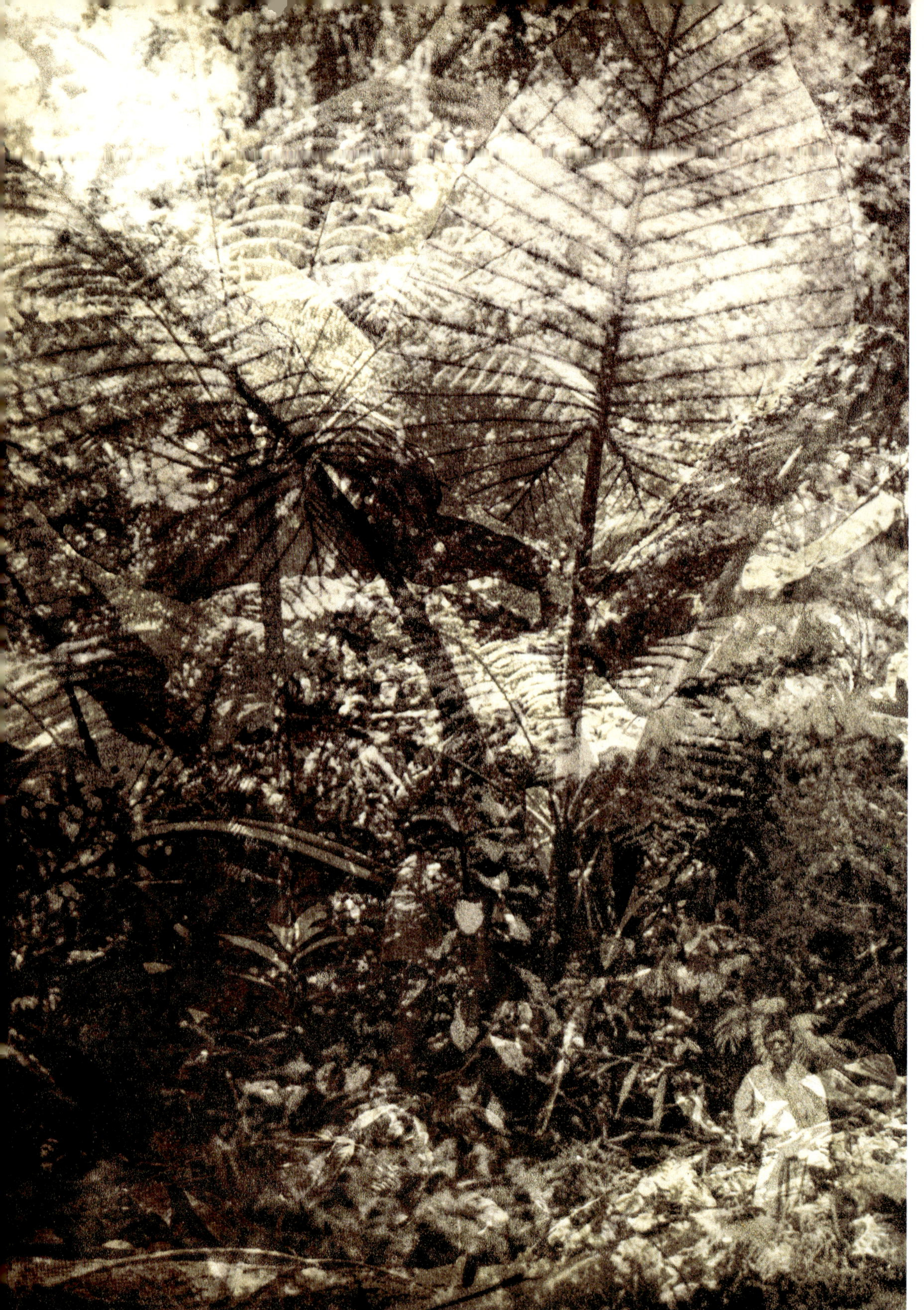

 "Whooo!" he says, turning to Johnson. But Johnson, along with Dassoud and every-one in sight, is bolting headlong in the opposite direction. He stands there, puzzled. "What's the rush?" he shouts. "It's nothing but a little breeze." The wind whistles. The sky goes dark. A hut skitters by. And then he hears it – a harsh sibilance, a spitting ticking release of air, as if all Edinburgh, Glasgow and the Borderlands had turned out to hiss the villain in a melodrama. All at once he's terrified. He takes to his legs – but too late! WHOMP! The horse blows down. And then he is himself knocked to his knees, suddenly stung in every pore of his body as if he'd blundered into a hive of bees. Sand! It's a sandstorm! T. Coraghessan Boyle, Water Music

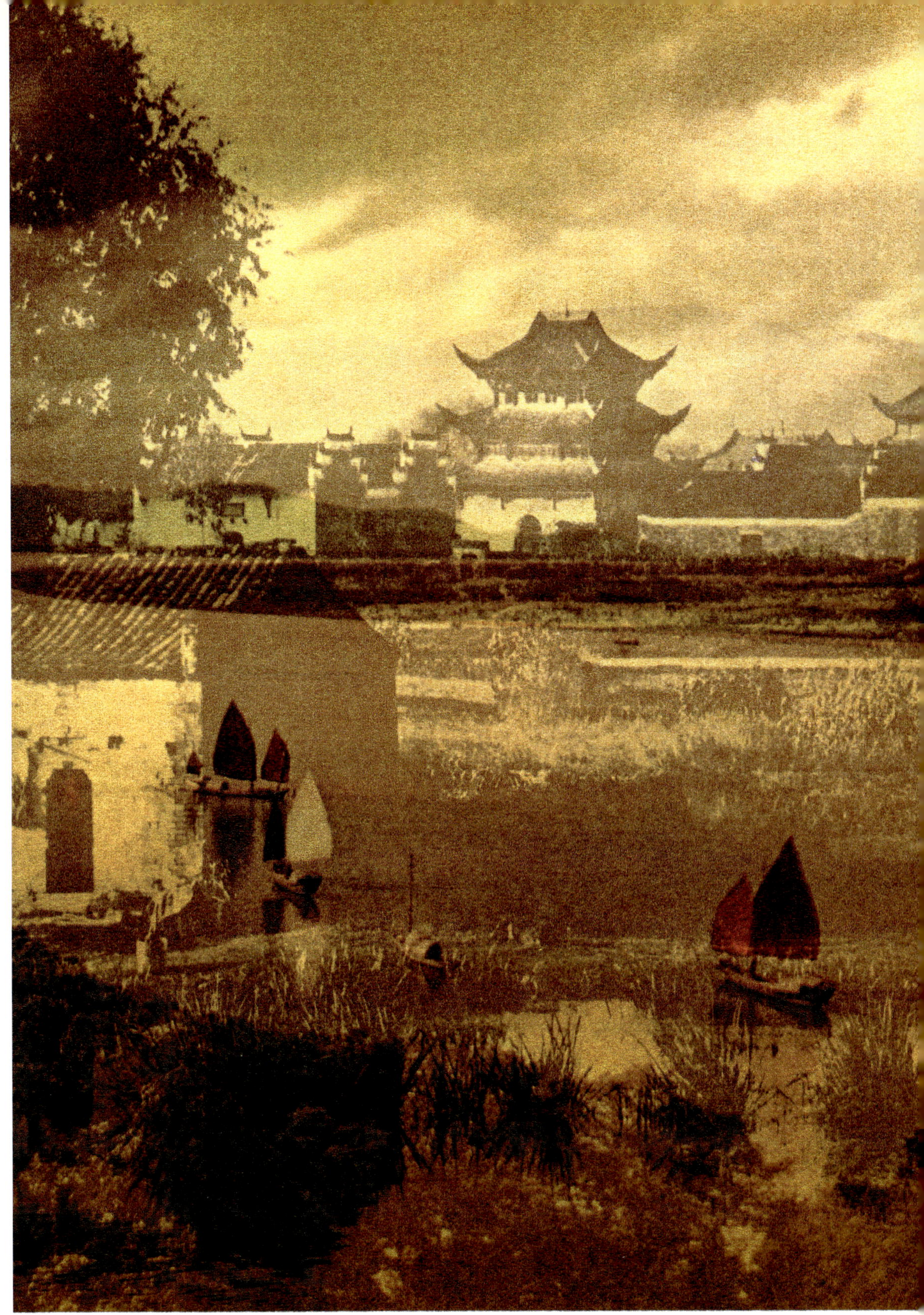

"In the Arabian desert. We are lost. I write your name in the sand. I love the desert. There is so much space to write your name. We're very thirsty but the mood is good. Indeed all explorers are agreed that one is always rescued at the very last minute. I hope your Mother is not suffering unduly from the dampness." Romain Gary, *Grüße vom Kilimandscharo* The extravagance of gesture, precipitating of every act, abruptness in issuing orders, baseless fears, and a desire to rush along the road, as though pursued by some phantom, all are evidence of the change that is being wrought, and are symptoms of the malady known as African spleen. Hermengildo Capelo & Roberto Ivens, in: Johannes Fabian, *Out of Our Minds* The black and white stripes of the zebra are like a

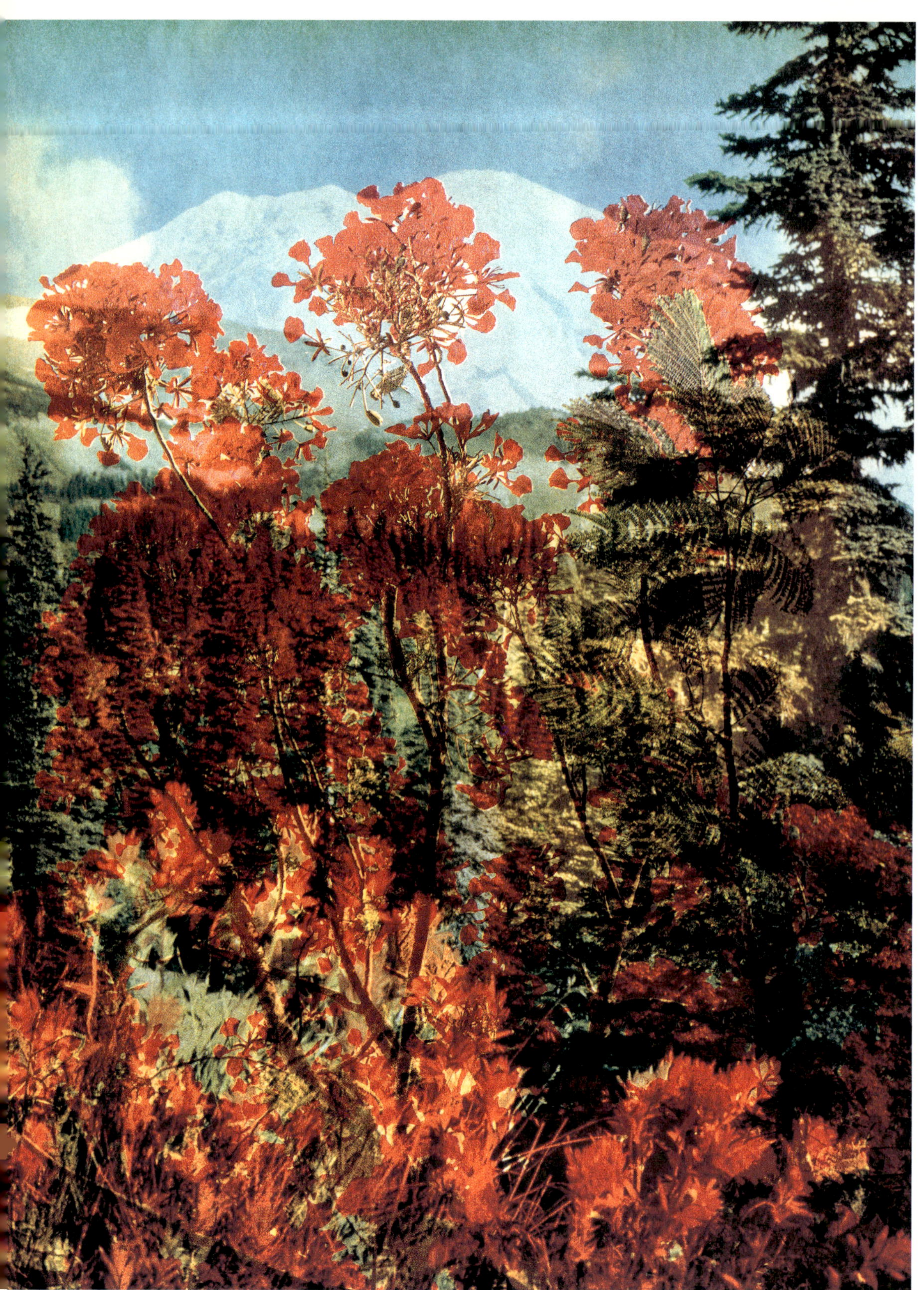

butterfly's wings, where two fingers pressed too hard are sufficient to destroy its colours. At last our cares succeeded in keeping these bewitched fellows in order, though it was no less difficult to keep the command of ourselves. One single Frenchman, who was my cook, having found means to escape against my orders, soon returned more dead than alive. He had hardly set his feet on shore, with the fair whom he had chosen, when he was immediately surrounded by a croud of Indians, who undressed him from head to feet. Around 1560, Rouen, Montaigne met three Brazilian Indians who had been brought back by a navigator, and he asked one of them what privileges the chief

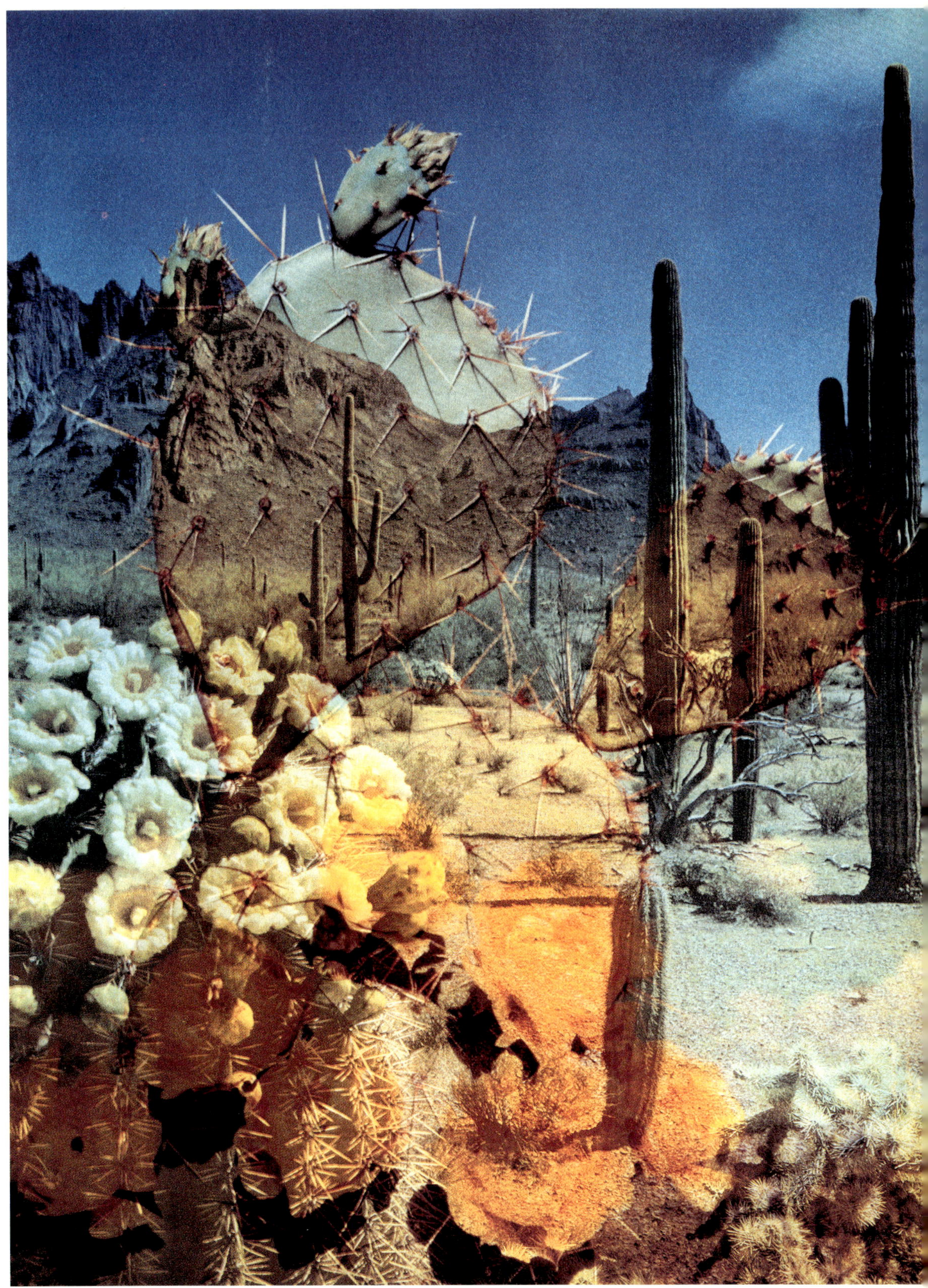

(he used the term 'king') enjoyed in his country; the native, who was himself a chief, replied that 'it was to march foremost in any charge of warre'. Claude Lévi-Strauss, *Tristes Tropiques*   The garrison the Jesuits maintained on this rock was there not merely to protect the missions against Caribbean incursions; they were used also for offensives or – as they say here – for the conquest of souls. The soldiers, spurred on by offers of pecuniary rewards, conducted armed attacks or entradas into the territory of independent Indians. Whoever dared to resist was put to death; huts were burned to the ground; plantations destroyed; and the old were taken captive as were women and children. Alexander von Humboldt, *Auf Steppen und Strömen Südamerikas*

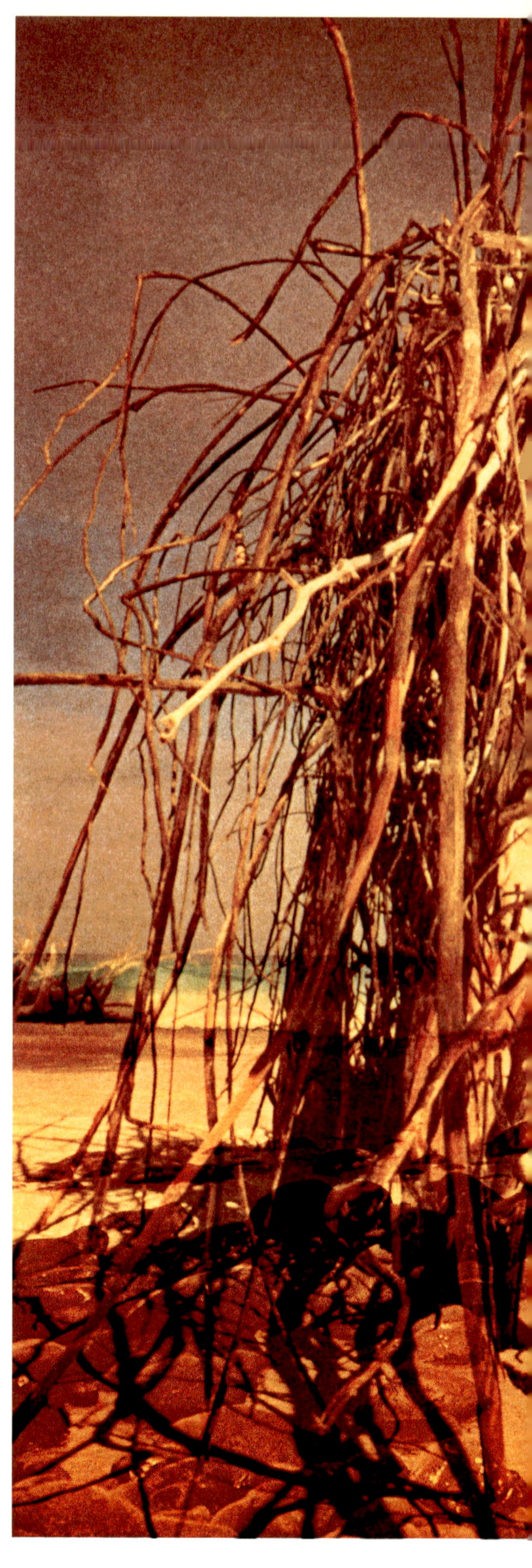

My ancestors stole land from the Indians. They got more from the government and cheated other settlers too, so I became heir to a great estate. Saul Bellow, *Henderson the Rain King* The mason who finishes the cornice of the palace returns at night perchance to a hut not so good as a wigwam. It is a mistake to suppose that, in a country where the usual evidences of civilization exist, the condition of a very large body of the inhabitants may not be as degraded as that of savages. Henry David Thoreau, *Walden* During precolonial times, and hence not so long ago, more than ten thousand little states, kingdoms, ethnic unions, and federations existed in Africa. Roland Oliver, a historian at the University of London, draws attention to a general paradox in

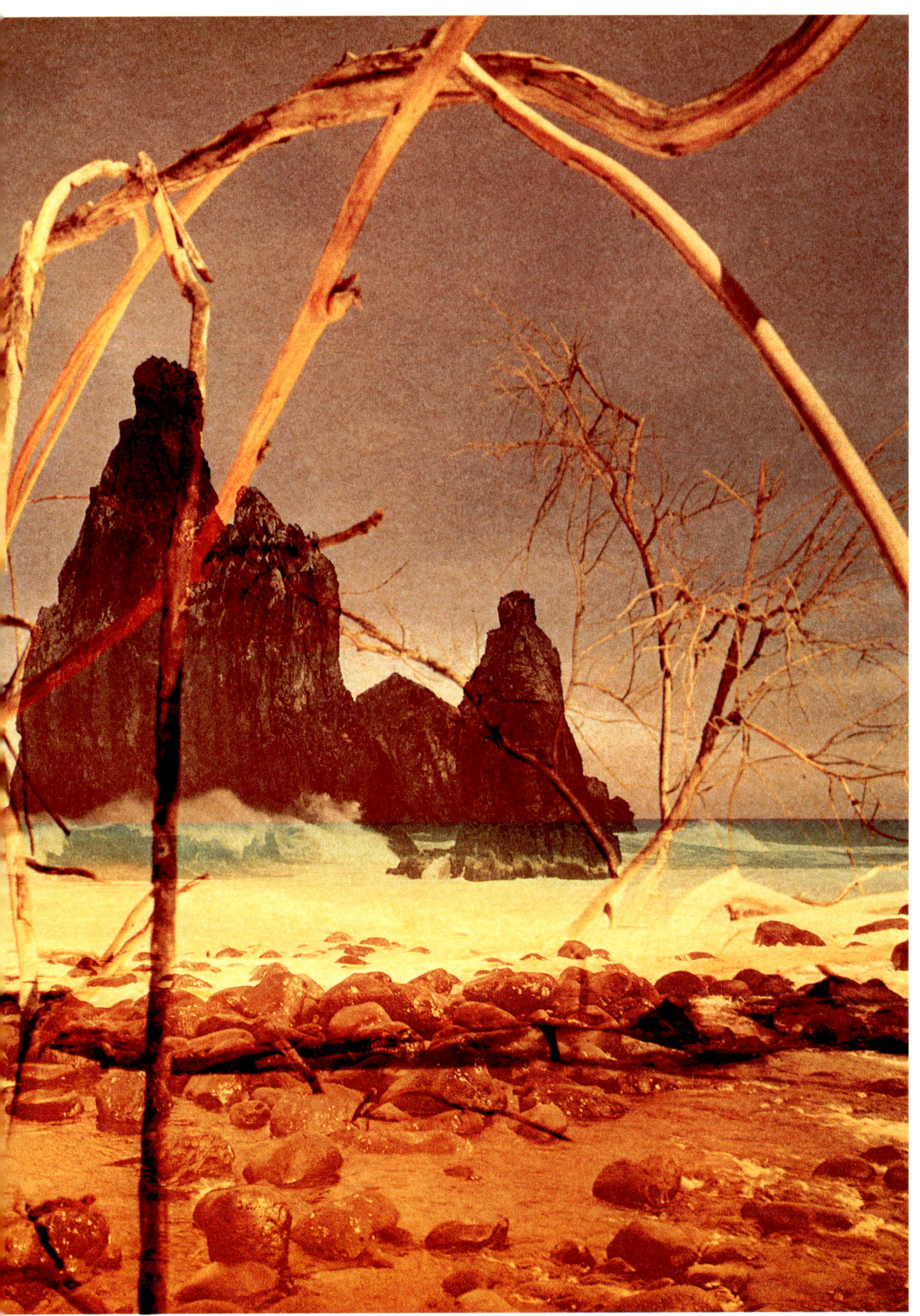

his book, *The African Experience* (1991): it has become common parlance to say that European colonialists partitioned Africa. Partitioned? Oliver marvels. Colonialism was a brutal unification, brought about by fire and sword! Ten thousand entities were reduced to fifty. Ryszard Kapuściński, *The Shadow of the Sun* When Moor's blacksmith, no longer a prisoner of war, returned home from Africa that stark autumn, Bering could say about three dozen words, but with greater enthusiasm he could cry recognizable imitations of several birdcalls – he *was* a chicken, was a collared dove, was a screech-owl. This was in the second year of peace. Christoph Ransmayr, *The Dog King* When Girolamo Benzoni visited Las Palmas in 1541, there was one single Guanche left, eighty-

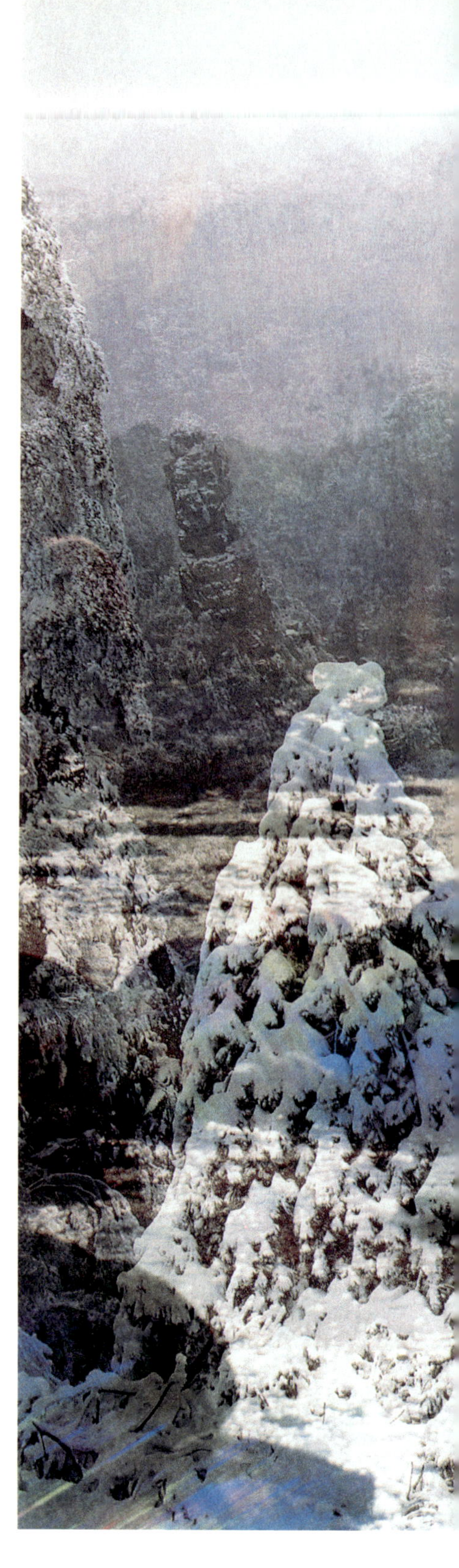

one years old and permanently drunk. The Guanches had gone under. This group of islands in the eastern Atlantic was the kindergarten for European imperialism. Beginners learned there that European people, plants, and animals manage very well even in areas where they did not exist by nature. They also learned that although the indigenous inhabitants are superior in numbers and put up bitter resistance, they are conquered, yes, exterminated – without anyone really knowing how it happened. Sven Lindqvist, *Exterminate All The Brutes* He would halt for a moment, to quench the sound of his own movement, when the silence about him would be absolute, complete, a wadded soundlessness, as it were, elsewhere all unknown. There was no stir of air,

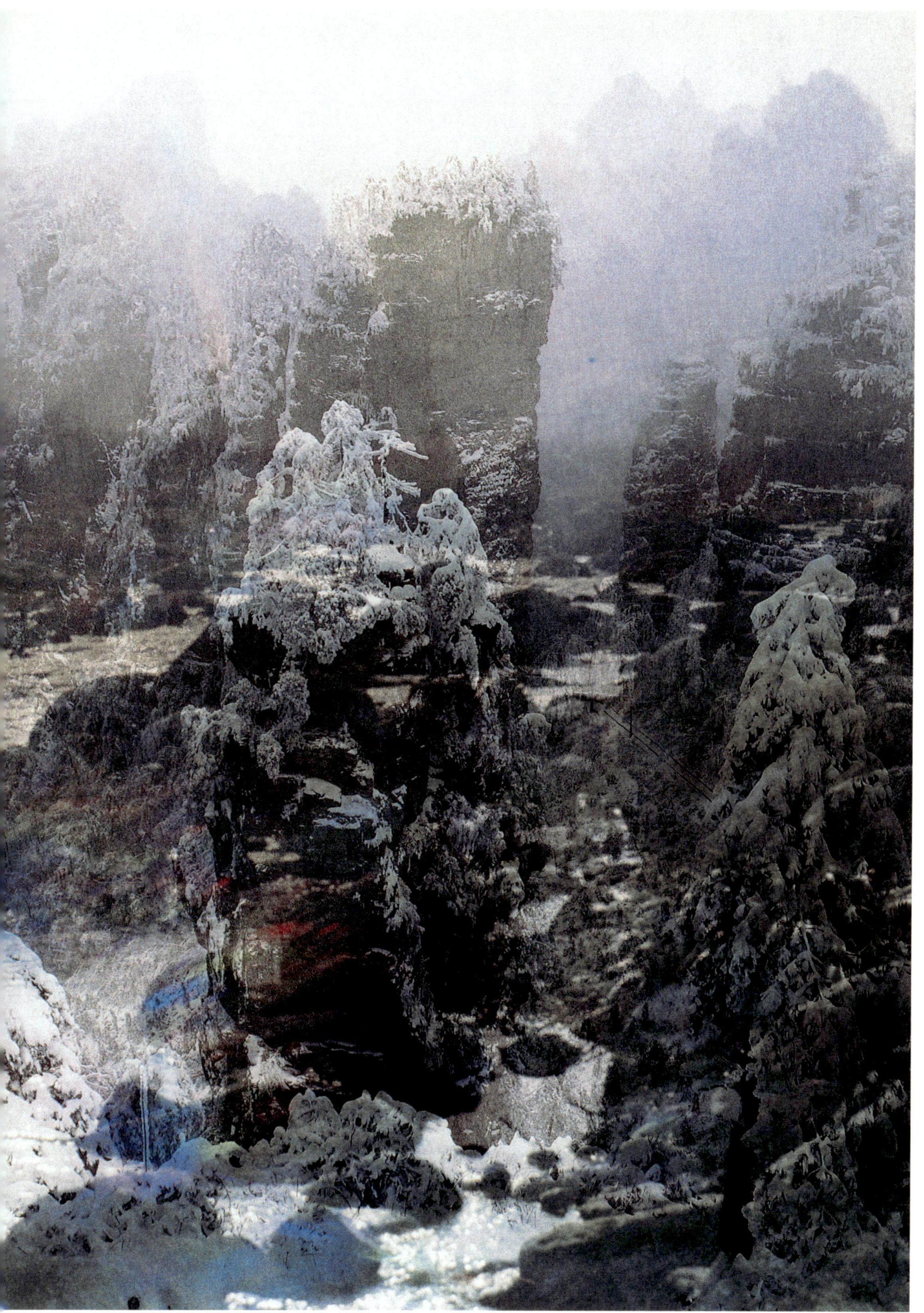

not so much as might even lightly sway the tree-boughs; there was not a rustle, nor the voice of a bird. It was primeval silence to which Hans Castorp hearkened, when he leaned thus on his staff, his head on one side, his mouth open. And always it snowed, snowed without pause, endlessly, gently, soundlessly falling. Thomas Mann, *The Magic Mountain* Indeed we soon came upon a small grey-black hut which had been built utterly artlessly into the hillside, out of stacked stones. The front of the hut rose up barely man-high above the ground; there were no windows, but a low door. Out of it there stepped a man, Robinson Crusoe-like in appearance, clad in animal skins, hair tousled, unwashed, perhaps for many moons. He appeared most

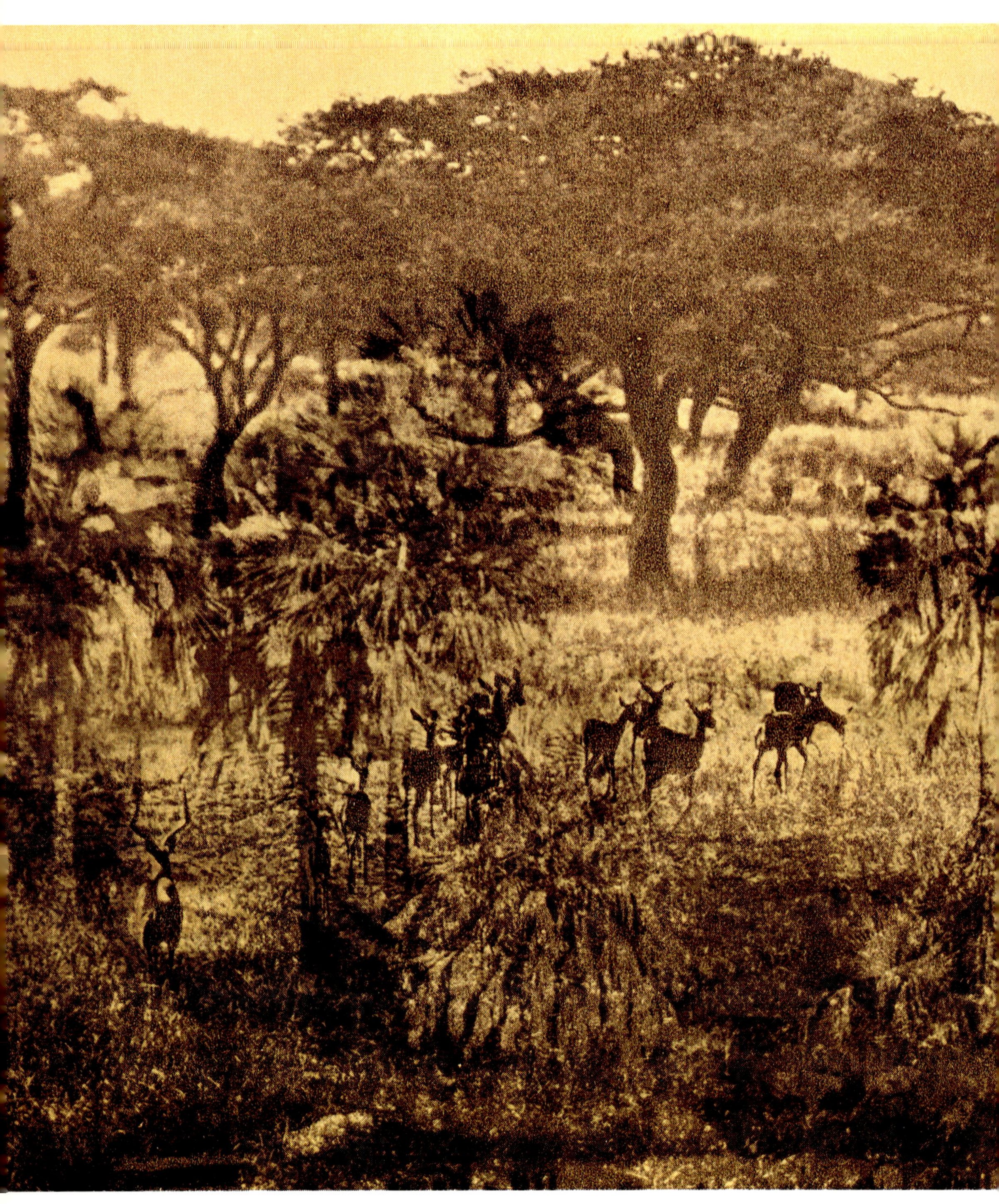

pleased that we had made the arduous journey to reach him, and we were no less pleased to make such a pleasant impression upon him. At first we had stopped short at the sight of him; yet he was another glorious example that a most noble heart could beat under such a humble smock, for not only did he greet us most warmly and with the broadest of smiles, he promptly offered us a dirty bowlful of milk. Ludwig Steub, Alpenreisen   His hut, a triumph of contemporary mud-and-wattle architecture, shared a common wall with the stockade erected round the factory, and the firelight lit the tips of the pointed timbers till they glowed like a row of filed teeth. T. Coraghessan Boyle, Water Music   The young African states know that besides the sun, they can sell their

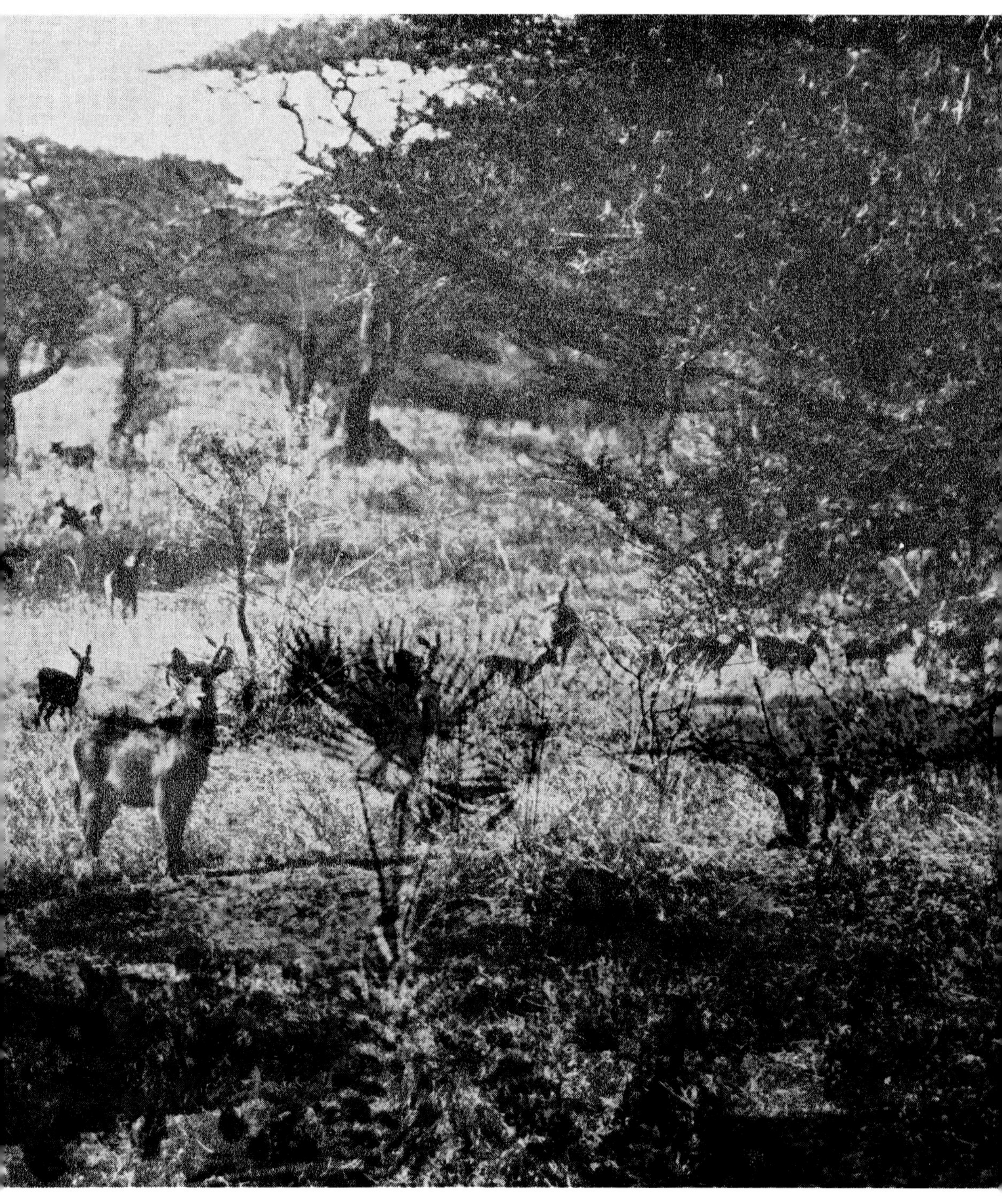

fauna in exchange for a strong currency. This is how the number of safaris, which allow some rich guy from Via Montenapoleone or Fifth Avenue to murder (murder being the operative word in this case, given the beauty, greatness and innocence of the animal which poses no risk to the hunter) an elephant or a leopard, will increase. Until the total extinction of the species. In short, Africa is disappearing for ever. Just the change of terminology used to describe Africa is proof of this. A century ago Africa was "mysterious". Today it is simply "depressed". Alberto Moravia, *A quale tribù appartieni?* The people are rather disgruntled with their behaviour. They remember the atrocities they committed, in the dens of T'ien-tsin; where women from the realm of the

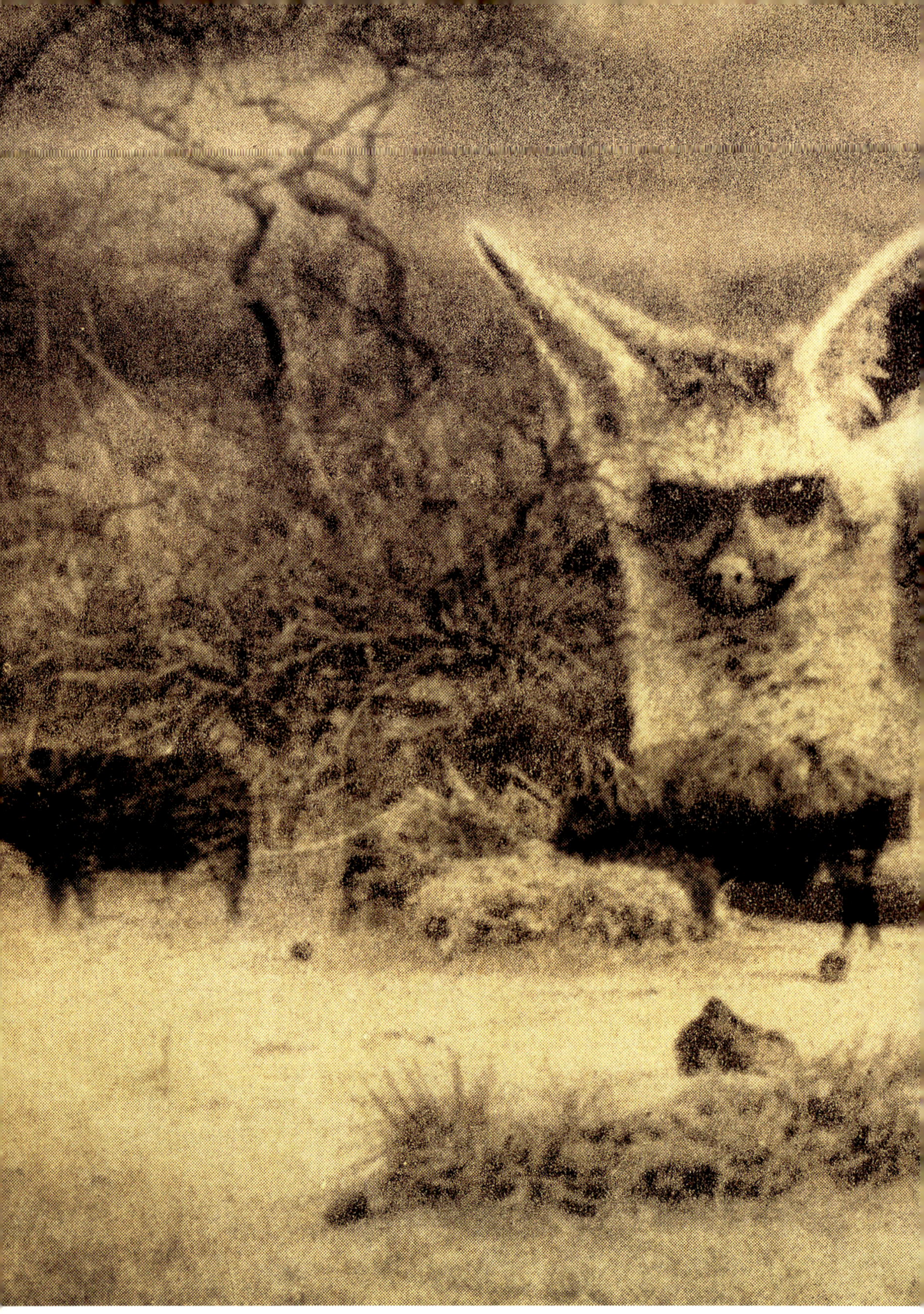

Franks, consecrated to a virginhood that no single triumphal arch or oath of consecration had marked, picked up begging children and plucked out their eyes. Thereafter they hardened the eyes, and used them in those truly ingenious instruments that allow one to see over vast distances. – No doubt, when they were massacred, no blind children were found among them. Without a doubt they had been killed. – That is what the people say. Victor Segalen, *Le fils du ciel*
Cornelius Vroom, the Patriarch of this restless House-hold, is an Admirer of the legendary Botha brothers, a pair of gin-drinking, pipe-smoking Nimrods of the generation previous whose great Joy and accomplishment lay in the hunting and slaughter of animals much larger than

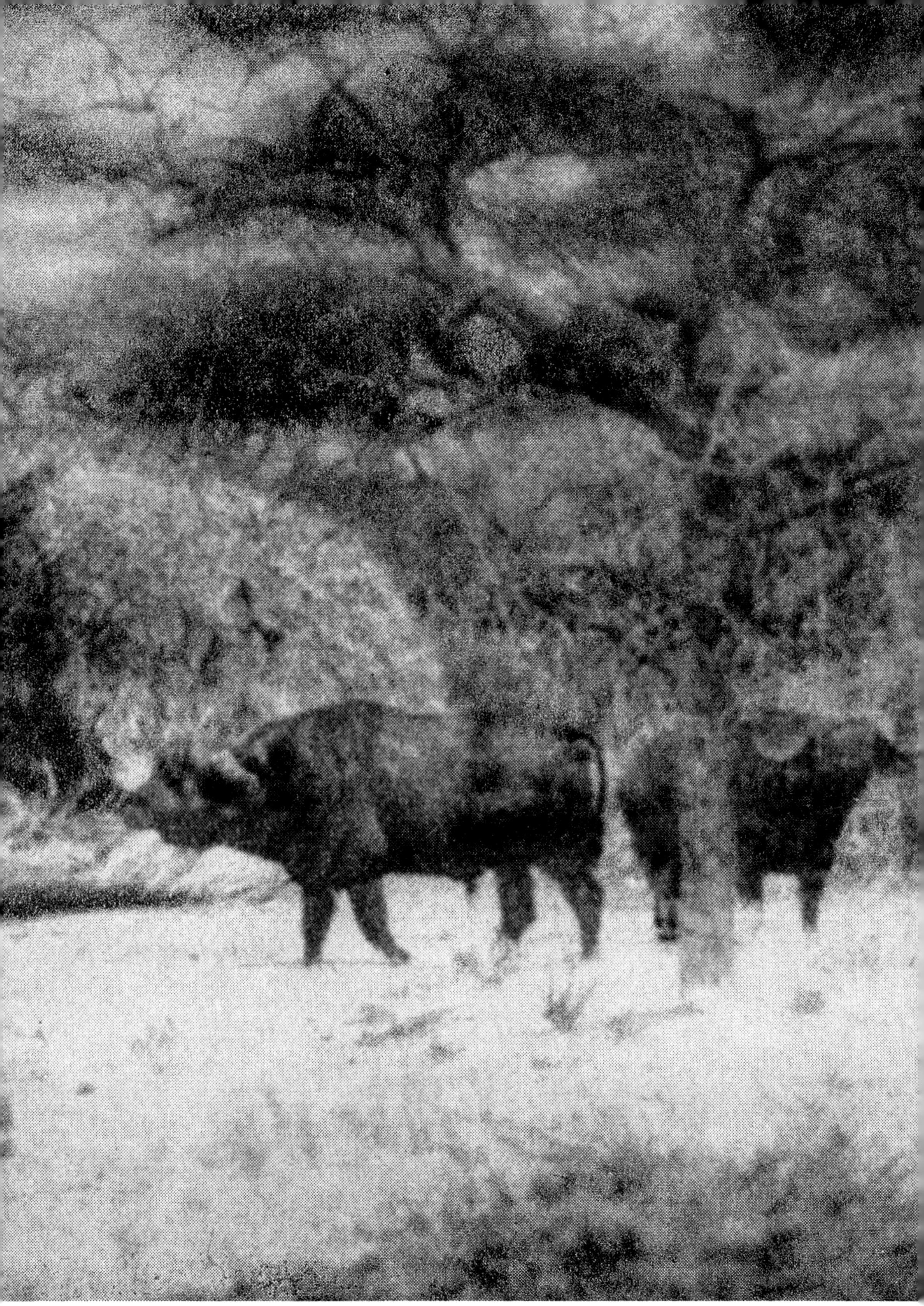

they. Vroom is a bottomless archive of epic adventures out in the unmapped wilds of Hottentot Land, some of which may even hold a gleam of truth, in among the narrative rubbish-tip of this Arm-chair Commando, wherein the mad Rhino forever rolls his eye, the killer Trunk stands erect and a-bellow, and the cowardly Kaffirs turn and flee, whilst the Dutchman lights his Pipe, and stands his Ground. Thomas Pynchon, *Mason & Dixon*   There were four goats, a parrot and a cage full of monkeys in the canoe, in addition to six other passengers and a dozen earthenware jars of produce. When Mungo asked what the monkeys were for, the ferryman grinned to display a gleaming mouthful of teeth. "Bake them," he said. "Make monkey bread." T. Coraghessan Boyle, *Water Music*

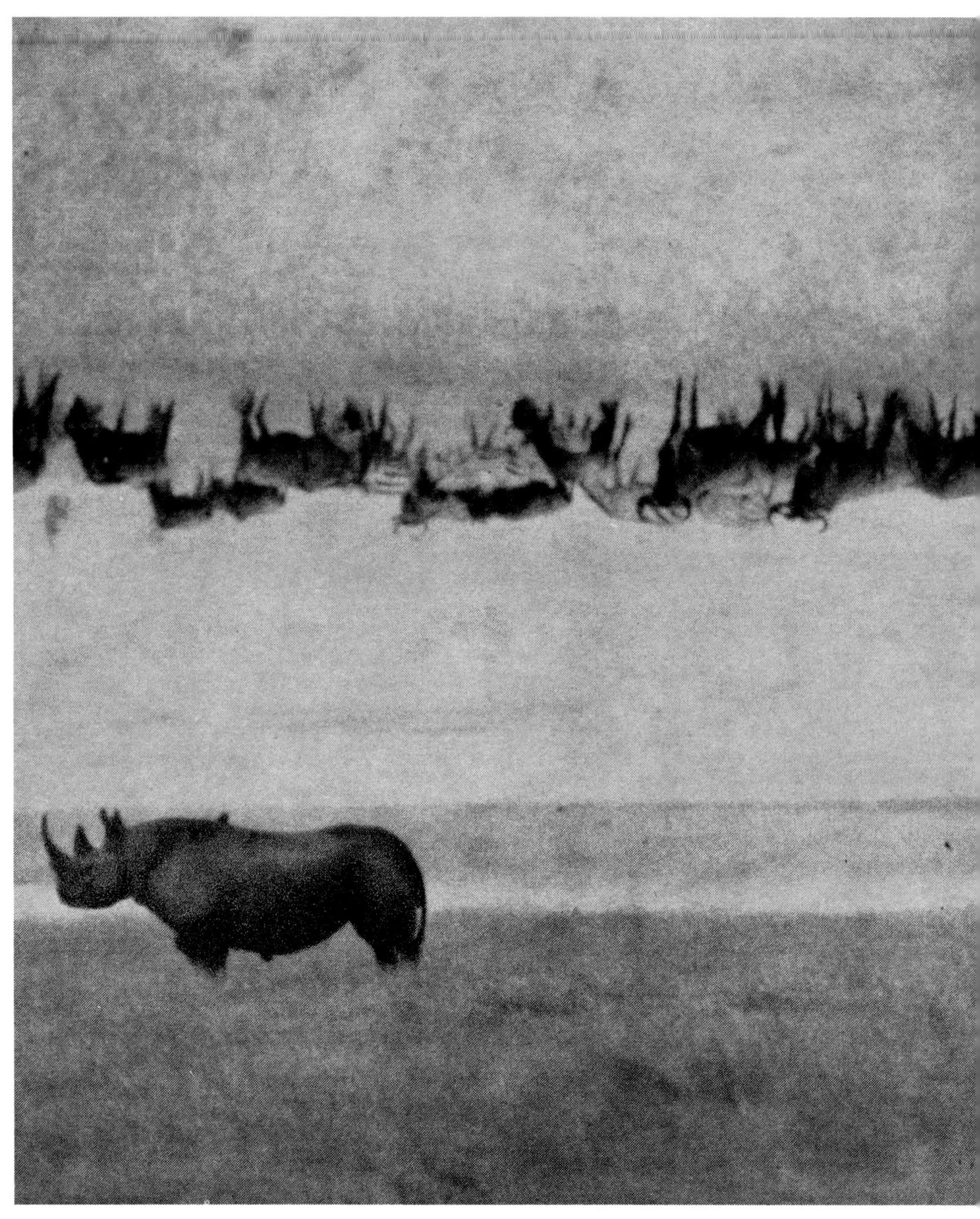

It was no longer necessary to send out dirty yokels in coonskin caps to chart the wilderness, kill the abos, and clear-cut the groves; now all you needed was a hot young geotect, a start matter compiler, and a jumbo Source. Neal Stephenson, *The Diamond Age* It's not true, I am told, that Bokassa (who today is the guest of the President of the Ivory Coast, yet another puppet who runs the country on behalf of French multinationals) ate only children. The Emperor preferred the twenty-year-olds at his court. If he had his eye on a new recruit, he would have him well fed so that whenever he saw him standing to attention, his mouth would start to water, and then he would promote him to the rank of sergeant. From that moment onwards the

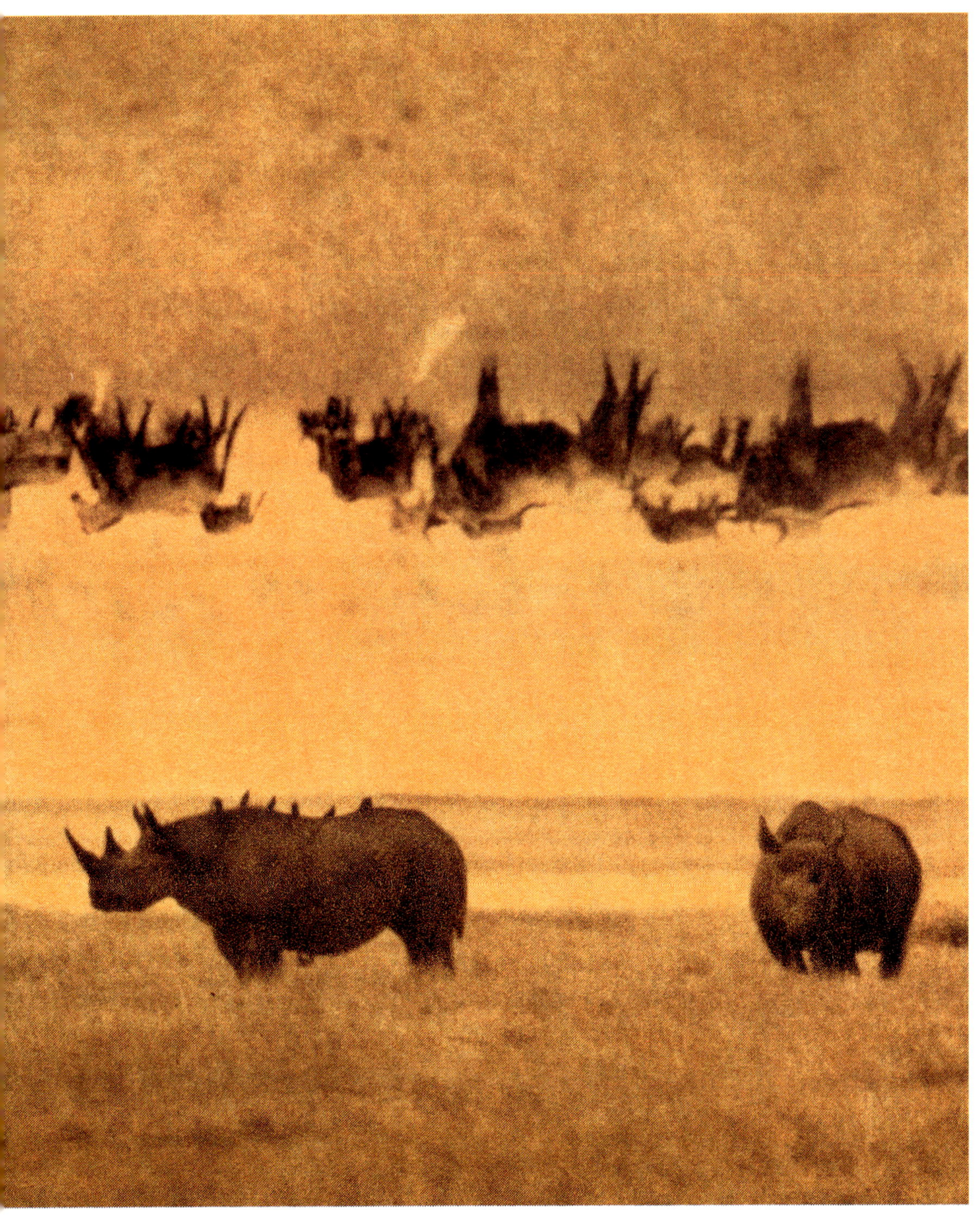

sergeant was virtually already in the frying pan. On the first demeanour Bokassa would have
him thrown into prison. And it was only a stone's throw from the prison cell to the freezer cell.
Sergio Saviane, *Auf Safari in Bokassaland* About five million of the indigenous American population lived in
what is now the United States. At the beginning of the nineteenth century, half a million still
remained. In 1891, at the time of Wounded Knee – the last great massacre of Indians in the
United States – the native population reached rock bottom: a quarter of a million, or 5 percent
of the original number of Indians. Sven Lindqvist, *Exterminate All The Brutes* "Indianapolis, Indiana," said
Constant, "is the first place in the United States of America where a white man was hanged

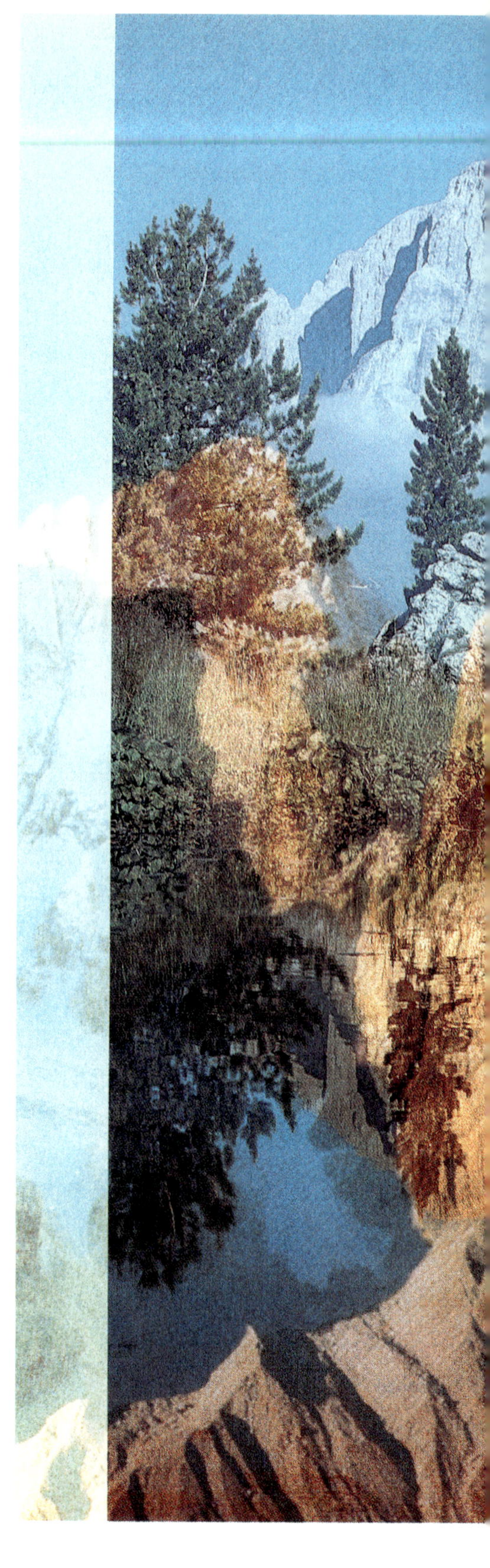

for the murder of an Indian. The kind of people who'll hang a white man for murdering an Indian –" said Constant, "that's the kind of people for me." Kurt Vonnegut, *The Sirens of the Titan* After having studied the sources, I no longer think opiates alone could carry the story of ecstasis in exploration. Myriads of causes made travelers lose control, if that is the point of searching for ecstatic elements in the production of knowledge. As such evidence accumulates, drugs – a problematic term under any circumstances – lose some of their fascination. Johannes Fabian, *Out of Our Minds* The acme, however, of all earthly enjoyments would seem to be *meat*. "Meat! meat!" is the watchword that resounds in all their campaigns. Georg Schweinfurth, *The Heart of Africa* Sometimes

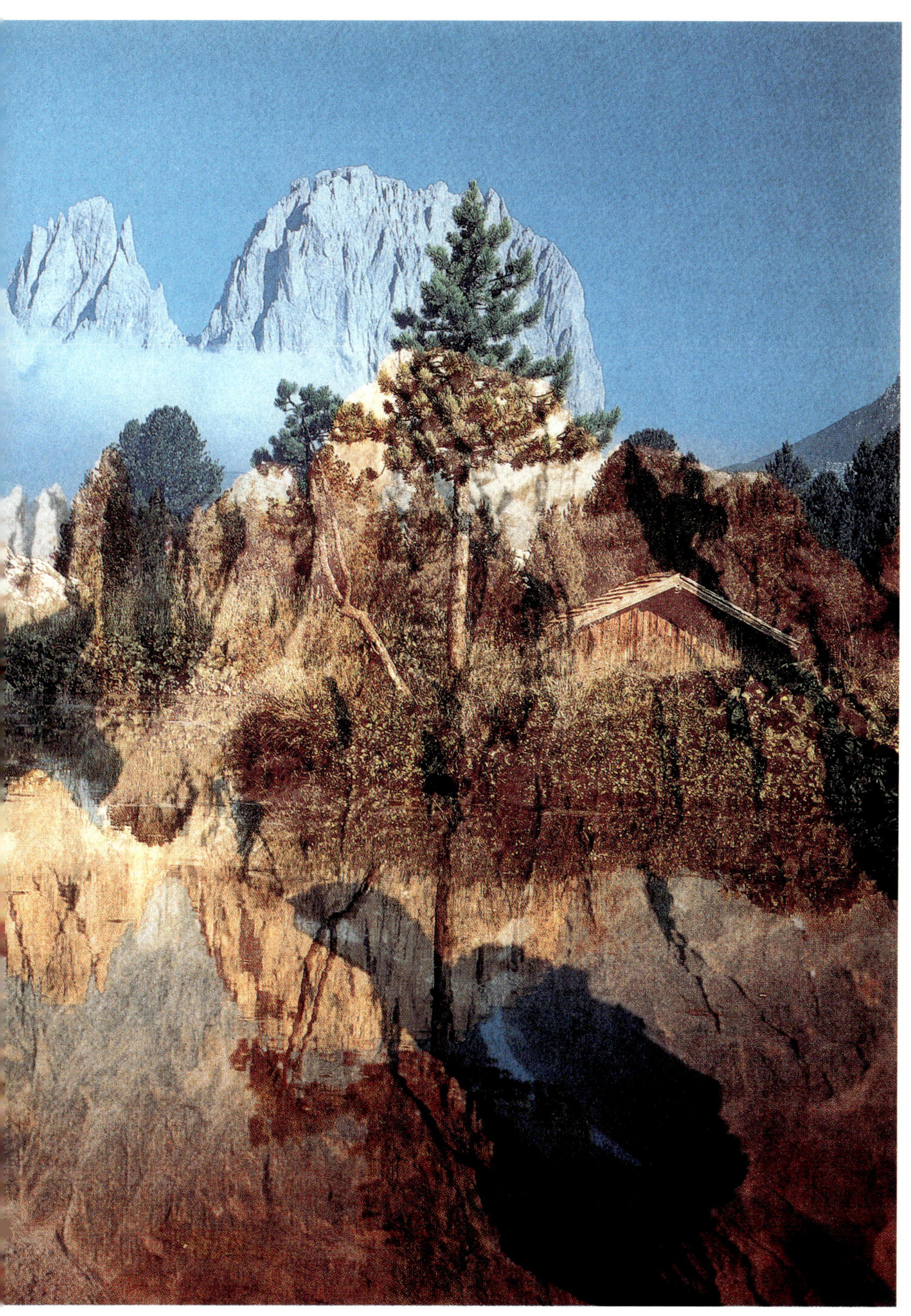

a nobleman beckons to his wedding celebrations one of their most reputable masters together with all his pupils. As they enter the guest room they sing religious songs and prayers yet by the close of the banquet the older ones begin to pull off their gowns and to dance. When one of the aged falls, one of the young pupils helps him up and kisses him, often in an unseemly way. This has given rise to a saying that everyone in Fez refers to: The banquet of the marabouts. It implies that after the feast each of these boys and youths becomes the consort of his teacher, for they are not permitted to marry. Johann Leo Africanus, *Beschreibung Afrikas* It is pleasing to observe, that there is now a benevolent association in England for the express purpose

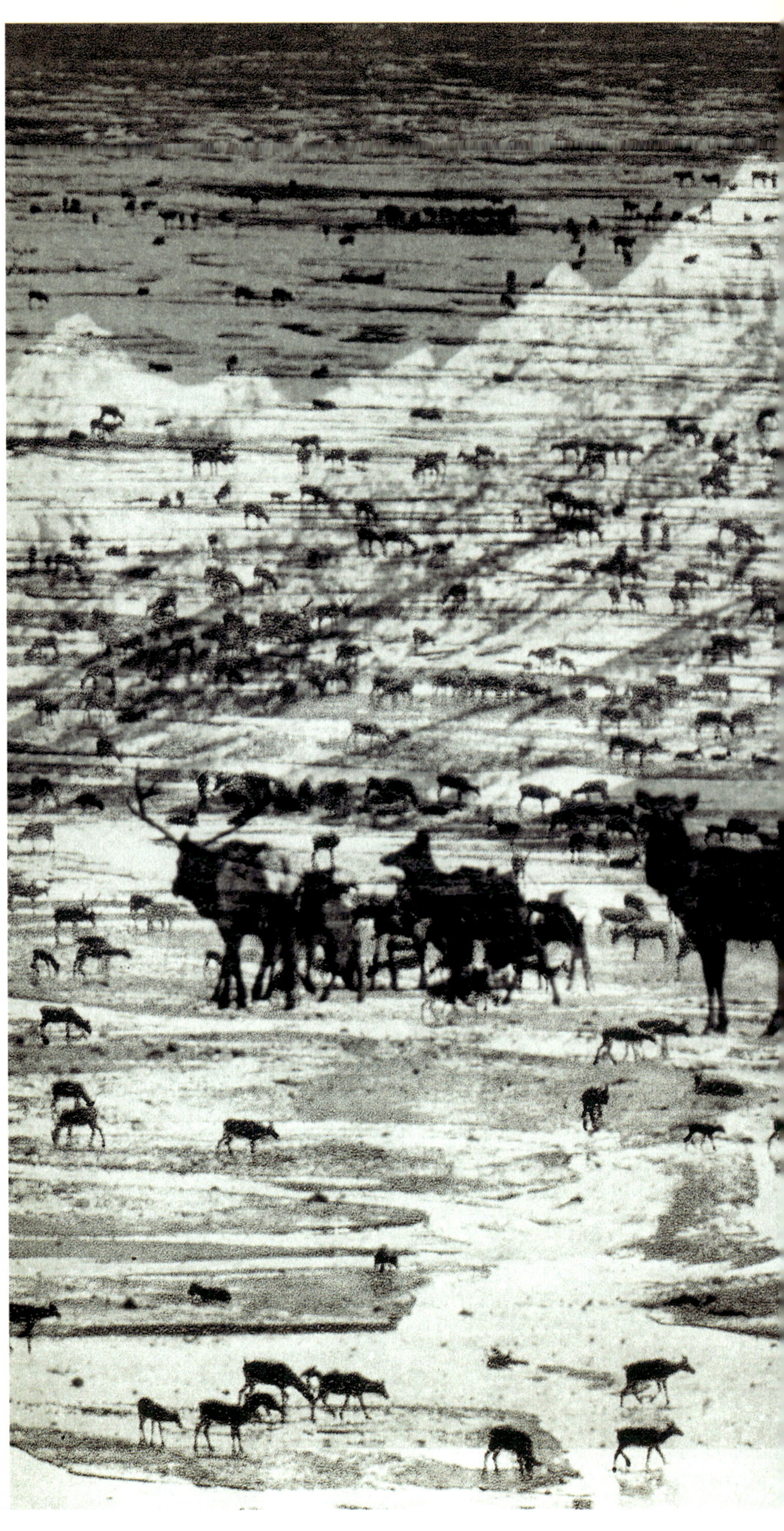

of instructing Chinese females at Malacca. *Charles Gutzlaff, Journal of Three Voyages Along the Coast of China*   Since the last war with the English the hatred against Europeans has been on the increase, and it has been embittered against the women by a Chinese prophecy, which declares that a woman shall one day conquer the Celestial Empire. I feared, therefore, that it would be to little purpose for me to remain in Canton … *Ida Pfeiffer, A Lady's Voyage Round the World*   The explorer thought to himself: It's always a ticklish matter to intervene decisively in other people's affairs. He was neither a member of the penal colony nor a citizen of the state to which it belonged. Were he to denounce this execution or actually try to stop it, they could say to him: You are a foreigner,

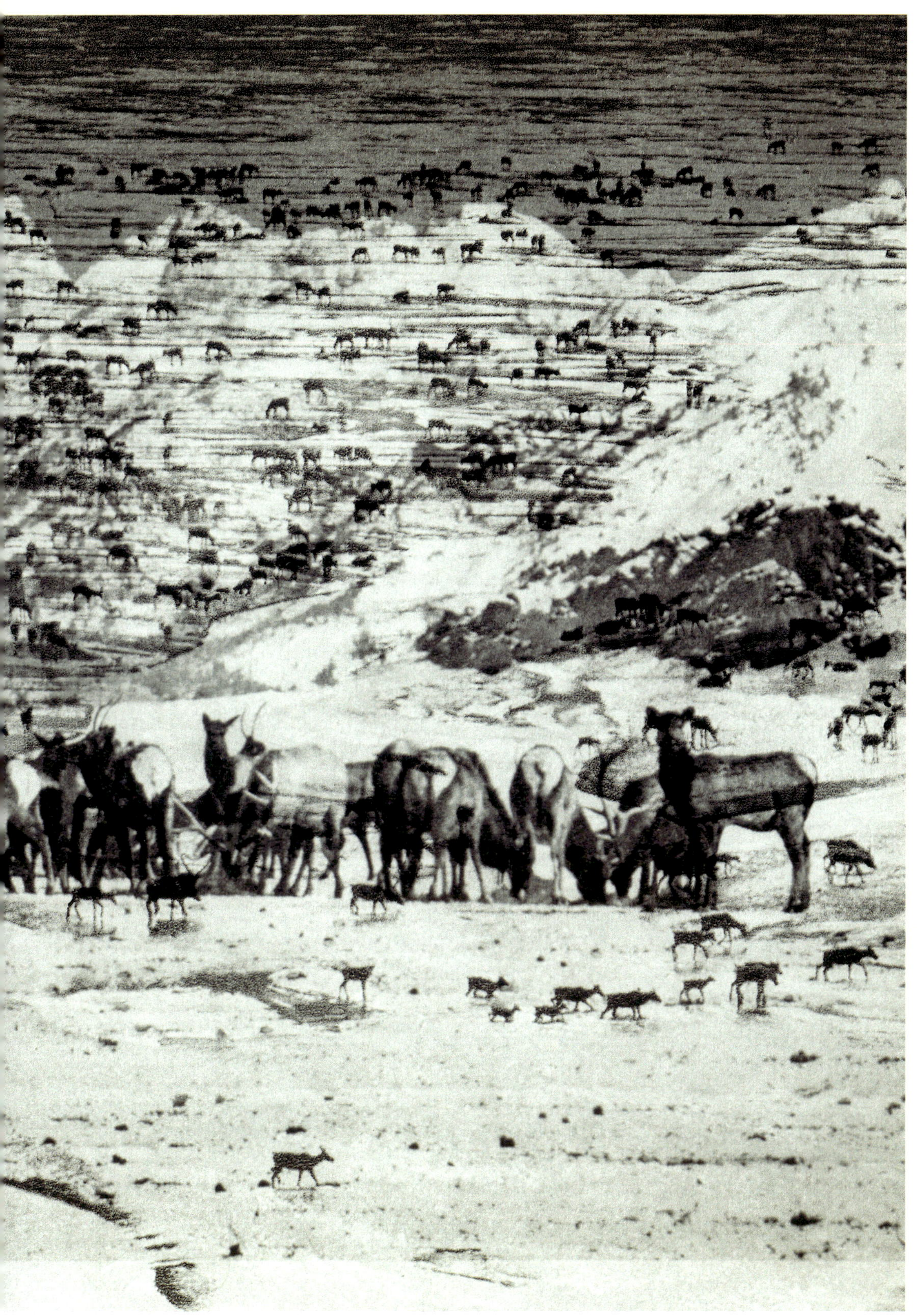

mind your own business. He could make no answer to that, unless he was to add that he was amazed at himself in this connection, for he traveled only as an observer, with no intention at all of altering other people's methods of administering justice. Franz Kafka, The Penal Colony Everywhere in the world where knowledge is being suppressed, knowledge that, if it were made known, would shatter our image of the world and force us to question ourselves – everywhere there, *Heart of Darkness* is being enacted. Sven Lindqvist, Exterminate All The Brutes The slave traders (mainly the Portuguese, the Dutch, English, French, Americans, Arabs, and their African partners) depopulated the continent and condemned it to a vegetative apathy: up to the present day,

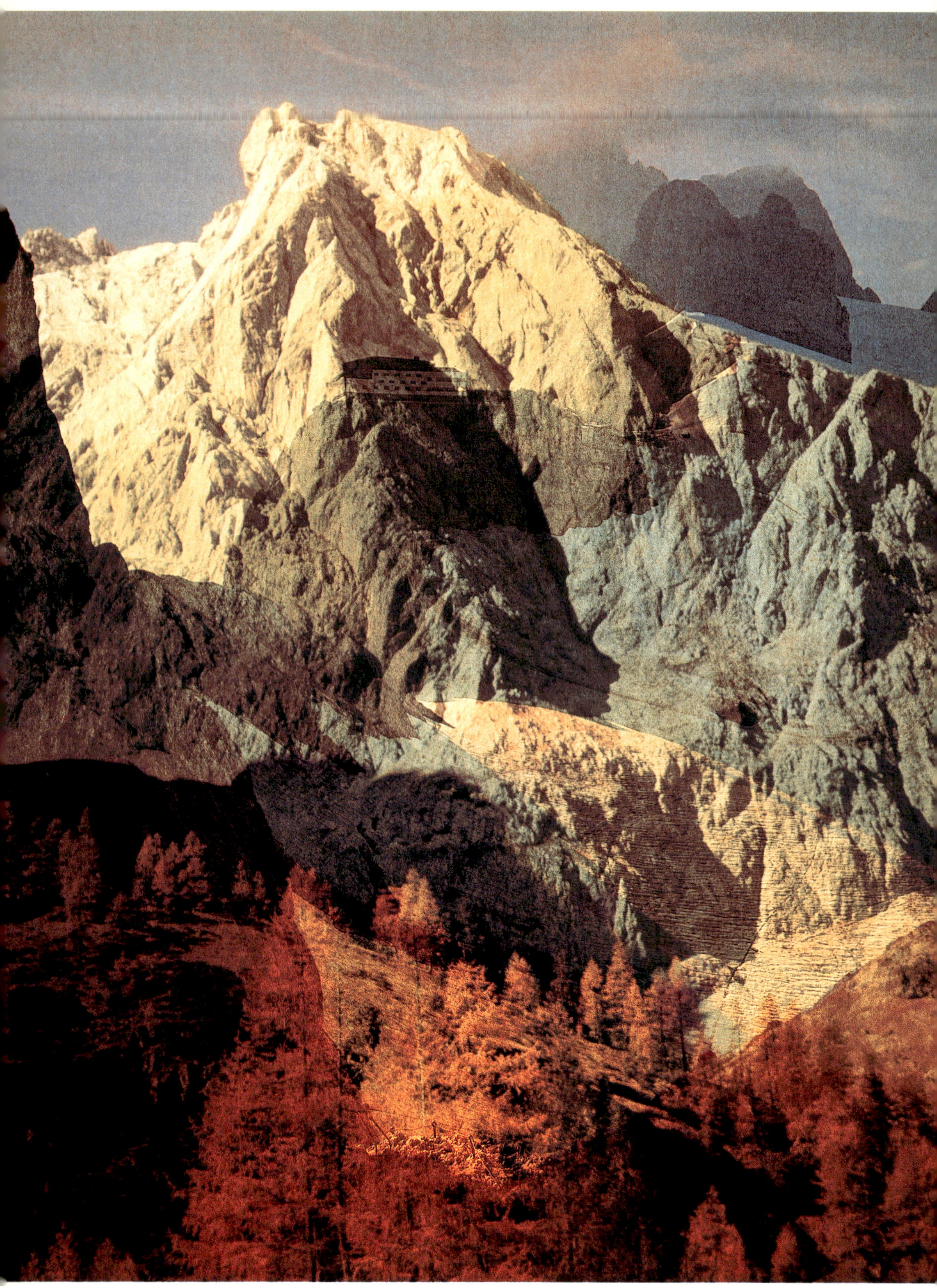

large stretches remain desolate, transformed into desert. To this day Africa has not recovered from this misfortune, from this nightmare. Ryszard Kapuściński, *The Shadow of the Sun* President Doumer has been assassinated. The Welsh captain, a very distracted person, suddenly announced it, and fetched the dispatches, which he'd received yesterday but had forgotten to tell us. Nothing new as far as the elections are concerned. Michel Leiris, *L'Afrique fantôme* Racism, hatred and contempt for others, and the desire to exterminate them, have their roots in African colonial relations. Everything was invented and honed there centuries before totalitarian systems grafted those grim and disgraceful impulses onto twentieth-century Europe. Ryszard Kapuściński, *The Shadow of the Sun*

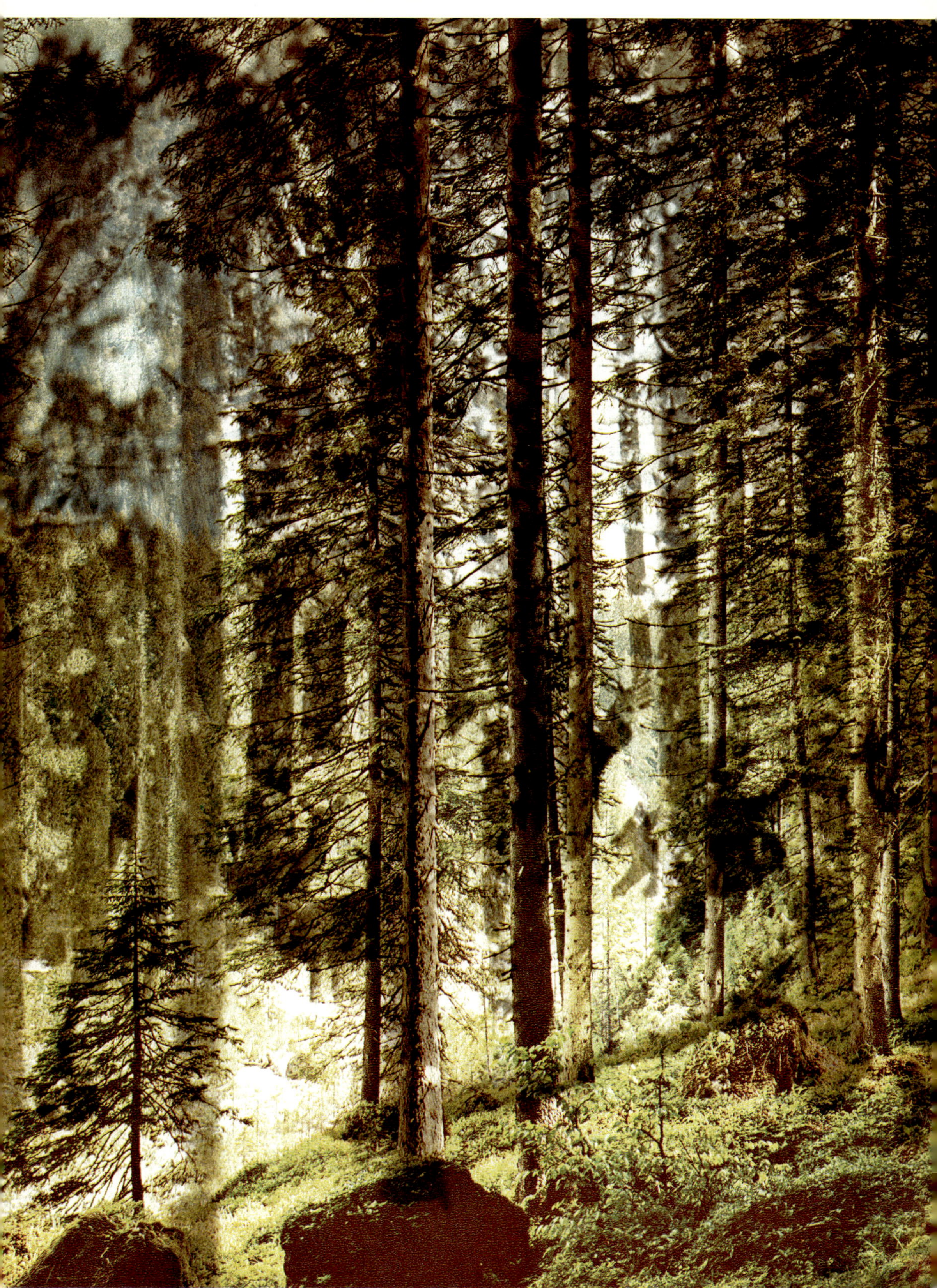

Congratulations on the Petromax lamp. Now we will not have to go to bed with Mr. Morrison's precious chickens. You should not have bought the evening gown. You will have no opportunity to wear it here. You are sadly mistaken if you think that people like the Rubenses will invite us to their parties. First, there is already a huge gap between the old, well-established, rich Jews and us poor refugees, and second, the Rubens family lives in Nairobi and that is further from Rongai than Breslau from Sohrau. Stefanie Zweig, *Nowhere in Africa*   "… They wanted something to take back to England where a reward is being offered for news of you. They were very pleased with it. And they took some photographs of the little cross I put up to commemorate your

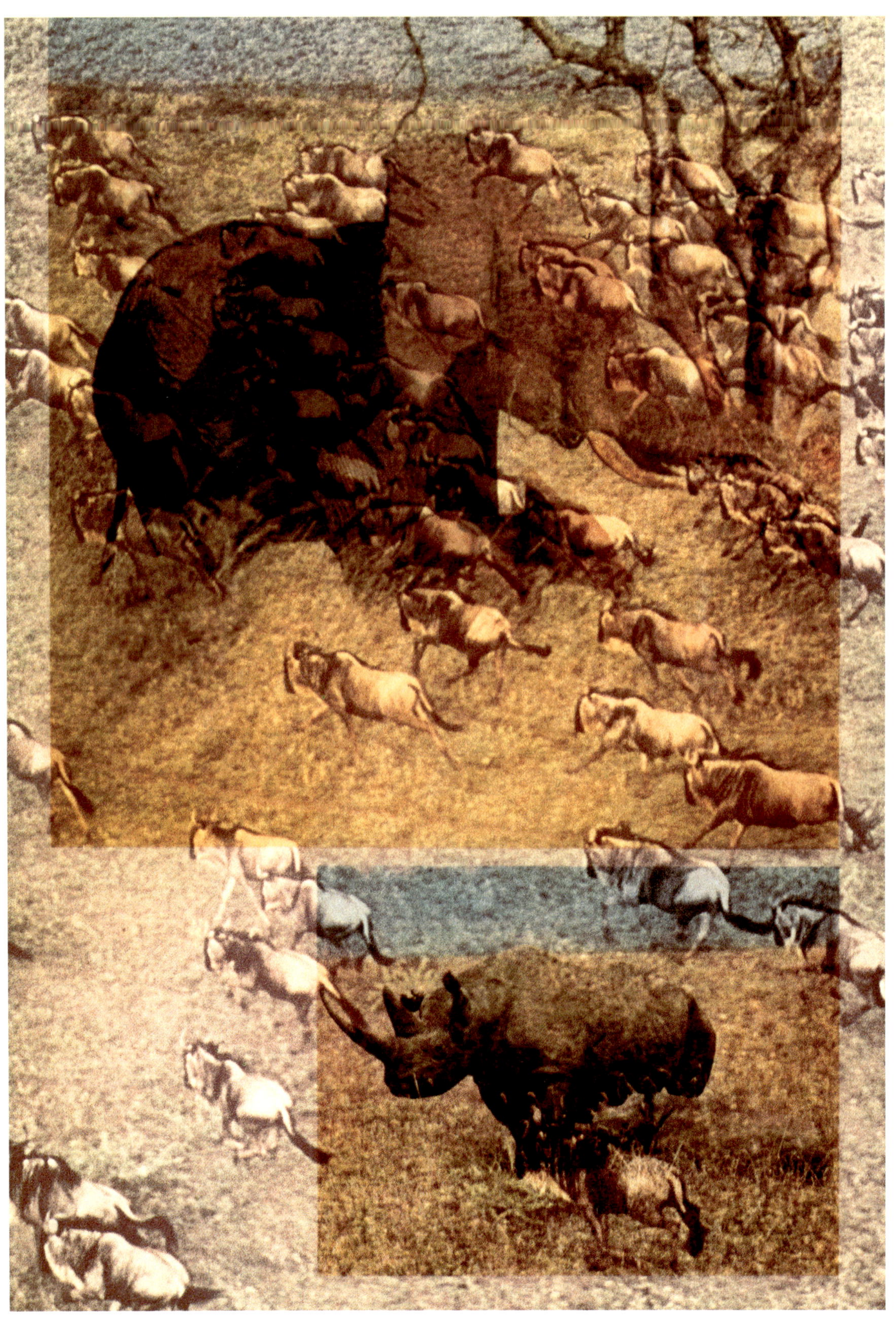

coming. They were pleased with that, too. They were very easily pleased. But I do not suppose they will visit us again, our life here is so retired … no pleasures except reading … I do not suppose we shall ever have visitors again … well, well, I will get you some medicine to make you feel better. Your head aches, does it not? … We will not have any Dickens today … but tomorrow, and the day after that, and the day after that. Let us read *Little Dorrit* again. There are passages in that book I can never hear without the temptation to weep." Evelyn Waugh, *A Handful of Dust* What had brought everything to such an abrupt halt was the discovery of the chrono-synclastic infundibula. They had been discovered mathematically, on the basis of bizarre

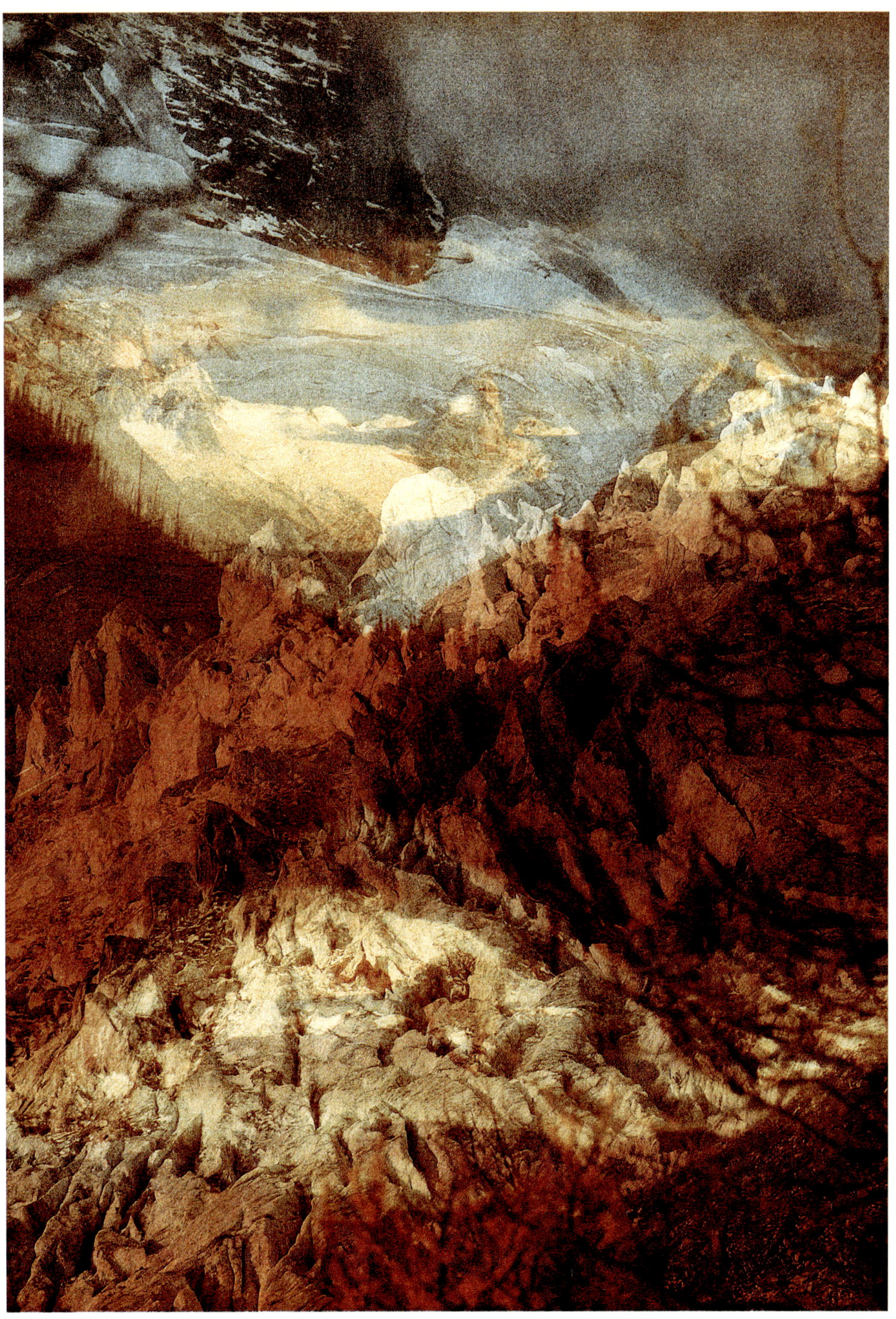

flight patterns of unmanned ships sent out, supposedly, in advance of men. The discovery of the chrono-synclastic infundibula said to mankind in effect: *What makes you think you're going anywhere?* Kurt Vonnegut, *The Sirens of The Titan* We penetrated deeper and deeper into the heart of darkness. It was very quiet there. At night sometimes the roll of drums behind the curtain of trees would run up the river and remain sustained faintly, as if hovering in the air high over our heads, till the first break of day. Whether it meant war, peace, or prayer we could not tell. Joseph Conrad, *Heart of Darkness* The *Asie's* crane sets to work picking up packing-cases out of the hold in a wide-meshed net and then empties them into the landing-barge. The natives receive them with

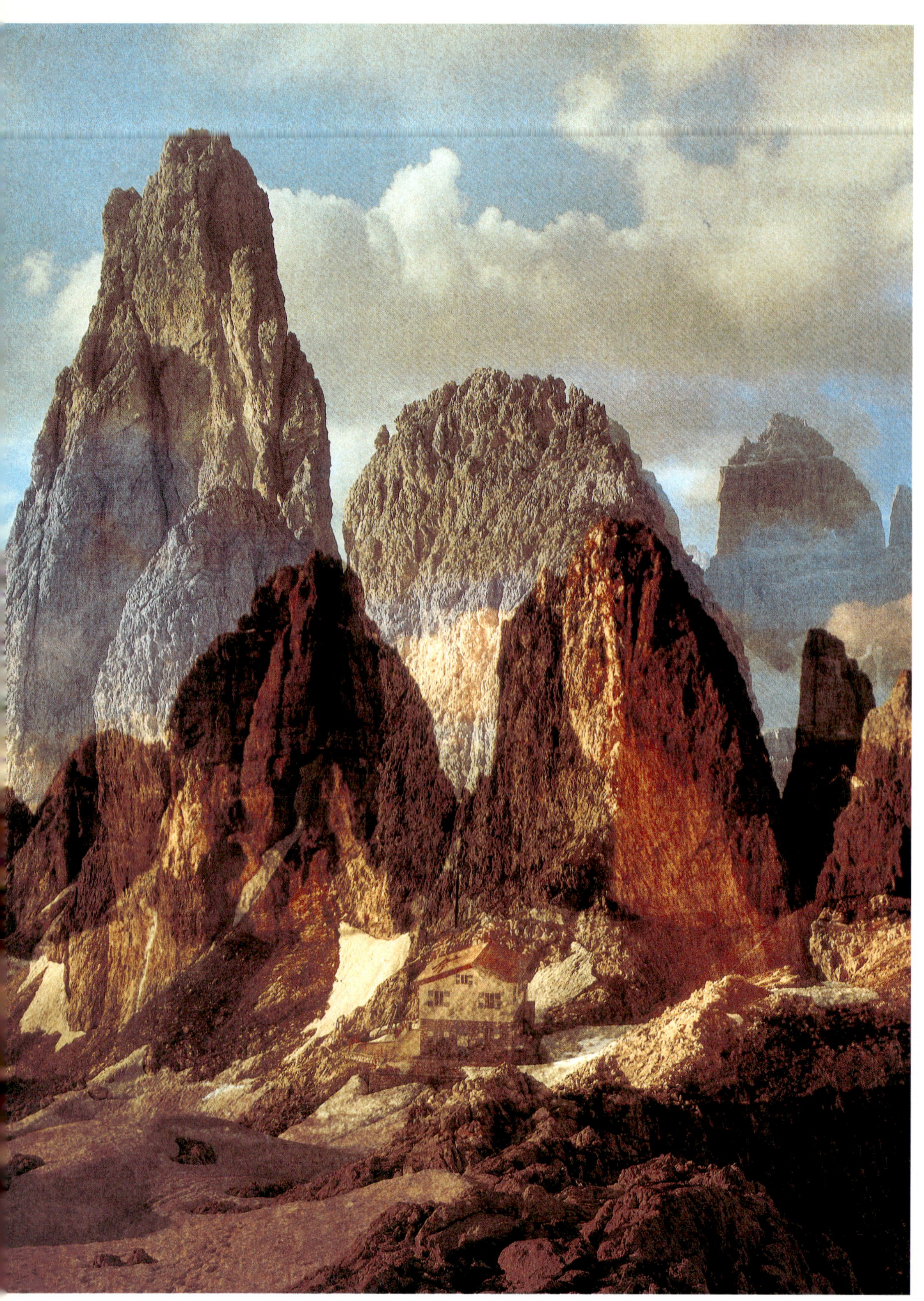

a great deal of shouting and bustling. It is a miracle that any of the cases get landed intact –
squashed and banged and flung about as they are. Some of them burst open like pods and
shed their contents of tins like seeds. I picked up one of these tins and showed it to F., the chief
agent of a food-supply business, who recognized the trademark and assured me that it was
one of a lot of damaged goods which it had been impossible to sell on the Bordeaux market.
André Gide, Travels in the Congo   I was after all to encounter thousands of the Nubians who had settled
there, and not once was I ever insulted through words or unseemly conduct. Not once did I feel
the need to give any one of them my hand; never did I sleep other than alone and lonely in my

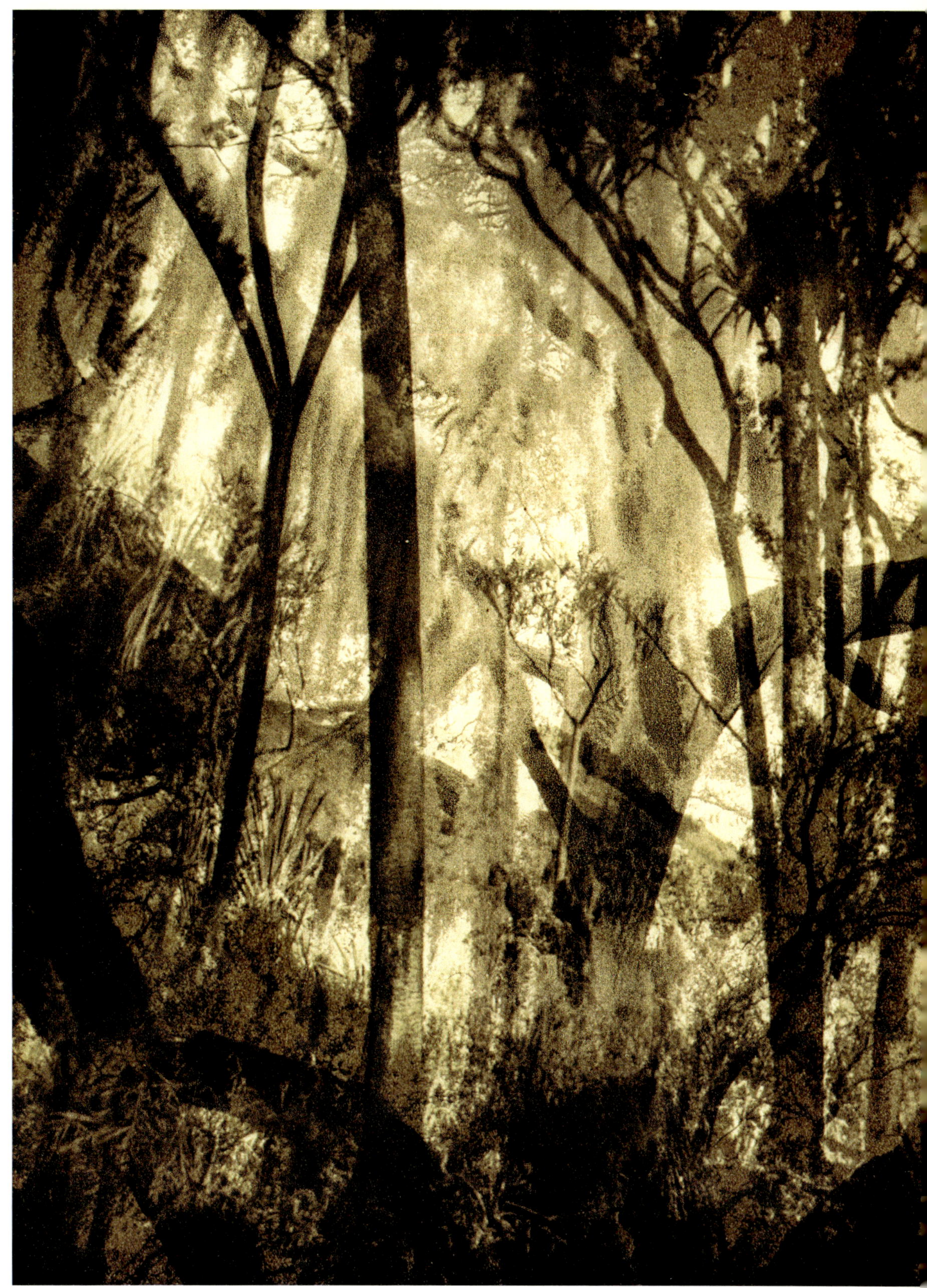

hut, nor dine other than alone in my own company. Georg Schweinfurth, *Im Herzen von Afrika* He flings the boots, paws at the buttons, jerks at his *jubbah*. Moist and mountainous, she waits for him, eyes aglow, veil lowered, her flesh smoldering like Vesuvius. He wheezes with haste and anticipation. It's a dream, an attack of fever: no mere mortal could approach this magnificence! He scrambles atop her, feeling for toeholds – so much terrain to explore – mountains, valleys and rifts, new continents, ancient rivers. T. Coraghessan Boyle, *Water Music* It would take an expert to gauge from available information the composition of these pharmacies, dosages recommended and actually taken, or the extent to which travelers spent their days more or less drugged. The

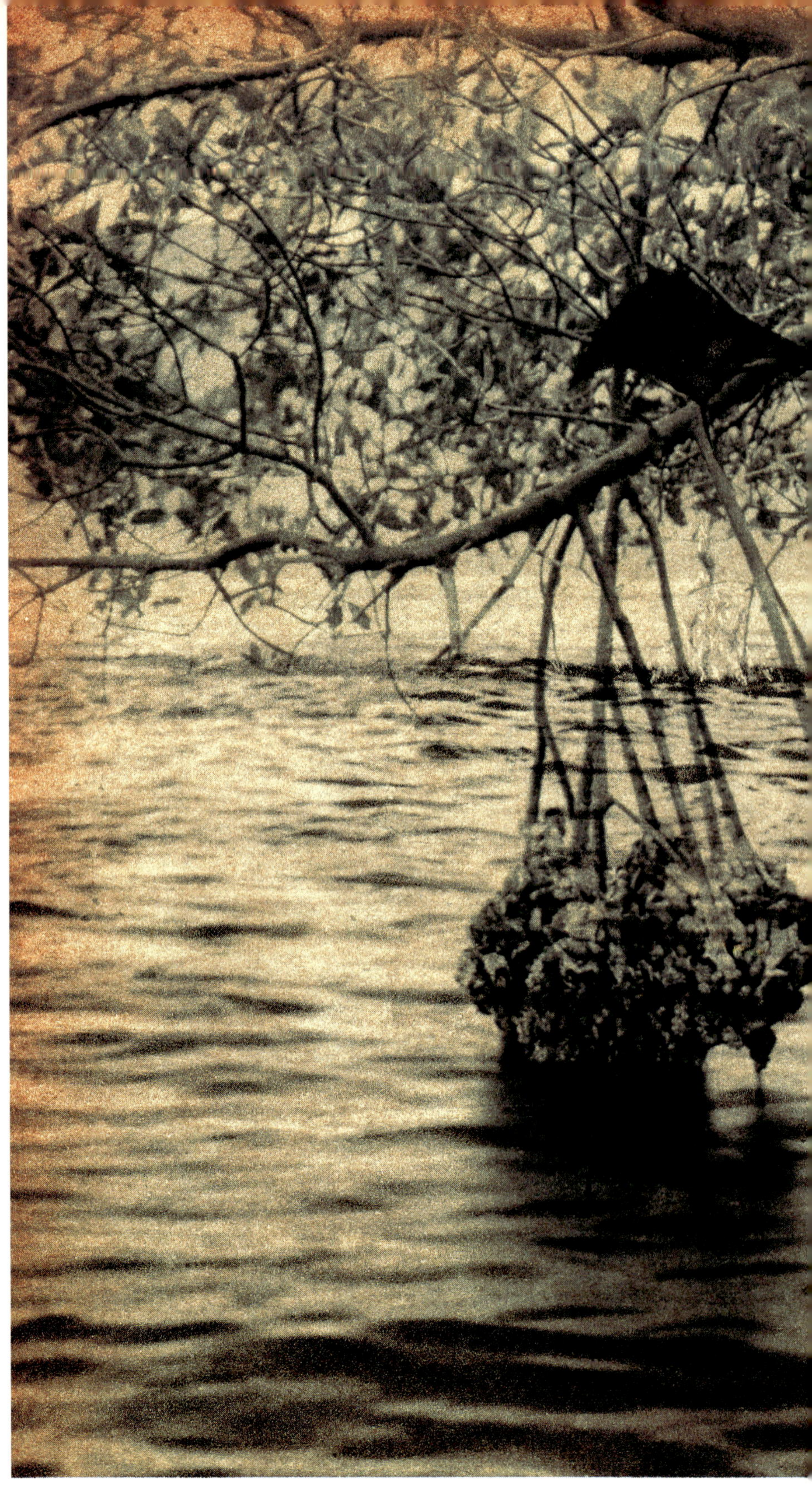

three or four substances mentioned most often were the ominous arsenic, quinine, and opium, the latter either as laudanum (an opium and alcohol tincture) or as morphine. Morphine was injected. Johannes Fabian, *Out of Our Minds* As for evening drinks, I managed to get away with just a whisky and water, two gin bitters and water, and one sherry – impossible to get away with less however. Michel Leiris, *L'Afrique fantôme* Fix and Passepartout saw that they were in a smoking house haunted by those wretched, cadaverous, idiotic creatures to whom every year the English merchants sell one million four hundred thousand pounds of the miserable drug called opium to the tune of millions spent on one of the most despicable vices which afflict humanity!

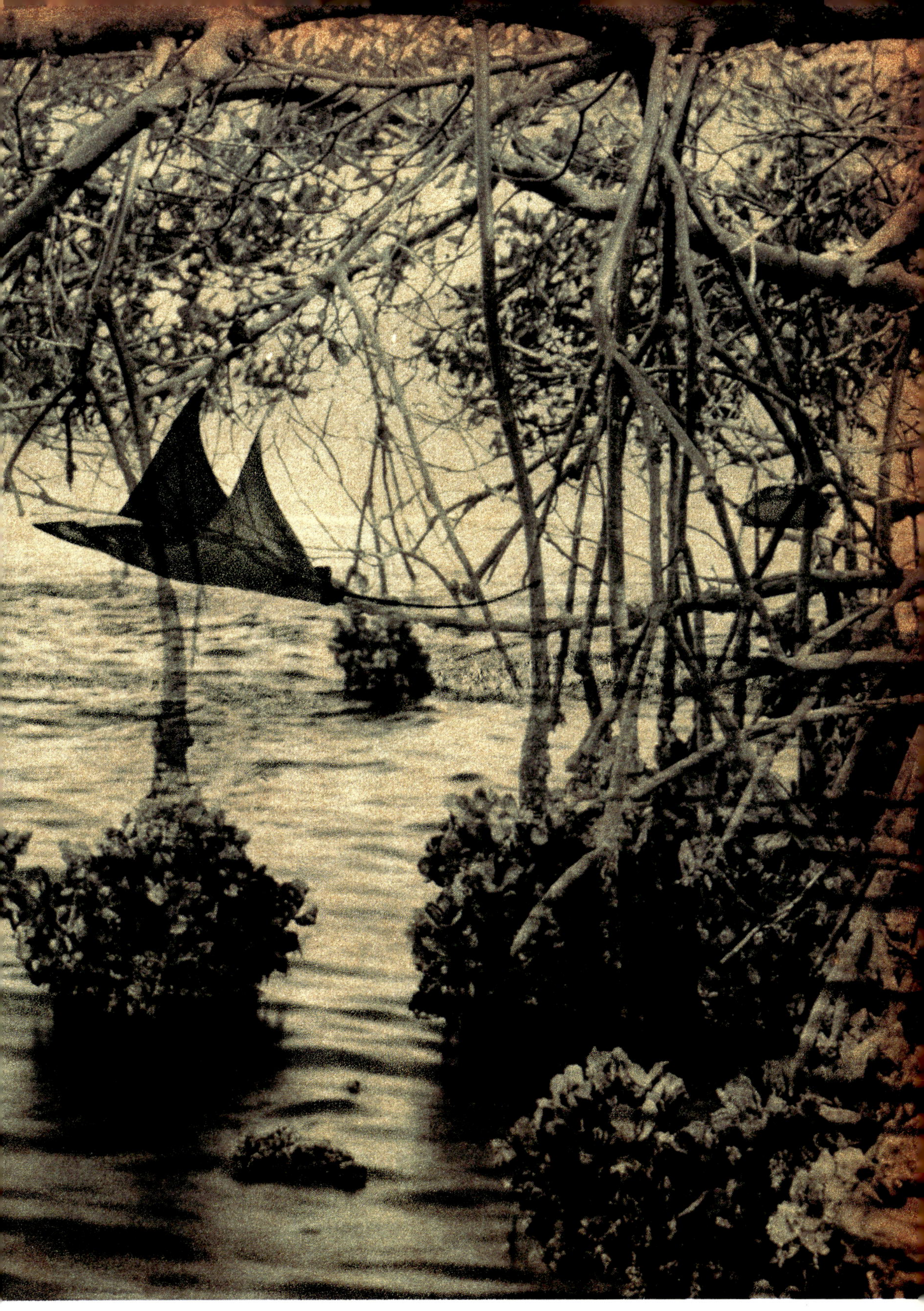

Rum has the advantage that you don't break into a sweat as after every glass of beer; on the other hand you wake up with a headache next morning, when the incomprehensible noise starts off again, half piano, half machine gun, and accompanied by singing – it went on every day between 6 and 7 A.M., and every day I decided to look into it, but I always forgot about it as the day wore on. Max Frisch, *Homo Faber*   And there was something exasperating about the unbroken sameness of the scenery on the banks. He had break-fasted on a can of tepid *pâté* and a slice of stale bread. But he had already drunk two glasses of whisky and water. Georges Simenon, *Tropic Moon*   'What was the subject?' I asked. 'I scarcely know. It

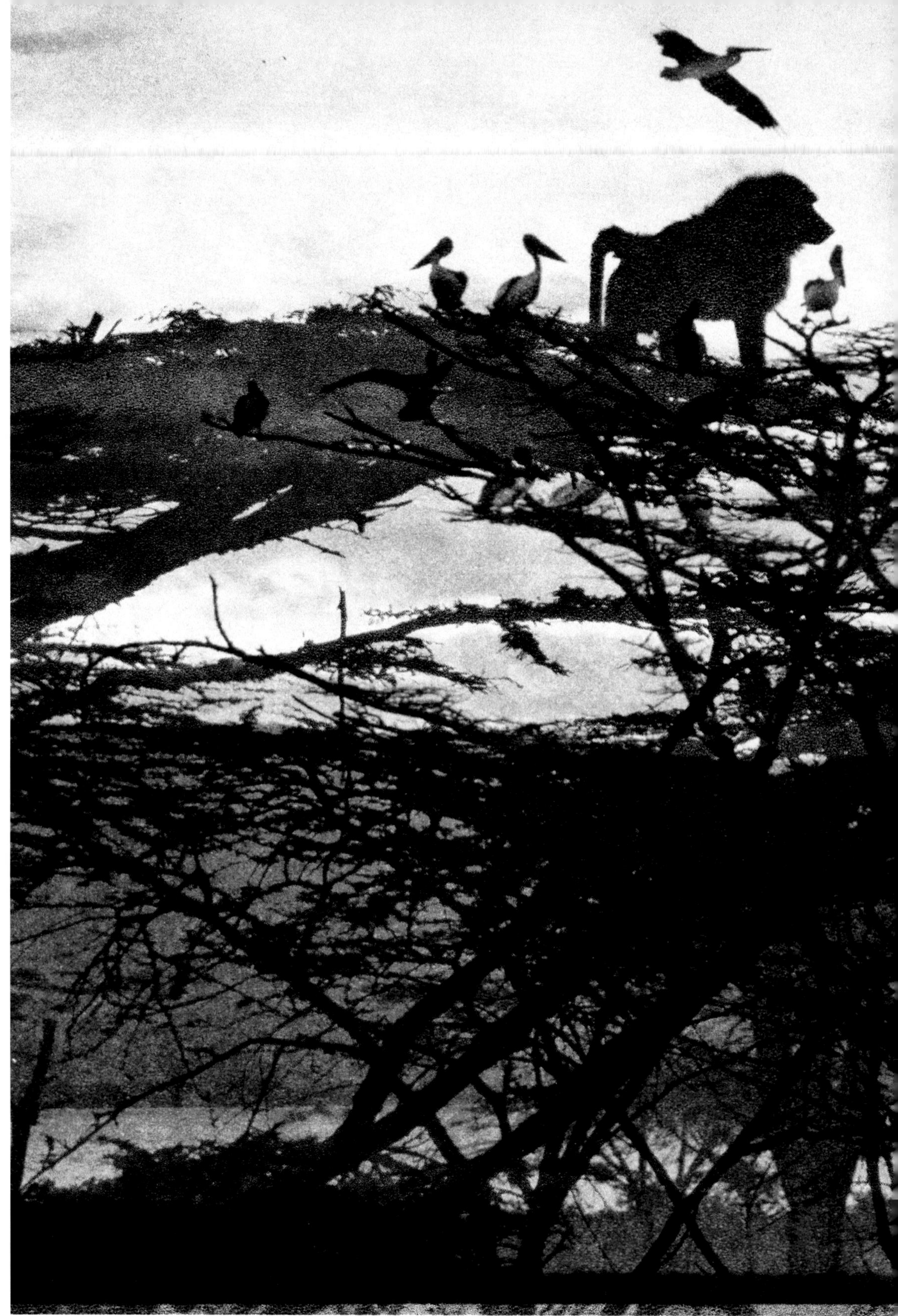

was strange and fantastic. It was a vision of the beginnings of the world, the Garden of Eden, with Adam and Eve – *que sais-je?* – it was a hymn to the beauty of the human form, male and female, and the praise of Nature, sublime, indifferent, lovely, and cruel. It gave you an awful sense of the infinity of space and of the endlessness of time. Because he painted the trees I see about me every day, the coconuts, the banyans, the flamboyants, the alligator pears, I have seen them ever since differently, as though there were in them a spirit and a mystery which I am ever on the point of seizing and which for ever escapes me. The colours were the colours familiar to me, and yet they were different. They had a significance which was all their own. And

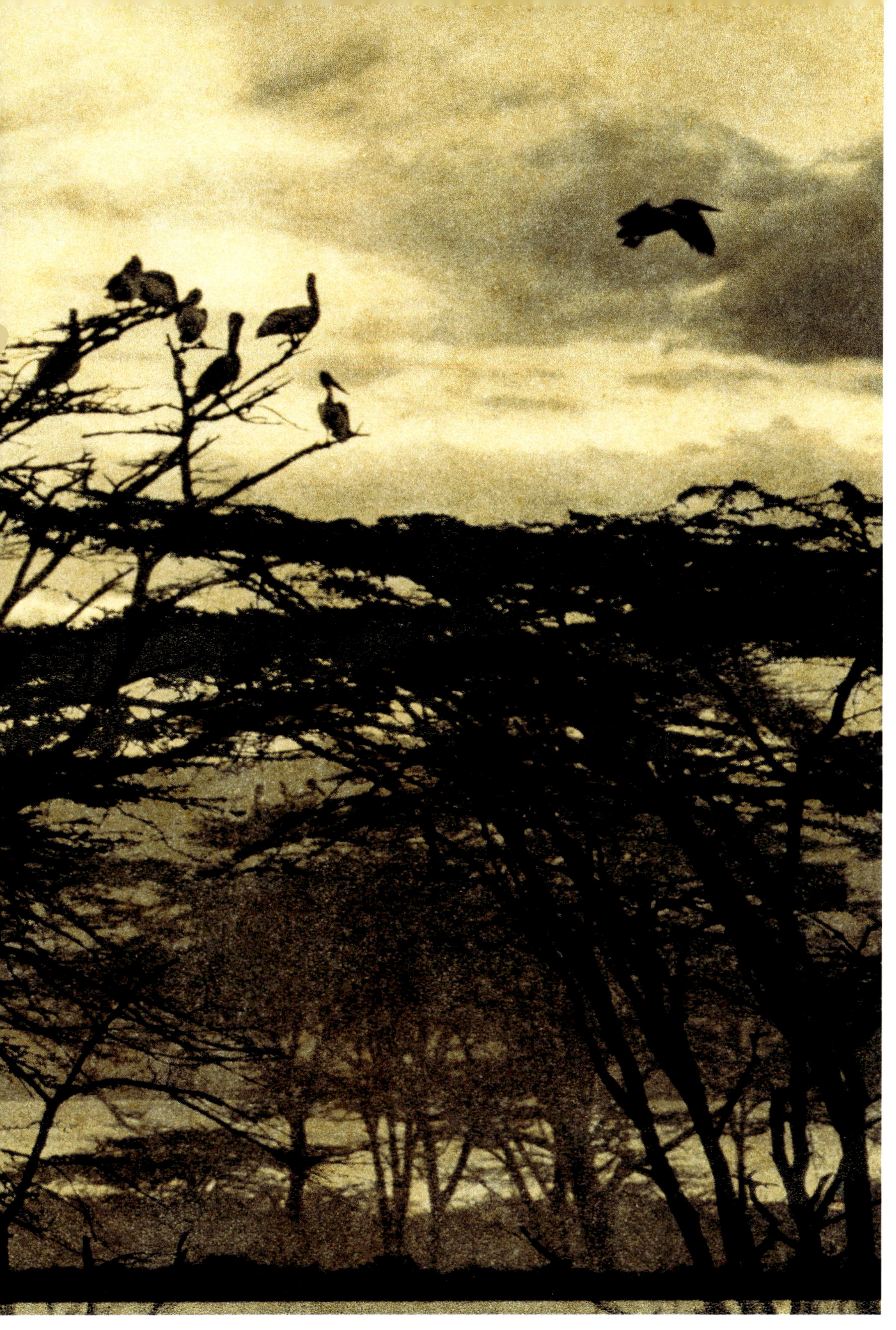

those nude men and women. They were of the earth, the clay of which they were created, and at the same time something divine. You saw man in the nakedness of his primeval instincts, and you were afraid, for you saw yourself.' W. Somerset Maugham, *The Moon and Sixpence*   Saturday 2 – at midday we saw several crocodiles at the tip of an islet – they slip silently into the water like huge slugs as the cangia approaches – for an hour we walked around the islet of sand without finding anything. At the end of the islet, I killed a small vulture. Gustave Flaubert, *Voyage en Égypte*   At the end of the celebration he had his first drink of *natema*, the sweet hallucinogenic liqueur prepared by boiling the roots of the *yahuasca plant*, and in the dream that followed he saw himself as an

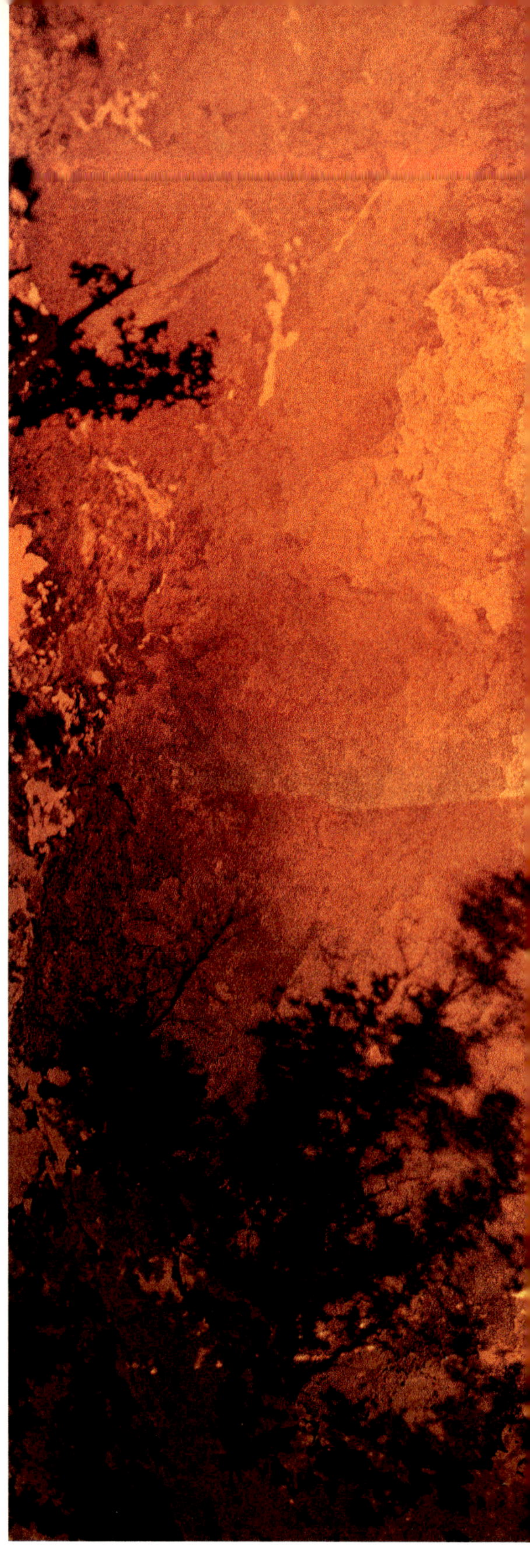

inseparable part of those perpetually changing places, like one more hair on that infinite green body, thinking and feeling like a Shuar; then, wearing the garb of a skilled hunter, he was following the tracks of a mysterious animal, without shape or substance, smell or sound, but endowed with two bright yellow eyes. *Luis Sepúlveda, The Old Man Who Read Love Stories*   Each mission has at least two interpreters. They are Indians with whose help the missionaries communicate with the newly baptised, as they rarely take the trouble of learning the language of the country. These interpreters accompany us on our botanising. While they appear to understand Spanish, they cannot speak it. Many were the times we had to call upon several interpreters to communicate

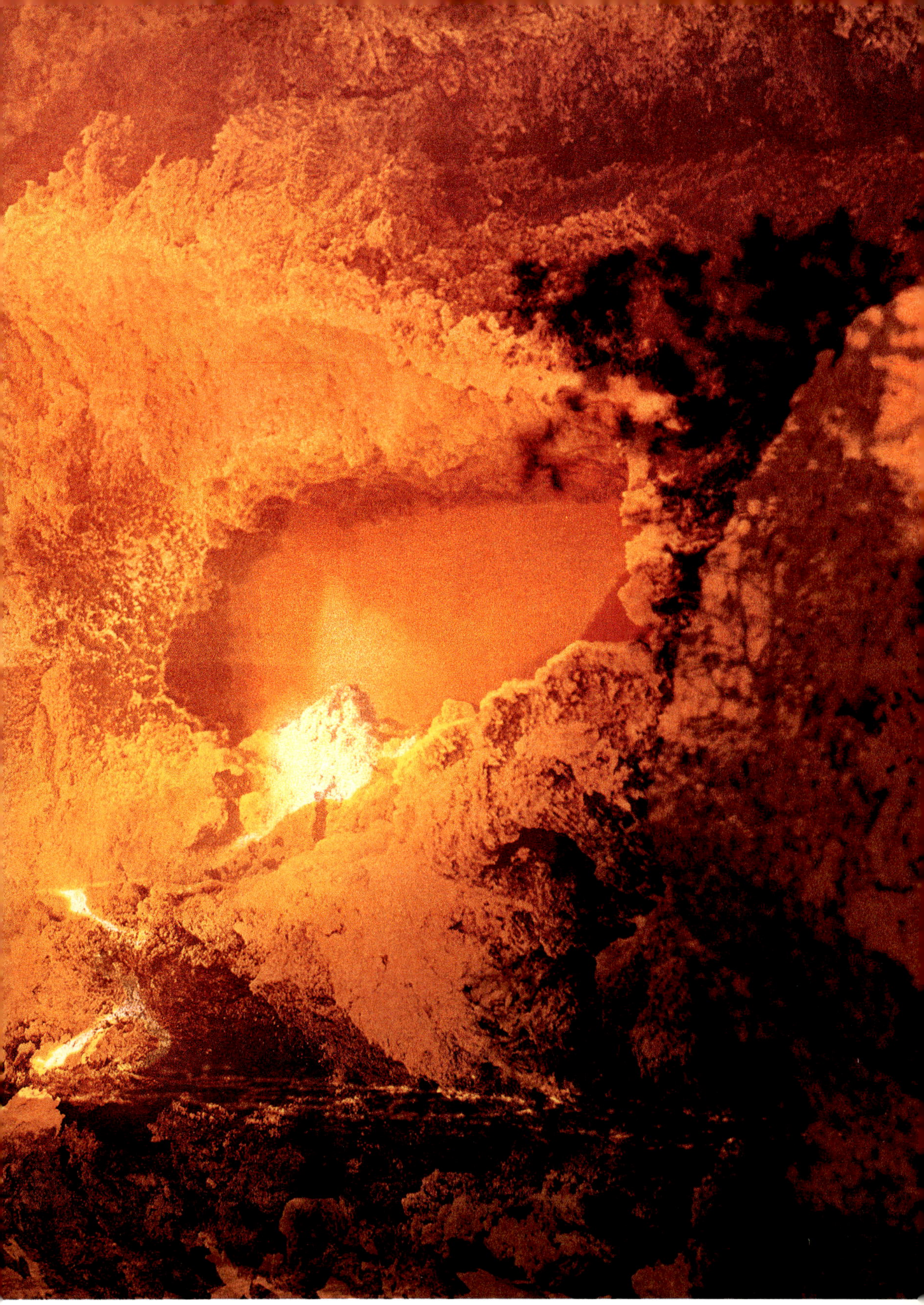

with the natives, so that the same sentence had to be translated several times. Alexander von Humboldt, *Auf Steppen und Strömen Südamerikas* The result of this failure of attention to the other's language is predictable: indeed, throughout the first voyage, before the Indians taken back to Spain have learned "to speak", the situation is one of total incomprehension; or, as Las Casas says in the margin of Columbus's journal: "They were all groping in darkness, because they did not understand what the Indians were saying." Tzvetan Todorov, *The Conquest of America* Having taught the gesture of writing to a Nambikwara chief who learned without comprehension, the anthropologist understands what he has taught and induces the lesson of writing. Jacques Derrida,

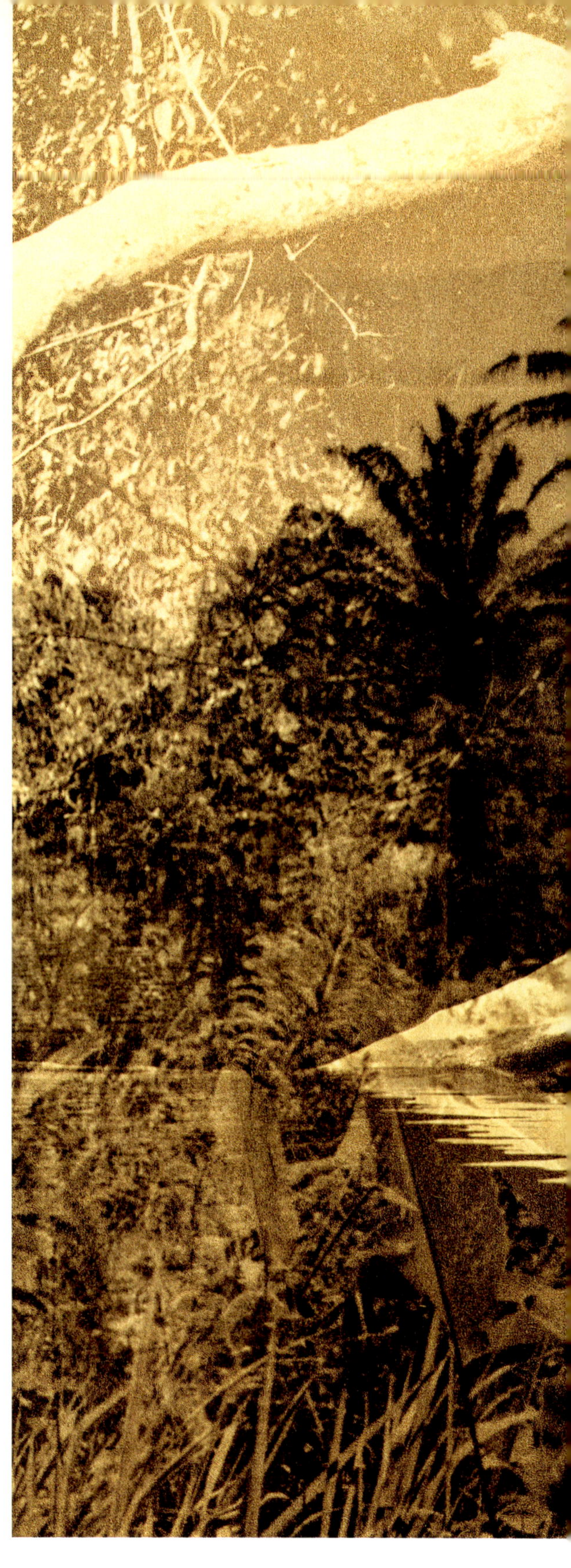

 "Automatically one had the impression how unnatural and sick our color looks under this hot sun and among our brothers with their more or less dark brown and velvety skin!" Richard Büttner, in: Johannes Fabian, *Out of Our Minds*   And Black is beautiful – certainly; yet does the author have to claim three times that the newborns were black, black, black, like their mothers? – Anyone who has been present at the birth of an Afro-American knows that Negroes are born fair-skinned. Hubert Fichte, *Petersilie*   I wish to say at this place that the beauty of King Dahfu's person prevailed with me as much as his words, if not more. His black skin shone as if with the moisture that gathers on plants when they reach their prime. His back was long and muscular. His

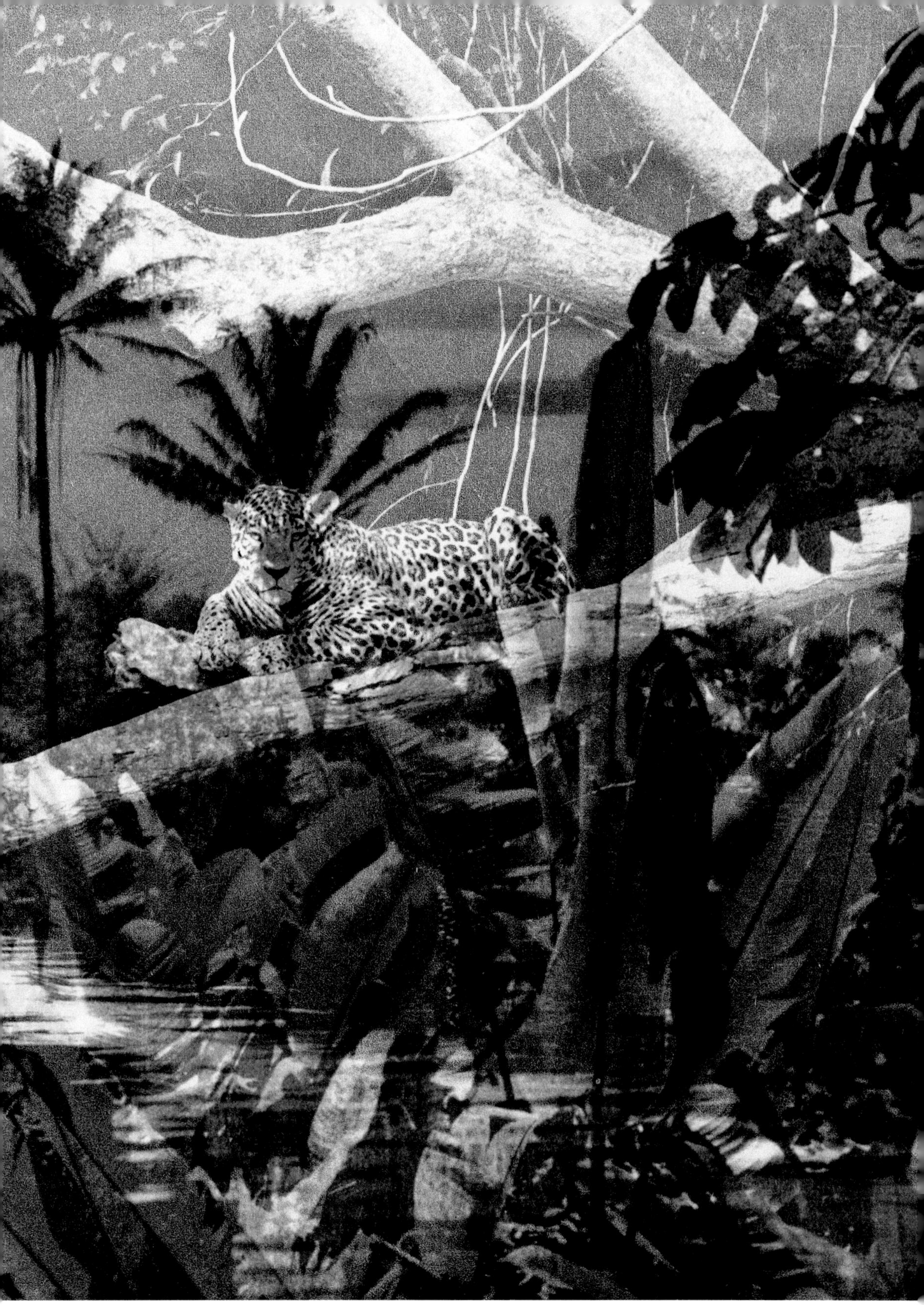

high-rising lips were a strong red. Human perfections are short-lived, and we love them more than we should, maybe. But I couldn't help it. The thing was involuntary. Saul Bellow, *Henderson the Rain King* It was more out of pity than anything else that Miller, the German-American, took him into his office; but he was a business man, and though Lawson's financial skill made him valuable, the circumstances were such that he could hardly refuse a smaller salary than he had before, and Miller did not hesitate to offer it to him. Ethel and Brevald blamed him for taking it, since Pedersen, the half-caste, offered him more. But he resented bitterly the thought of being under the orders of a half-caste. When Ethel nagged him he burst out furiously: "I'll see myself dead

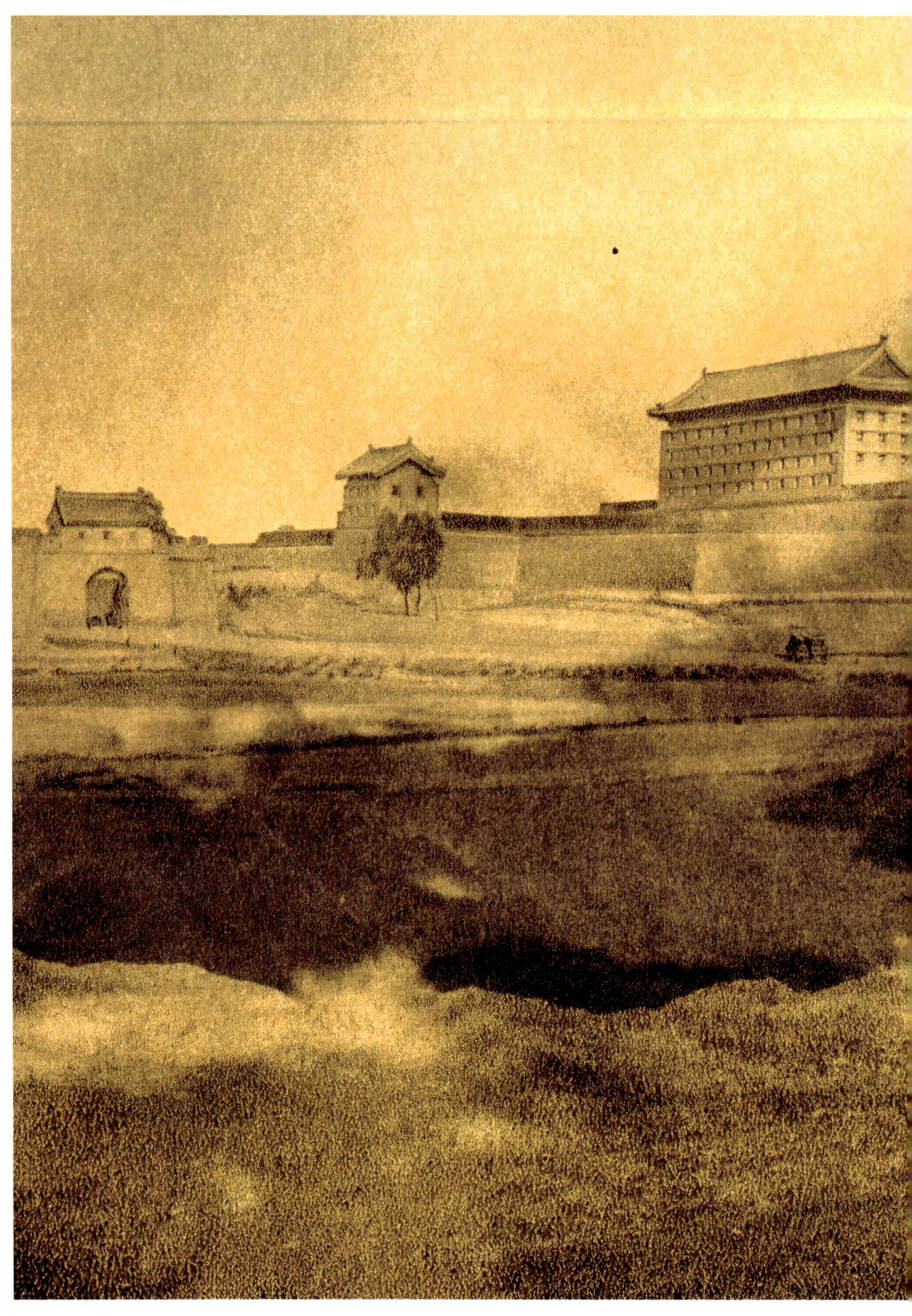

before I work for a nigger." "You may have to," she said. W. Somerset Maugham, *The Trembling of A Leaf*   "All that the Mistress prizes of you is your Whiteness, understand? Don't feel disparag'd,– ev'ry white male who comes to this Town is approach'd by ev'ry Dutch Wife, upon the same Topick. The baby, being fairer than its mother, will fetch more upon the Market,– there it begins, there it ends." Thomas Pynchon, *Mason & Dixon*   Lydia willed herself not to believe the stories of "bone-pointing" and of sorcerers who could "sing" men to their doom. All the same, she had an idea that the Aboriginals, with their terrifying immobility, had somehow got Australia by the throat. There was an awesome power in these apparently passive people who would sit, watch, wait

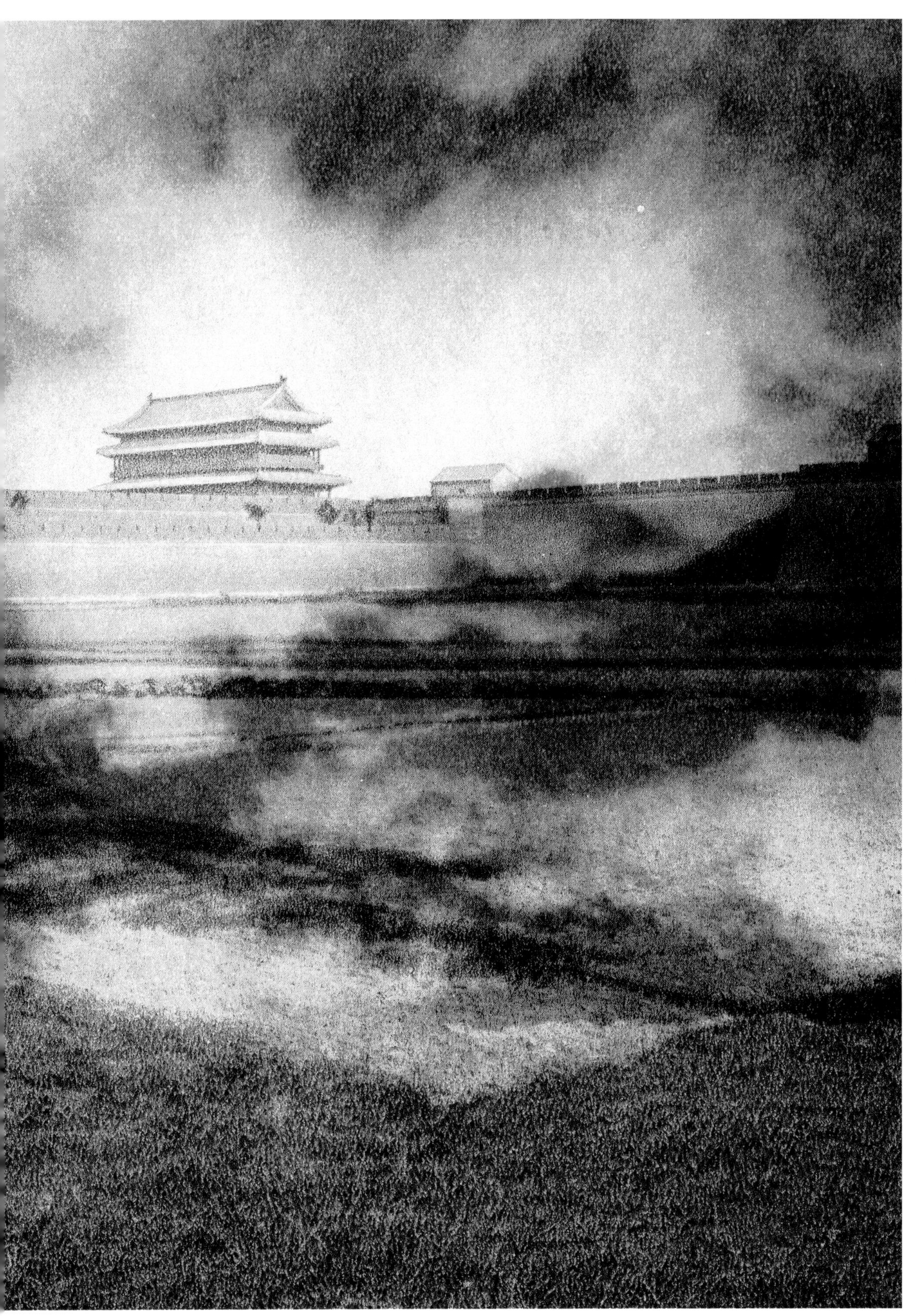

and manipulate the white man's guilt. Bruce Chatwin, *Songlines*   I put the broom back where it was. Now I kick it and make it fall over. I look at the broom lying on the ground and then at my outstretched leg. How white my skin is. What untold suffering we have spread about the world and continue to spread with our colonial expansion, our missions and our economic interests. It's damned unpleasant belonging to this of all races and classes. Florence Weiss, *Vor dem Vulkanausbruch* He watched them walking around quite unconcernedly under the blazing sun, whereas the mere thought of facing even the milder glare on the veranda made him shudder. How different he was from Adèle, who seemed so thoroughly in her element here, so brisk and at ease in her

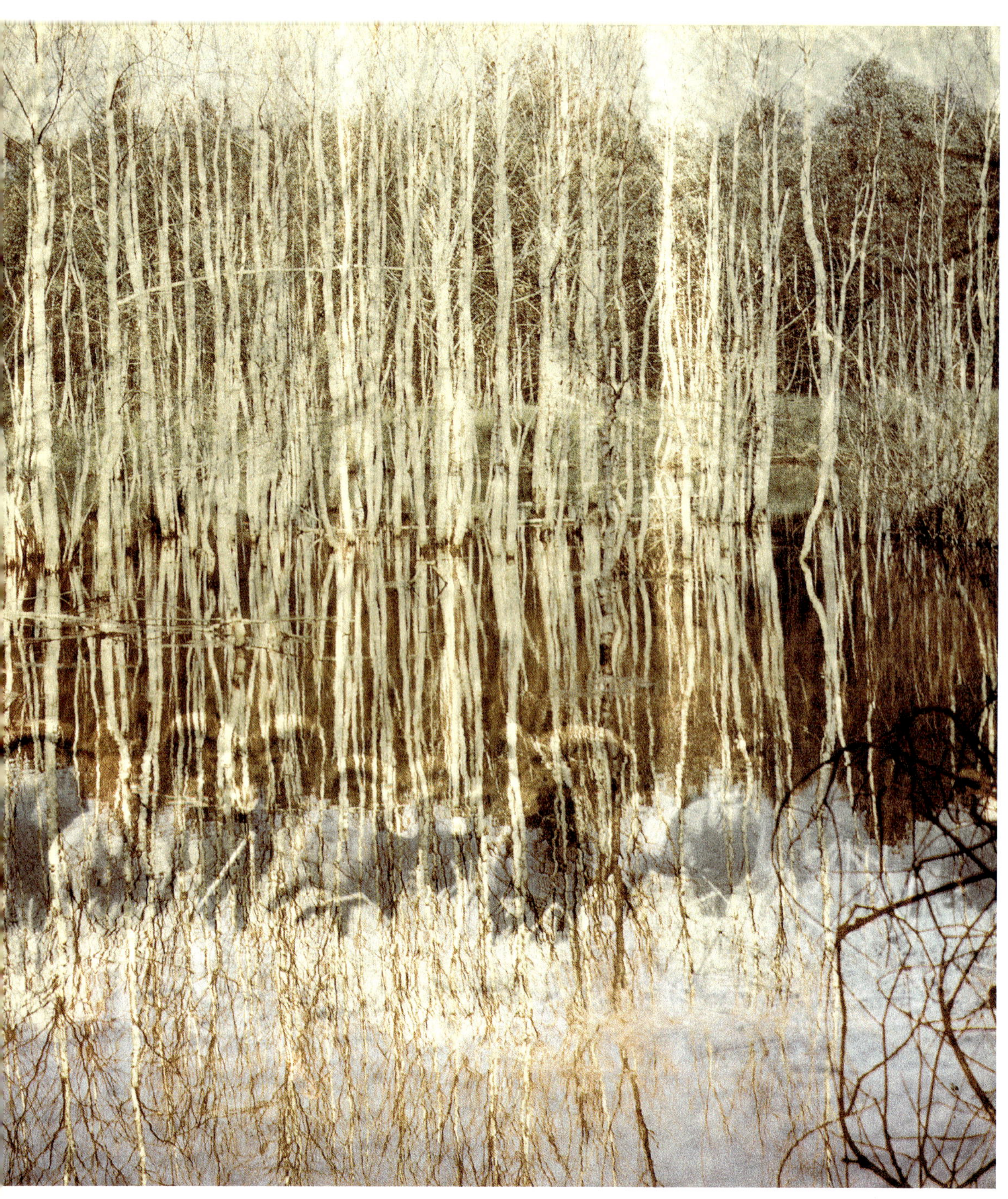

black silk dress, white sun helmet, doeskin boots! She chattered away with the blacks in their own language and handled them as if she'd spent her life among them. Georges Simenon, *Tropic Moon* "Nudity with a black skin never strikes me as strange or noteworthy; but with a white skin it is different. Indeed, I almost developed a morbid disinclination to look at myself, and once or twice I have even blushed to see my white skin. I became so afraid of being seen bathing even by men, that it was only with the utmost secrecy that I ever attempted it." Joseph Thomson, in: Johannes Fabian, *Out of Our Minds* Dowayos have a rich series of odd sounds to describe smells, conventionalized but not strictly part of the language, rather like our 'ouch' or 'bang'. A hot debate

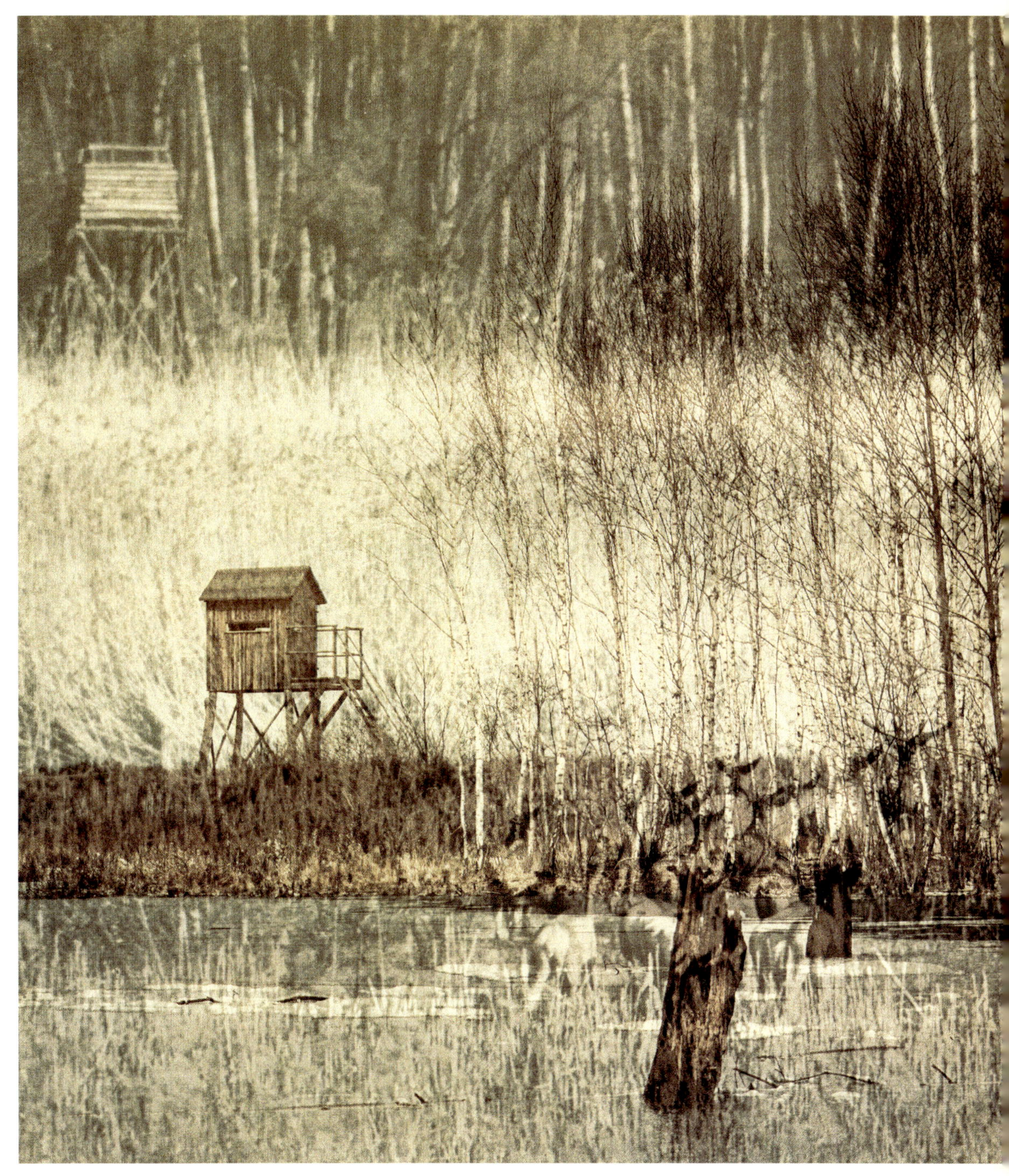

arose as to whether I was *sok, sok, sok* (like rotten meat, Matthieu helpfully explained) or *virrr* (stale milk), to which all lustily contributed. Nigel Barley, *A Plague of Caterpillars* The Prime Minister of Mandadipa, who had long since been changed into a parrot, exercised his official functions from his high perch right up to his death; and the gates of the first capital were guarded for years only by ghouls or converted goblins – so recently repentant and so confused they were still devouring laggard travellers. Nicolas Bouvier, *The Scorpion-Fish* One ought to mention that, after four hours of talks and twelve hours of rites, all of which in the heat, ethnologists start to lose the plot. Hubert Fichte, *Das Haus der Mina in São Luiz de Maranhão* To be sure, it would still remain to be asked if

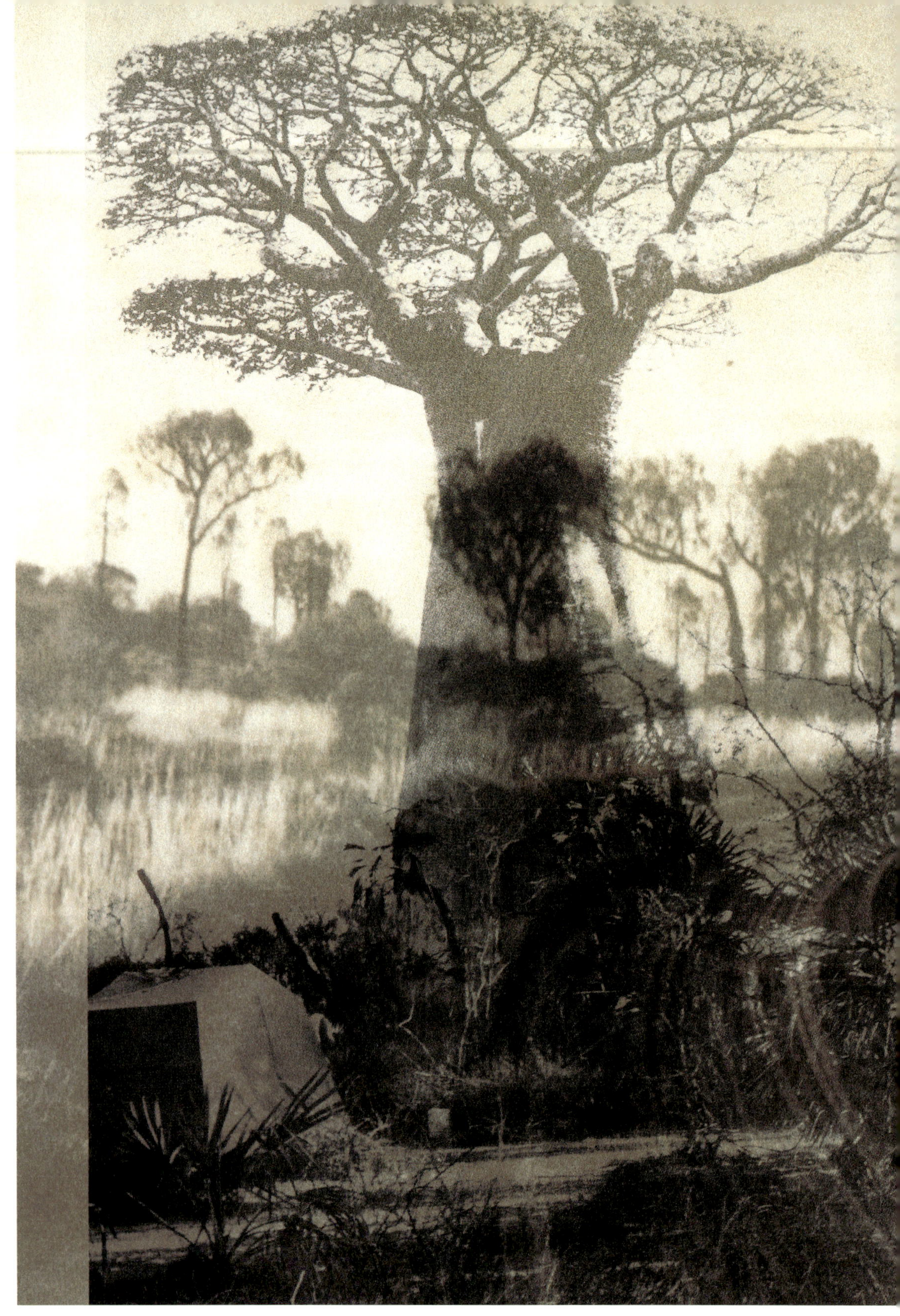

the anthropologist considers himself "engineer" or *bricoleur*. Jacques Derrida, *Of Grammatology* "Only three months ago this here," said Pankraz, nudging the fur with his foot, "was a live lion, before I killed it. This chap taught me and converted me, and preached to me so forcefully for twelve hours that I, poor fellow that I am, was finally healed for ever of all sullenness and maliciousness. In memory of this, his fur shall no longer leave my side. That was a fine story indeed!" he added, with a sigh. Gottfried Keller, *Pankraz der Schmoller* "Their religion, their only fetish, is hemp, *liamba*; they broke their poisoned arrows and no longer keep idols; everyone who wants to belong to the tribe must smoke liamba, and if he doesn't want to, he is expelled" Otto H. Schütt,

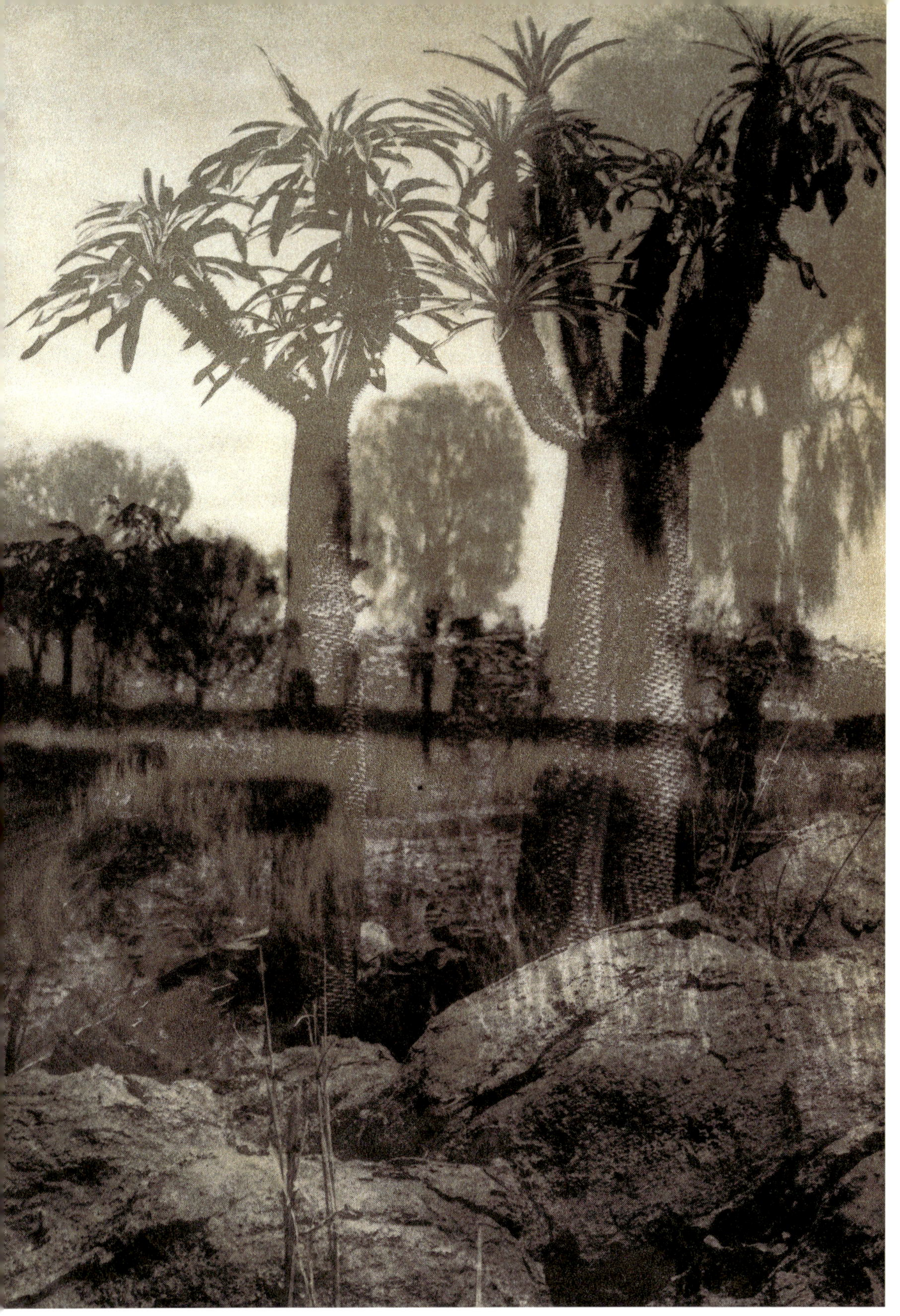

in: Johannes Fabian, *Out of Our Minds* The Otomacs are restless, noisy, and extreme in their passions. They not only adore the fermented liquors of cassava, maize and palm wine, but also get very drunk, to the point of madness, with *niopo* powder. They gather the long pods of a mimosa, which we have made known as *Acacia niopo*; they cut them into little pieces, dampen them and let them ferment. When the macerated plants turn black they are crushed into a paste and mixed with cassava flour and lime obtained from burning the shell of a helix. They cook this mass on a grill of hardwood above a fire. The hardened pâté looks like little cakes. When they want to use it they crumble it into a powder and put it on a small plate. The Otomac holds

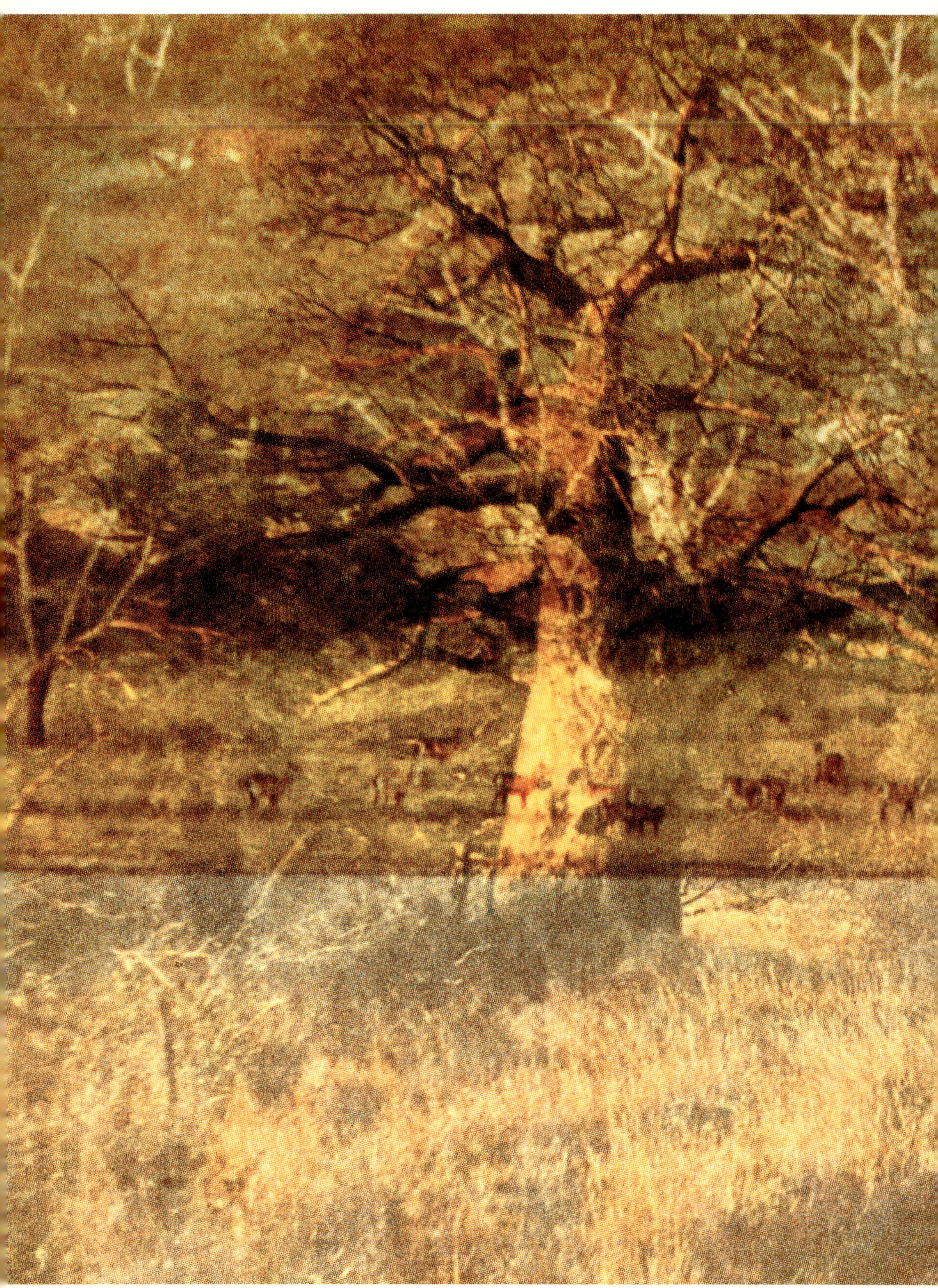

this plate with one hand while through his nose, along the forked bone of a bird whose two extremities end up in his nostrils, he breathes in the *niopo*. Alexander von Humboldt, *Personal Narrative of a Journey to the Equinoctial Regions of the New Continent*   Malkam Ayyahou presents the first chicken to the woman Fantay, who slowly dances the *gourri*, then places the chicken under her *chamma* gown. She is hidden. The female zar *Dira*, descended on to her, swears that he accepts the blood, and once again Fantay performs the *gourri* dance. Michel Leiris, *L'Afrique fantôme*   The name Niam-niam is borrowed from the dialect of the Dinka, and means "eaters", or rather "great eaters", manifestly betokening a reference to the cannibal propensities of the people. Georg Schweinfurth, *The Heart of Africa*   The groom

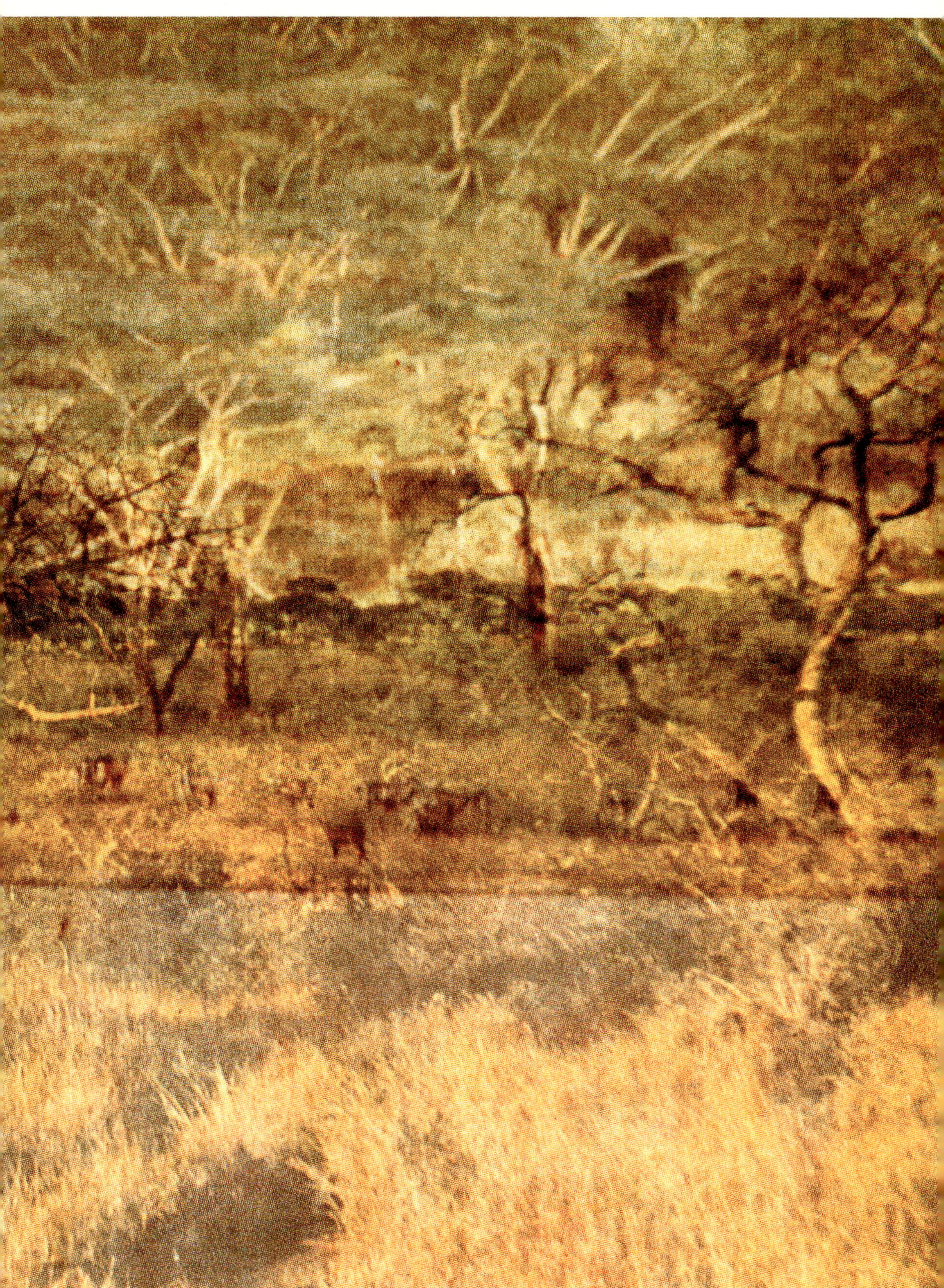

wore slippers with upturned toes. He was accompanied by a retinue of Mussulmen in embroidered burnooses and a cordon of slaves leading goats and bullocks, and carrying a tent. At an appointed spot the tent was struck, the goats and bullocks slaughtered, a fire ignited in a depression in the earth. There was a feast. Beef and mutton, songbirds, roasted larvae and other delicacies. There was dancing, songs were sung and tales told. And then there was the pièce de résistance: a whole baked camel. T. Coraghessan Boyle, *Water Music* What could she have been up to in that hut? And why now this all too obvious eagerness to please and humor him? Georges Simenon, *Tropic Moon* In former times, men wore a loin-cloth that would be unfastened to allow

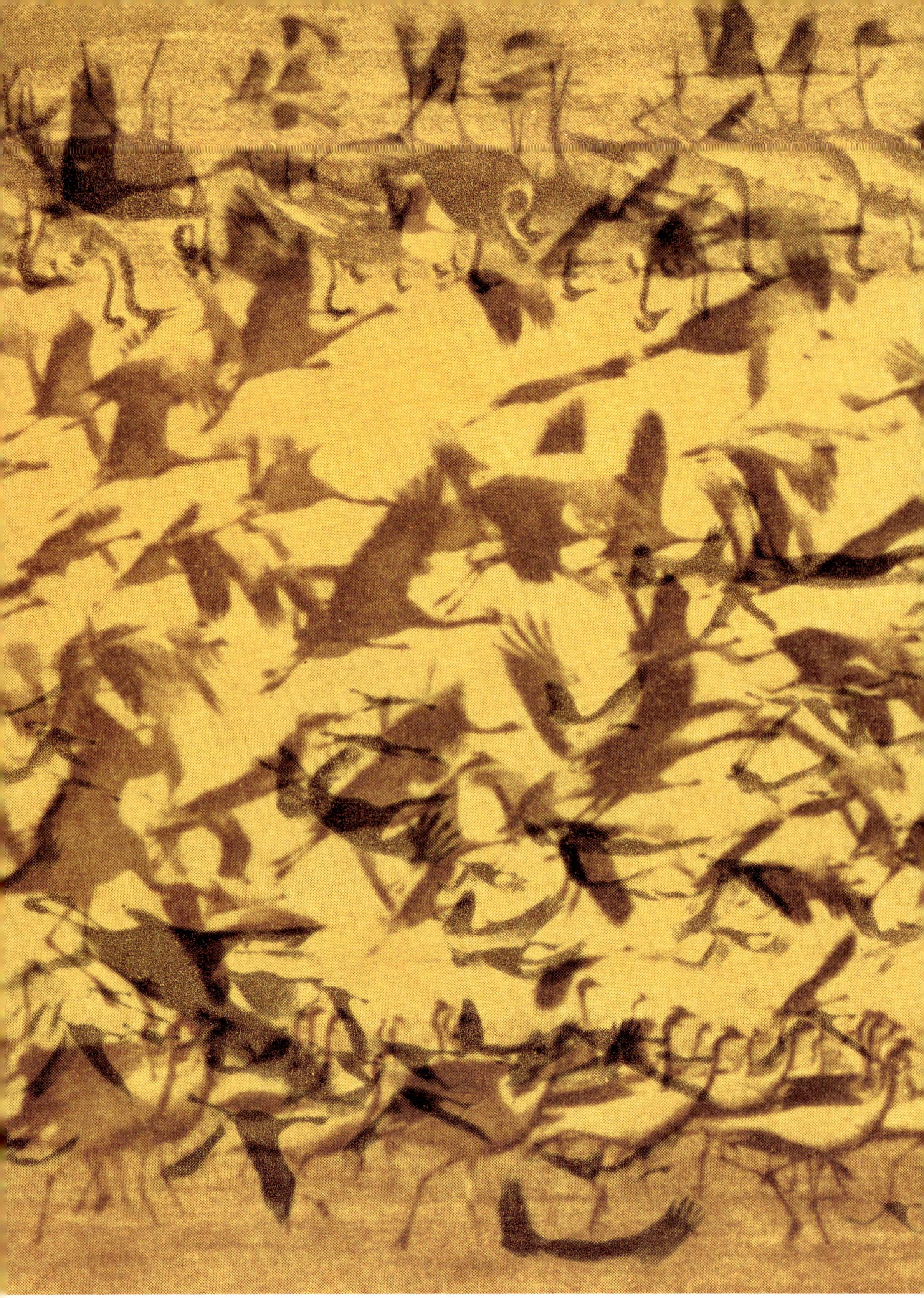

removal of the gourd penis-sheath that was required for the circumcised. Nowadays shorts are the fashion and only old men or those engaged in ritual activity wear sheaths. As a joke, women make with their cheeks the plopping sound of a male privy member being removed from a sheath; this sound also serves as a coy euphemism for the sexual act itself. Nigel Barley, *The Innocent Anthropologist* I possessed neither boots nor shoes, guns nor ammunition, paper nor instruments, and even my watches, which were so essential to me, were gone; what use then to think any further of a journey to unknown countries under such circumstances as these? Convinced of the vanity of any attempt to proceed, I was therefore obliged with a heavy heart,

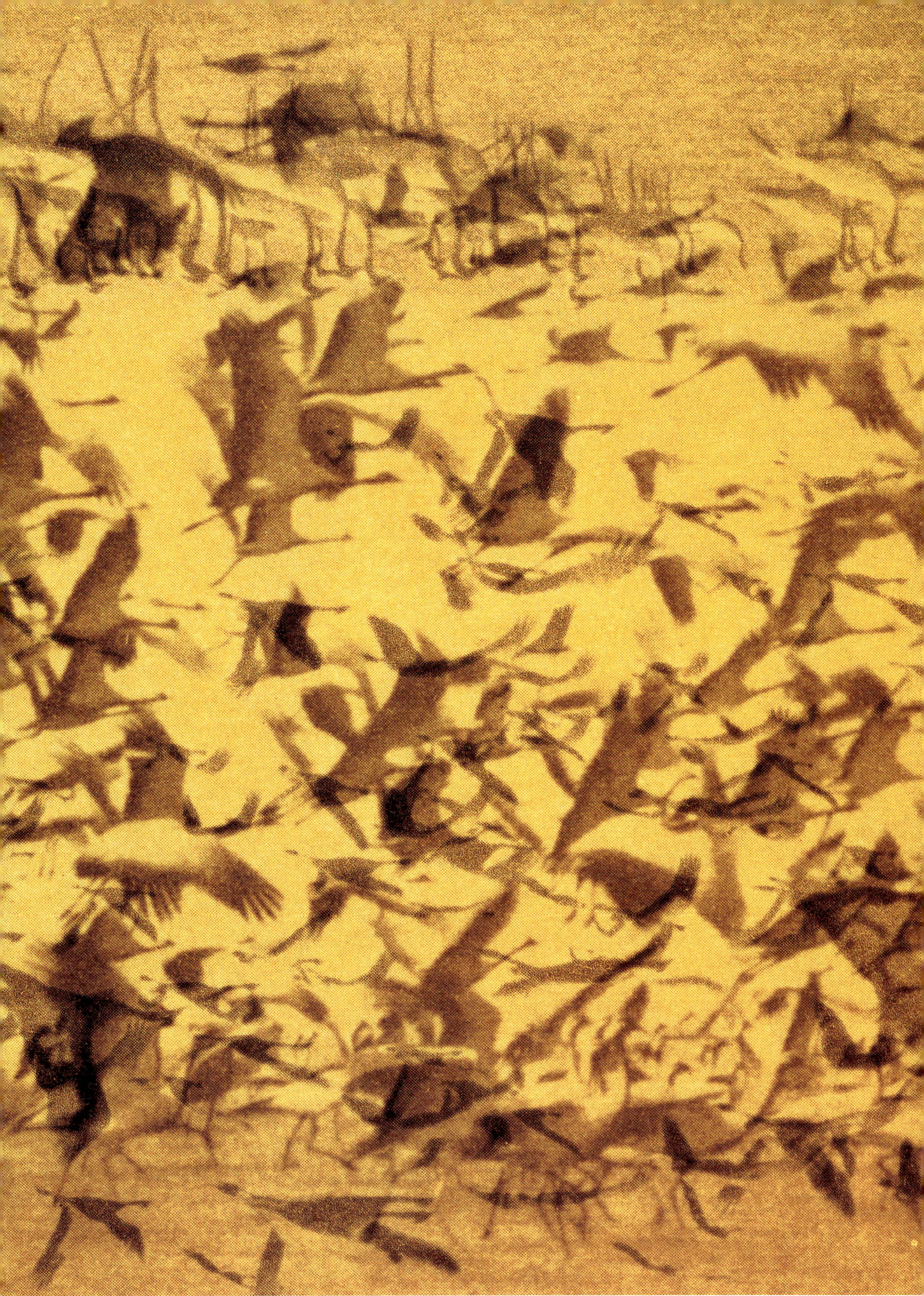

to turn my thoughts towards Europe. Georg Schweinfurth, *The Heart of Africa* It does take a very long time before one does understand the mentality of the people here, but they are lovable and certainly also smart. Above all, they would never conceive the idea of imprisoning people or chasing them out of the country. They do not care that we are Jews or refugees or, unhappily, both. On a good day I sometimes believe that I could get used to this country. Maybe black people have some medicine (called *dawa* here) against memories. Stefanie Zweig, *Nowhere in Africa* All for monuments, all for shrines and memorial plaques – that had always been the slogan when-ever the largest blocks of granite had been dragged off from Moor Quarry down to the lowlands, back when the granite had still been flawlessly thick, not brittle and banded with fragile streaks. All for peace. All for the grand memorial enterprise. ... Bullshit.

 His head burned, his body was wet with clammy sweat, he was plagued by intolerable thirst. He looked about for refreshment, of whatever sort, and found a little fruit-shop where he bought some strawberries. They were overripe and soft; he ate them as he went. It was well past midnight. I pinched myself to make sure I wasn't dreaming, cupped my hands round my mouth and called out in a tone of scarce-concealed defeat: 'Father, pray for me. I can't remember anything anymore, it's too hot.' 'My son,' replied

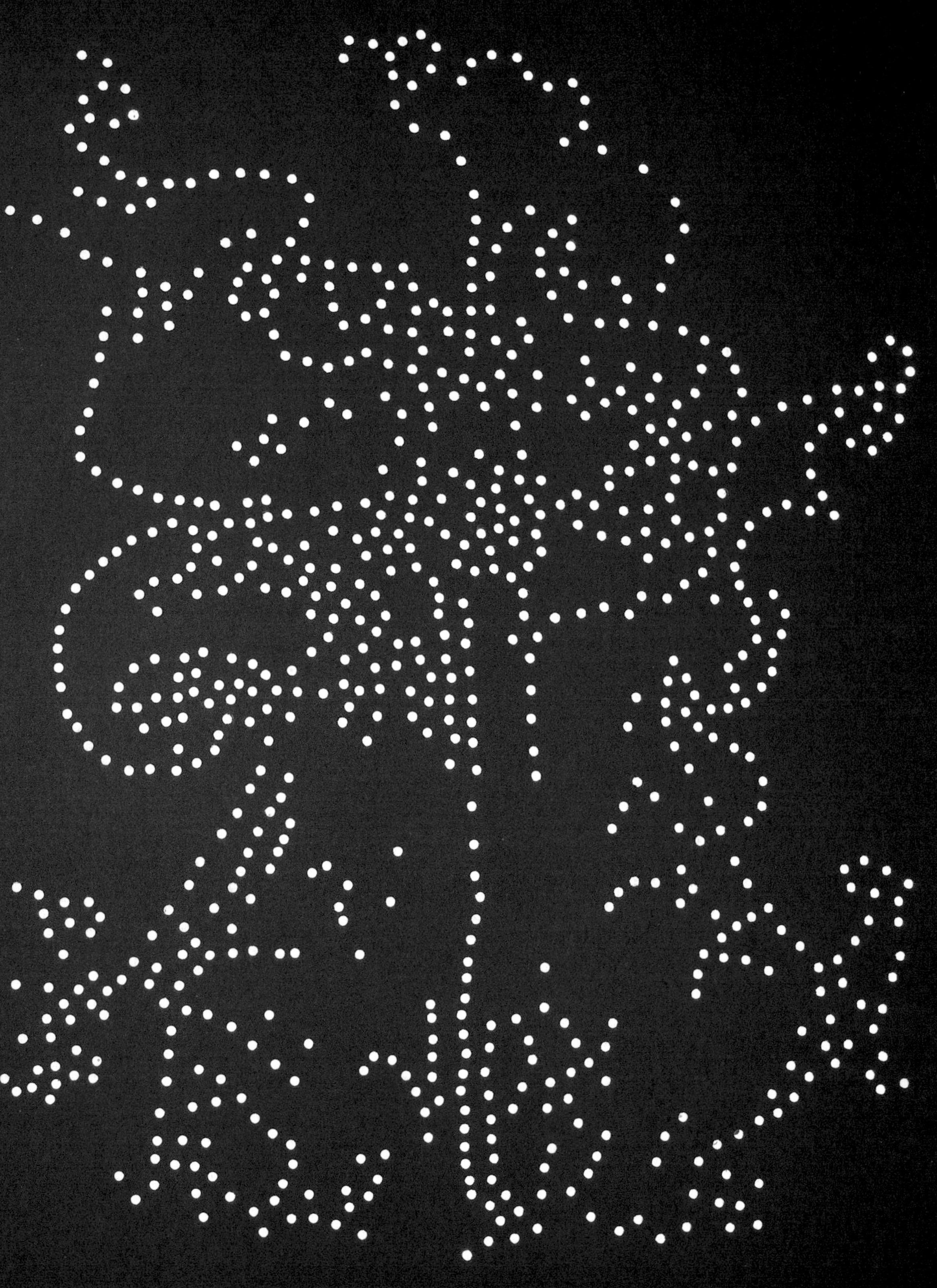

the apparition at once, 'I've been too hot to pray for a very long time.' Nicolas Bouvier, The Scorpion-Fish

The Waniamwesi are in many respects on a much higher level than any population of the interior, perhaps with the exception of the Bashilange, though quite amazingly they are, like the Bashilange, more addicted to hemp smoking than any other tribes known to me. I am convinced that hemp has a domesticating effect on the negro, that the narcotic weed mitigates their restless savagery, the pervasive inclination of staying away from external influence. It makes the negro more approachable and more useful for culture and civilization, without denying certain harmfulness to their physical constitution; a fact that is probably exaggerated

American people called the Bororo; this they connected with the name applied generally to the nomadic Fulani, the Mbororo. It was further proof that Fulanis hailed from South America and had here colonized these inferior races. Several young men offered me this theory worthy of a Thor Heyerdahl. It explained their light skin and long, non-frizzy hair, their straight noses and thin lips. They were often at great pains to point out that my exposed parts, brown from the sun, were the same colour as theirs, pale from wear.

The dry season development that most delighted the Dowayos was the arrival of my fridge. I had long sought to buy a paraffin refrigerator, regarding them wistfully in the city shops, but they cost more than I could afford and the difficulty of transporting them put the whole matter out of the question. In the abandoned house of the Dutch linguists who had worked on the language of the Dowayos there lingered such a machine. One day I had the good fortune to bump into them at N'gaoundere and they offered to lend it to me. I could not believe my luck; I should have cold water and fresh meat. My reliance on tinned food would be reduced; and some of the pressure on my finances would be relieved. I set it up outside my fine new house, the roof of which was just being completed. It was considered a great joke when I asked why they had left off the normal spikes that protect a house-dweller against witchcraft. Everyone knew that a white man was not subject to attacks from witchcraft just as everyone knew that he must live in a square, not a round house. My own house was consequently built square and, instead of witchcraft remedies, an empty beer bottle was placed on top.

To celebrate, Jon and Jeannie came out and we drank cold beer with an ecstatic Zuuldibo. My 'cold granary' was a source of great wonder to everyone. It baffled them – as it rather did me – how a fire in my 'granary' made it cold. I could not resist the temptation of showing them ice, which none but the greatest sophisticates had previously encountered. They were terrified. Never having experienced such extreme temperature difference, Dowayos would insist that ice felt 'hot'; if they touched it, it would burn them. I never fully convinced them that it was merely water in another form. Watching it melt in the sun, they would say, 'The cold matter has gone away. Only the warm is left.' Even the Old Man of Kpan was obliged to come and see this wonder, in accordance with his role of keeper of the mysteries.

This enabled me to re-establish contact with him and remind him of his promise that I might visit him. The trip was arranged for the following week. His son would come to guide us.

To my great surprise, the boy arrived on the appointed day and Zuuldibo insisted on accompanying us. The trek was enlivened, as we approached the daunting mountains for the first time, by encounters with mountain dwellers. I was amused to note that the women here greeted me as their 'lover'. It was explained to me that this was a peculiarity of the area and much play was made of it. Having crossed the long, hot plains, dotted with salt-licks where wild beasts and cattle sought sustenance side by side, we began the climb. Temperatures at this time of year could be well over 110°F at noon, and both Matthieu and I were soon bathed in sweat. I had brought drinking water which he piously declined, but he was unable to avail himself of the only stream we passed since – as I have mentioned – highland water is forbidden to lowland Dowayos unless offered by a local resident. The Old Man's 'son' turned out to be some sort of a cousin and was not empowered to make the offering. The path climbed steadily through patchy trees. At whatever time of year one travelled, it was at grave risk to life and limb. In the wet season one could hang on to vegetation while clambering up rock-faces, but the ground was covered with grass and occasionally one foot would simply shoot off into space as the path became a dotted line on the cliff wall. In the dry season one could see the surface and better place the feet, but there were no handholds to rectify a mistake.

We shared our journey with jibbering baboons who sent loose shale cascading down on us from above. Beneath was a sheer drop of three hundred feet or more to a river which hissed through granite boulders. We all laughed nervously when Zuuldibo remarked on his fear of falling as he did not know how to swim. After several hours' rough passage we came onto an plateau with fantastic views over the whole of Dowayoland laid away

The banner text of quotations and excerpts running through the publication was compiled by Rémy Markowitsch and Maya Roos. The authors and publishers cited hold the copyrights to the texts. The mix of quotations has been read and recorded by the artist for the *On Travel* exhibition, and incorporated as an audio installation.
♀ The sources marked were translated by Stephen B. Grynwasser for Apostroph AG, Translations, Lucerne.

AFRICANUS, Johann Leo, *Beschreibung Afrikas* (Leipzig: F.A. Brockhaus, 1984), p.126 ▸ 84/85. ♀
© Bibliographisches Institut & F.A. Brockhaus AG Mannheim.

ALTENBERG, Peter, "Ashantee", in: Altenberg, Peter, *Diogenes in Wien: Aphorismen, Skizzen und Geschichten*, vol.1 (Berlin: Volk & Welt, 1979), p.57 ▸ 21. ♀

BARLEY, Nigel, *The Innocent Anthropologist: Notes from a Mud Hut* (London: Penguin Books, 1986), p.73 ▸ 5, 77 ▸ 109/110, 152 ▸ 123.
© 1983 Nigel Barley.

—— *Native Land* (London: Penguin Books, 1990), p.55 ▸ 14.
© 1989 Nigel Barley.

—— *A Plague of Caterpillars: A Return to the African Bush* (London: Penguin Books, 1987), p.22 ▸ 119/120, 114 ▸ 104/105.
© 1986 Nigel Barley.

BELLOW, Saul, *Henderson the Rain King* (Harmondsworth, Middlesex: Penguin Books, 1979), p.24 ▸ 74, 157 ▸ 5/6, 201 ▸ 100/101, 187 ▸ 50/51, 229 ▸ 11/12.
© 1958, 1959, renewed 1986, 1987 Saul Bellow. Used by permission of Viking Penguin, a division of Penguin Group (USA) Inc.

BOTTON, Alain de, *The Art of Travel* (London: Hamish Hamilton, 2002), p.98 ▸ 21/22.
© 2002 Alain de Botton.

BOUGAINVILLE, Lewis de, *A Voyage Round the World* (London: Da Capo Press, 1967), p.219 ▸ 72, 251 ▸ 56/57, 252 ▸ 30/31.

BOUVIER, Nicolas, *The Scorpion-Fish*, trans. Robyn Marsack (Manchester: Carcanet Press Limited, 1987), p.37 ▸ 16/17, 39 ▸ 9, 48 ▸ 30, 55 ▸ 105, 96 ▸ 112/113, 105 ▸ 49/50.

BOYLE, T. Coraghessan, *Water Music* (London: Granta Books, 1993), p.4 ▸ 40/41, 5 ▸ 37/38, 54 ▸ 108/109, 58 ▸ 93, 67 ▸ 70, 123 ▸ 121/122, 173 ▸ 81, 319 ▸ 78.

BRAUN, Christina von, *Der Einbruch der Wohnstube in die Fremde* (Bern: Benteli, 1987), p.22 ▸ 6/7, 35 ▸ 9/10, 37 ▸ 22/23. ♀

BURGER, Hermann, *Schilten* (Frankfurt am Main: Fischer, 2002), p.294 ▸ 28/29. ♀

CHAMISSO, Adelbert von, *Peter Schlemiel: The Man Who Sold His Shadow* (New York: International Publishing Corporation, 1993), p.77 ▸ 17/18, 79 ▸ 68/69.

CHATWIN, Bruce, *What Am I Doing Here* (London: Pan Books, 1990), p.23f ▸ 10/11.

—— *The Songlines* (New York: Penguin Books, 1988), p.78 ▸ 69, 141 ▸ 102/103.
© 1987 Bruce Chatwin. Used by permission of Viking Penguin, a division of Penguin Group (USA) Inc.

CONRAD, Joseph, *Heart of Darkness* (London: Penguin Books, 1994), p.9 ▸ 27/28, 10 ▸ 41, 17 ▸ 128/Backcover, 43 ▸ 7/8, 50 ▸ 91, 51 ▸ 29, 72 ▸ 126.

DEFOE, Daniel, *Robinson Crusoe* (New York: Oxford University Press, 1999), p.221 ▸ 67/68.
By permission of Oxford University Press.

DERRIDA, Jacques, *Of Grammatology* (Baltimore: The Johns Hopkins University Press, 1997), p.104f ▸ 105/106, 122 ▸ 99.
© English Translation 1974, 1976 The Johns Hopkins University Press. Originally published in French as *De la Grammatologie* © 1967 Les Editions de Minuit. Reprinted by permission of Georges Borchardt, Inc., for Les Editions de Minuit.

---

but nevertheless must be admitted. Hermann von Wissmann, in: Johannes Fabian, *Out of Our Minds* People still stared at him uneasily, as he walked by. He felt so calm, his brain was working now so smoothly, with such logical precision, that he couldn't resist the temptation of mystifying them a bit, playing to the gallery. With twinkling, fever-bright eyes he watched their faces as he said out loud: "But there's no such place as Africa." For a quarter of an hour more, as he paced the deck methodically, he kept on repeating in a calm, clear tone: "There's no such place as Africa. No such place." Georges Simenon, *Tropic Moon* A fairy-tale wood of ancient larches, feathery with new green, spread over an emerald slope. Under the moss there might be living crystals, mauve

FABIAN, Johannes, *Out of Our Minds: Reason and Madness in the Exploration of Central Africa* (Berkeley: University of California Press, 2000), p.33 ▸ 25/26, 63 ▸ 4/5,8, 64 ▸ 71, 65 ▸ 93/94, 66f ▸ 84,120, 67f ▸ 36/37, 154 ▸ 106, 171 ▸ 113/116, 235f ▸ 100,104.

FICHTE, Hubert, *Das Haus der Mina in São Luiz de Maranhão: Materialien zum Studium des religiösen Verhaltens* (Frankfurt am Main: S. Fischer, 1989), p.17 ▸ 39/40,105. ♀
© 1989 S. Fischer Verlag GmbH, Frankfurt am Main. Reprinted by kind permission of S. Fischer Verlag GmbH, Frankfurt am Main.

—— *Petersilie: Die afroamerikanischen Religionen IV* (Frankfurt am Main: Fischer, 1980), p.47 ▸ 33, 360 ▸ 21, 368 ▸ 100. ♀
© 1980 S. Fischer Verlag GmbH, Frankfurt am Main. Reprinted by kind permission of S. Fischer Verlag GmbH, Frankfurt am Main.

FLAUBERT, Gustave, *Voyage en Égypte* (Paris: B. Grasset, 1991), p.269 ▸ 23,97, 295 ▸ 5. ♀

FLETCHER, Robert James, *Isles of Illusion: Letters from the South Seas*, ed. Bohun Lynch (Boston: Small, Maynard & Company, 1923), p.32f ▸ 3/4, 78 ▸ 23, 91f ▸ 66, 308f ▸ 57.

FRISCH, Max, *Homo Faber* (Orlando: Harcourt Brace & Company, 1959), p.36 ▸ 124/125, 40 ▸ 95.
© 1959, renewed 1987 Michael Bullock. Reprinted by permission of Harcourt, Inc.

GARY, Romain, "Grüße vom Kilimandscharo", in: Märtin, Ralf-Peter (ed.), *Lust am Reisen: Ein Lesebuch* (München: Piper, 1990), p.269 ▸ 49,71. ♀
Originally published in French as *Les racines du ciel* © Editions Gallimard, Paris.

GIDE, André, *Travels in the Congo* (Harmondsworth, Middlesex: Penguin Books, 1986), p.8 ▸ 91/92, 20 ▸ 4.
Originally published in French as *Voyage au Congo* © Editions Gallimard, Paris.

GUTZLAFF, Charles, *Journal of Three Voyages Along the Coast of China in 1831, 1832, and 1833, with Notices of Siam, Korea, and Loo-Choo Islands* (Taipei: Ch'Eng-Wen Publishing Company, 1968), p.147f ▸ 19/20, 155 ▸ 66, 175 ▸ 85/86.

HUMBOLDT, Alexander von, *Personal Narrative of a Journey to the Equinoctial Regions of the New Continent* (Harmondsworth, Middlesex: Penguin Books, 1995), p.268 ▸ 107/108.

—— *Auf Steppen und Strömen Südamerikas* (Leipzig: F.A. Brockhaus, 1968), p.217 ▸ 32/33, 221f ▸ 73, 223 ▸ 98/99, 326 ▸ 39. ♀
© Bibliographisches Institut & F.A. Brockhaus AG Mannheim.

KAFKA, Franz, *The Penal Colony, Stories and Short Pieces*, (New York: Schocken Books, 1948), p.192 ▸ 29/30, 206 ▸ 86/87.

KAPUŚCIŃSKI, Ryszard, *The Shadow of the Sun: My African Life* (London: Penguin Books, 2002), p.82 ▸ 87/88, 311 ▸ 58/59, 322 ▸ 88, 323 ▸ 74/75.

KELLER, Gottfried, *Pankraz der Schmoller* (Stuttgart: Reclam, 1980), p.16 ▸ 106. ♀

KRAMER, Fritz, *Verkehrte Welten: Zur imaginären Ethnographie des 19. Jahrhunderts* (Frankfurt am Main: Syndikat, 1981), p.95 ▸ 48/49,56, 105 ▸ 26/27. ♀
Reprinted by kind permission of Sabine Groenewold Verlage, Hamburg.

LEIRIS, Michel, *Manhood. A Journey from Childhood into the Fierce Order of Virility*, trans. Richard Howard (Chicago/London: University of Chicago Press, 2001), p.140 ▸ 12.
© Translation 1963, 1984 Richard Howard.
© Translator's Note 1983 Richard Howard.
Originally published in French as *L'Age d'homme* © 1939, 1946 Editions Gallimard, Paris.

—— *L'Afrique fantôme* (Paris: Editions Gallimard, 1981), p.299 ▸ 94, 304 ▸ 88, 390 ▸ 5, 411 ▸ 26, 506 ▸ 19, 507 ▸ 108. ♀
© Editions Gallimard, Paris.

and white. The stream in the midst of the wood somewhere ran over a boulder, falling so that it looked like a big silver comb. He no longer answered his wife's letters. Here, amid the secrets of Nature, their belonging together was only one secret more. There was a tender scarlet flower, one that existed in no other man's world, only in his, and thus God had ordered things, wholly as a wonder. There was a place in the body that was kept hidden away, and no one might see it lest he should die: only one man. At this moment it seemed to him as wonderfully senseless and unpractical as only profound religious feeling can be. And only now did he realise what he had done in cutting himself off for this summer and letting himself drift on his

LÉVI-STRAUSS, Claude, *Tristes Tropiques*
(New York: Penguin Books, 1992), p.75 ▸ 31/32,
82 ▸ 20, 86 ▸ 15/16, 87 ▸ 1, 185 ▸ 53/55, 309 ▸ 72/73,
347 ▸ 122/123, 383 ▸ 118/119, 390 ▸ 51/52, 405 ▸ 59,
414f ▸ 126/128.
Originally published in French as *Tristes Tropiques*
© 1955 Librairie Plon, Paris. Reprinted by
permission of Georges Borchardt, Inc., for Librairie
Plon, Paris. © English translation, 1973 Jonathan
Cape, Ltd.
LINDQVIST, Sven, *Exterminate All the Brutes*
(New York: New Press, 1996), p.7 ▸ 13, 48 ▸ 38,
111 ▸ 75/76, 112 ▸ 20/21, 114 ▸ 83, 133 ▸ 48, 141 ▸ 69,
172 ▸ 40,87.
MALINOWSKI, Bronislaw, *Argonauts of the Western
Pacific: An Account of Native Enterprise and
Adventure in the Archipelagoes of Melanesian New
Guinea* (London: Routledge & Kegan Paul, 1953)
p.4 ▸ 118, 34 ▸ 57/58.
MANN, Thomas, *Death in Venice* (London: Penguin
Books, 1971), p.5f ▸ Frontcover/1, 75 ▸ 112.
© Secker & Warburg. Used by permission of
The Random House Group Ltd.
—— *The Magic Mountain* (Harmondsworth, Middlesex:
Penguin Books, 1985), p.476 ▸ 76/77.
© Secker & Warburg. Used by permission of
The Random House Group Ltd.
MICHAUX, Henri, *A Barbarian in Asia*, trans. Sylvia
Beach (New York: New Directions, 1986),
p.8 ▸ 125/126, 120 ▸ 13/14.
© 1945 Librairie Gallimard; © 1949 New Directions
Publishing Corp. Reprinted by permission of New
Directions Publishing Corp.
—— *Ecuador. A Travel Journal*, trans. by Robin Magowan
(Evanston, Illinois: The Marlboro Press/North-
western, Northwestern University Press, 2001),
p.127 ▸ 55,56.
MIKLOUCHO-MACLAY, Nikolai, *New Guinea Diaries
1871–1883* (Madang: Kristen Pres, 1975), p.102 ▸ 41.
—— *Bei den Papuas: Die Reisetagebücher des Nikolai
Mikloucho-Maclay* (Berlin: Neues Leben, 1986),
p.86 ▸ 69. ♀

MORAVIA, Alberto, *A quale tribù appartieni?*
(Milano: Tascabili Bompiani, 1981),
p.77 ▸ 78/79, 143 ▸ 71/72. ♀
© 1972 RCS Libri SpA, Milano, Bompiani.
MÜLLER, Robert, *Tropen: Der Mythos der Reise:
Urkunden eines deutschen Ingenieurs* (Stuttgart:
Reclam, 1993), p.38 ▸ 35, 102 ▸ 25, 194 ▸ 16, 304 ▸ 8/9,
305 ▸ 2, 331 ▸ 12/13, 333 ▸ 1, 402 ▸ 125. ♀
© 1994-99 Igel Verlag, Uhlhornsweg 99a,
D-26129 Oldenburg.
MUSIL, Robert, "Grigia", in: Musil, Robert, *Five Women*
(Boston: Verba Mundi, David R. Godine Publisher,
1999), p.23 ▸ 24/25, 23f ▸ 116/118.
NABOKOV, Vladimir, "Terra Incognita", in:
The Stories of Vladimir Nabokov (New York: Vintage
International, 1997), p.297f ▸ 2/3, 300 ▸ 121.
© 1995 Dmitri Nabokov. Used by permission of
Alfred A. Knopf, a division of Random House, Inc.
NADOLNY, Sten, "Die Reise ins Eis", in: Märtin,
Ralf-Peter (ed.), *Lust am Reisen: Ein Lesebuch*
(München: Piper, 1990), p.441 ▸ 8. ♀
PFEIFFER, Ida, *A Lady's Voyage Round the World*
(London: Century, 1988) p.45 ▸ 86.
PYNCHON, Thomas, *Mason & Dixon* (London:
Jonathan Cape, 1997), p.60 ▸ 80/81, 65 ▸ 102.
© 1997 Thomas Pynchon. Reprinted by permission
of Melanie Jackson Agency, LLC. Reprinted by
permission of The Random House Group Ltd.
RANSMAYR, Christoph, *Der Weg nach Surabaya:
Reportagen und kleine Prosa* (Frankfurt am Main:
Fischer, 1999), p.219 ▸ 35/36. ♀
© 1997 S. Fischer Verlag GmbH, Frankfurt am
Main. Reprinted by permission of S. Fischer Verlag
GmbH, Frankfurt am Main.
—— *The Dog King* (New York: Vintage International,
1998), p.14 ▸ 75, 268 ▸ 111/112.
RYLE, John, "The Road to Abyei", in: *Granta 26*
(Spring 1989), p.89 ▸ 28.
© John Ryle, Chair of the Rift Valley Institute,
a network of regional specialists in Eastern Africa,
www.riftvalley.net.

own tide, this tide that had taken control of him. Among the trees with their arsenic-green beards he sank down on one knee and spread out his arms, a thing he had never done before in all his life, and it was as though in this moment someone lifted him out of his own embrace. *Robert Musil, Grigia* The feeling of hopelessness and despair after many obstinate but futile attempts had entirely failed to bring me into real touch with the natives, or supply me with any material. I had periods of despondency, when I buried myself in the reading of novels, as a man might take to drink in a fit of tropical depression and boredom. *Bronislaw Malinowski, Argonauts of the Western Pacific* The only justification for the dramatic fable described in the preceding chapter is

SAVIANE, Sergio, "Auf Safari in Bokassaland",
in: Enzensberger, Hans Magnus (ed.), *Nie wieder!*
Die schlimmsten Reisen der Welt (Frankfurt am Main:
Eichborn, 1997), p.271 ▸ 82/83. ♀

SCHWEINFURTH, Georg, *The Heart of Africa:*
Three Years' Travels and Adventures in the Unexplored
Regions of Central Africa: From 1868 to 1871
(London: Sampson Low, Marston, Low, and Searle,
1873), p.3 ▸ 108, 13f ▸ 120/121, 16f ▸ 84,
298 ▸ 110/111, 314 ▸ 36, 440 ▸ 53.
—— *Im Herzen von Afrika 1868–1871*
(Stuttgart: Edition Erdmann, 1984) p.330 ▸ 92/93. ♀
© 1984 Edition Erdmann, Lenningen.

SEGALEN, Victor, *Le fils du ciel* (Paris: Flammarion,
1975), p.24 ▸ 6, 93 ▸ 79/80. ♀
—— *Essay on Exoticism: An Aesthetics of Diversity*
(Durham/London: Duke University Press, 2002),
p.23 ▸ 16, 25 ▸ 1/2, 44 ▸ 125.

SEPÚLVEDA, Luis, *The Old Man Who Read Love Stories*
(London: Harcourt, Inc., 1993), p.38 ▸ 97/98.
© 1989 Luis Sepúlveda. © English translation, 1993
Peter Bush, Souvenir Press Ltd. and Harcourt, Inc.
Reprinted by permission of Harcourt, Inc.

SIMENON, Georges, "Tropic Moon", in: Simenon,
Georges, *African Trio* (New York/London:
Harcourt Brace Jovanovich, 1979), p.176 ▸ 95,109,
182 ▸ 103/104, 227 ▸ 116.
© Extract from the translation of *Tropic Moon* by
Georges Simenon reprinted with the kind
permission of Georges Simenon Ltd.
© 1933 Georges Simenon Ltd., a Chorion company.
All rights reserved.

SOMERSET MAUGHAM, William, *The Moon and*
Sixpence (New York: Penguin Books, 1944),
p.174 ▸ 27, 209 ▸ 95/97.
First published 1919. © the Royal Literary Fund.
—— *The Trembling of a Leaf* (Mililani, Hawaii: Booklines
Hawaii Ltd., 1985), p.157 ▸ 23/24, 182f ▸ 101/102.

STEPHENSON, Neal, *The Diamond Age*
(London: ROC, Penguin Books, 1996), p.19 ▸ 82.
© 1995 Neal Stephenson.

STERNE, Laurence, *Tristram Shandy*
(New York: Random House, 1928), p.484 ▸ 14/15.
STEUB, Ludwig, *Alpenreisen* (München: Heimeran,
1978), p.69 ▸ 77/78, 82 ▸ 123/124. ♀
THOREAU, Henry David, *Walden* (Oxford/
New York: Oxford University Press, 1997),
p.29 ▸ 25, 32 ▸ 74, 286 ▸ 2.
By permission of Oxford University Press.
TODOROV, Tzvetan, *The Conquest of America:*
The Question of the Other (Norman: Oklahoma
Paperbacks, University of Oklahoma Press, 1999),
p.31 ▸ 99, 200 ▸ 59/60.
© English translation, 1984 Harper & Row,
Publishers, Inc. Originally published in French as
La Conquete de l'Amérique © 1982 Editions du Seuil.
Reprinted by permission of Georges Borchardt, Inc.,
for Editions du Seuil.
TRAVEN, B., *The Bridge in the Jungle* (Chicago: Elephant
Paperback, 1994), p.7f ▸ 18/19, 191f ▸ 34/35.
VERNE, Jules, *Around the World in Eighty Days*
(London: Penguin Books, 1994), p.117 ▸ 94.
© 1987 Fischer Taschenbuch Verlag GmbH,
Frankfurt am Main. Reprinted by kind permission of
S. Fischer Verlag GmbH, Frankfurt am Main.
VOLTAIRE, *Candide or Optimism* (Hertfordshire:
Wordsworth Classics, 1993), p.42 ▸ 52/53.
VONNEGUT, Kurt, *The Sirens of the Titan*
(London: Victor Gollancz, 1972), p.30f ▸ 90/91,
169f ▸ 38/39, 314 ▸ 83/84.
WAUGH, Evelyn, *A Handful of Dust* (London: Penguin
Books, 2000), p.218 ▸ 50, 221 ▸ 89/90.
First published 1934. © 1934 Evelyn Waugh.
WEISS, Florence, *Vor dem Vulkanausbruch:*
Meine Freundinnen in Rabaul (Frankfurt am Main:
Fischer, 2001), p.313 ▸ 66/67, 315 ▸ 103. ♀
ZWEIG, Stefan, *Brazil: A Land of the Future*
(Riverside, CA: Ariadne Press, 2000), p.10 ▸ 12.
ZWEIG, Stefanie, *Nowhere in Africa*
(Madison, Wisconsin: The University of Wisconsin
Press, 2004), p.11 ▸ 89, 17 ▸ 111.
© 2004 Reprinted by permission of The University
of Wisconsin Press.

that it illustrates the mental disorder to which the traveller is exposed through abnormal living
conditions over a prolonged period. But the problem still remains: how can the anthropologist
overcome the contradiction resulting from the circumstances of his choice? He has in front
of him and available for study a given society – his own; why does he decide to spurn it and to
reserve for other societies – which are among the most remote and the most alien – a patience
and a devotion which his choice of vocation has deflected from his fellow-citizens? Claude Lévi-Strauss,
Tristes Tropiques The life style of Peace Corps members might reasonably be termed 'informal'.
Few return to the United States as clean-cut as when they arrive. Whatever contribution they

The photo work by Rémy Markowitsch reproduced here represents the outcome of his expeditions into the inner sanctum of travel and photography books.
The photographic transilluminations are based on pages of photographs printed on both sides which were taken from the publications listed below.

Frontcover ON TRAVEL 001, 2004
Source: Forrester, Bob, Mike Murray-Hudson, Lance Cherry, *The Swamp Book: Perspective and Description of the Natural Elements and Resources of the Okavango Delta* (Johannesburg: Southern Book Publishers, 1989).

Flyleaf *Fright figure: Englishman (Nicobars)*
Source: Lips, Eva, *Weisheit zwischen Eis und Urwald: Vom Humor der Naturvölker*, 2nd ed. (Leipzig: F. A. Brockhaus, 1959), p.162. Drawing by Inge Brüx.

Page 1 ON TRAVEL 059, 2004
Source: Dolder, Willi, *Tropenwelt: Fauna und Flora zwischen Wendekreisen* (Bern: Kümmerly & Frey, Geographischer Verlag, 1976).

Pages 2/3 BARLEY, 2004
Installation view, Museum zu Allerheiligen, Schaffhausen, 2004. Exterior view: wood material, paint, beer bottle. Photo: Jürg Fausch.

Pages 4/5 BARLEY, 2004
Installation view, Museum zu Allerheiligen, Schaffhausen, 2004. Interior view: wood material, paint, book, chicken claws. Photo: Jürg Fausch.

Pages 6/7 ON TRAVEL 104, 1998
Source: Boerschmann, Ernst, *Baukunst und Landschaft in China: Eine Reise durch zwölf Provinzen* (Berlin: Ernst Wasmuth, 1926).

Pages 8/9 ON TRAVEL 005, 2001
Source: Berg, Bengt, *Mit den Zugvögeln nach Afrika* (Berlin: Dietrich Reimer/Ernst Vohsen, 1932).

Pages 10/11 ON TRAVEL 114, 1998
Source: Yongnan, Shi, Wang Tianxing (ed.), *Famous Places in China* (Beijing: China Esperanto Press, 1997).

Page 12 ON TRAVEL 067, 2004
Source: Wyss, Max Albert, *Zauber der Berge: Eine Auswahl der schönsten Aufnahmen aus der europäischen Alpenwelt* (Lucerne/Frankfurt am Main: C. J. Bucher, 1966). (Published under licence for the Buchclub Ex Libris)

Page 13 ON TRAVEL 128, 2001
Source: Reisigel, Dr. Herbert, *Blumen-Paradiese der Welt: Aus dem Reich der Botaniker und Blumenfreunde* (Innsbruck: Pinguin-Verlag/Frankfurt am Main: Umschau Verlag, 1964).

Page 14 ON TRAVEL 065, 2001
Source: Frass, Hermann, *Wunderwelt der Dolomiten* (Bozen: Athesia, 1969).

Page 15 ON TRAVEL 066, 2003
Source: Brybycin, Georg, *Our Fragile Wilderness: The Splendor of Canada's Western Nature* (Calgary, Alberta: G.B. Publishing, 1980).

Pages 16/17 ON TRAVEL 016, 1998
Source: Roedelberg, Franz A., Vera Groschoff, *Belauschte Wildnis: Afrikas Tierwelt in 250 Bildern* (Frankfurt am Main/Vienna/Zurich: Büchergilde Gutenberg, 1964).

Pages 18/19 ON TRAVEL 041, 2004
Source: Roedelberg, Franz A., Vera Groschoff, *Ernte im Garten Eden: Eine Umweltschau in 250 Bildern aus der Lebensgemeinschaft der Pflanzen und Tiere* (Berlin: Safari Verlag Reinhard Jaspert, 1972).

Pages 20/21 ON TRAVEL 039, 2003
Source: Lindgens, Dr. Arthur, *Afrika aufs Korn genommen: Mit Büchse und Kamera durch Ostafrika* (Hamburg: Paul Parey, 1953).

Pages 22/23 ON TRAVEL 004, 2001
Source: Berg, Bengt, *Mit den Zugvögeln nach Afrika*.

Page 24 ON TRAVEL 120, 2003
Source: Wyss, Max Albert, *Zauber der Berge*.

Page 25 ON TRAVEL 030, 2002
Source: Dolder, Willi, *Tropenwelt*.

Page 26 ON TRAVEL 028, 2003
Source: Kümmerli, Walter, *Der Wald: Welt der Bäume, Bäume der Welt* (Bern: Kümmerly & Frey, Geographischer Verlag, 1970).

---

may or may not make to Third World development, they undergo rapid personal change. Nigel Barley, *A Plague of Caterpillars* At night, thinking that the place looked unusually peaceable, I resolved that I would try to get a really good night's sleep – a luxury I had been deprived of for several days. To allay the feverish excitement of my brain I took a good dose of laudanum, and turned into my tent. Jérôme Becker, in: Johannes Fabian, *Out of Our Minds* How large is the proportion of beer consumed by the Niam-niam may be estimated by simply observing the ordinary way in which they store their corn. As a regular rule, there are three granaries allotted to each dwelling, of which two are made to suffice for the supply which is to contribute the meal necessary for

Page 27 ON TRAVEL 069, 2004
  Source: Trenker, Luis, *Goldene Bergwelt*
  (Munich: F. Bruckmann, 1981).
Page 28 ON TRAVEL 061, 2004
  Source: Fishbein, Seymour L. (ed.),
  Wilderness U.S.A. (Washington D.C.: National
  Geographic Society, 1973).
Page 29 ON TRAVEL 060, 2004
  Source: Fishbein, Seymour L. (ed.):
  Wilderness U.S.A.
Pages 30/31 ON TRAVEL 094, 2004
  Source: *Amerikanische Nationalparks*
  (Stuttgart: Parkland, 1985).
Pages 32/33 ON TRAVEL 027, 2004
  Source: Roedelberg, Franz A., Vera Groschoff,
  Ernte im Garten Eden.
Pages 34/35 ON TRAVEL 109, 1998
  Source: Yongnan, Shi, Wang Tianxing (ed.),
  Famous Places in China.
Page 36 ON TRAVEL 122, 2004
  Source: Brybycin, Georg, *Our Fragile Wilderness*.
Page 37 ON TRAVEL 071, 2004
  Source: Trenker, Luis, *Goldene Bergwelt*.
Page 38 ON TRAVEL 013, 2004
  Source: Curry-Lindahl, Kai, *Knaurs Tierleben in
  Steppe und Savanne* (Munich/Zurich: Droemersche
  Verlagsanstalt Th. Knaur Nachf., 1981). (Published
  under licence for the Buchclub Ex Libris)
Page 39 ON TRAVEL 082, 2004
  Source: Brybycin, Georg, *Our Fragile Wilderness*.
Page 40 ON TRAVEL 127, 2001
  Source: Reisigel, Dr. Herbert, *Blumen-Paradiese
  der Welt*.
Page 41 ON TRAVEL 045, 2004
  Source: Curry-Lindahl, Kai, *Knaurs Tierleben
  in Steppe und Savanne*.
Pages 42/43 ON TRAVEL 049, 2004
  Source: Kümmerli, Walter, *Der Wald*.
Pages 44/45 ON TRAVEL 051, 2004
  Source: Kümmerli, Walter, *Der Wald*.
Pages 46/47 ON TRAVEL 050, 2004
  Source: Tosco, Uberto, *The Flowering Wilderness*
  (Novarra: Igeda/Orbis Publishing, 1972).

Page 48 ON TRAVEL: «TRISTES TROPIQUES» 02, 2004
  Source: Lévi-Strauss, Claude, *Traurige Tropen*
  (Frankfurt am Main: Suhrkamp, 1998). (Original
  edition: «Tristes Tropiques», Librairie Plon, 1955)
Page 49 ON TRAVEL: «TRISTES TROPIQUES» 01, 2004
  Source: Lévi-Strauss, Claude, *Traurige Tropen*.
Page 50 ON TRAVEL: «TRISTES TROPIQUES» 13, 2004
  Source: Lévi-Strauss, Claude, *Traurige Tropen*.
Page 51 ON TRAVEL: «TRISTES TROPIQUES» 12, 2004
  Source: Lévi-Strauss, Claude, *Traurige Tropen*.
Page 52 ON TRAVEL: «TRISTES TROPIQUES» 07, 2004
  Source: Lévi-Strauss, Claude, *Traurige Tropen*.
Page 53 ON TRAVEL: «TRISTES TROPIQUES» 03, 2004
  Source: Lévi-Strauss, Claude, *Traurige Tropen*.
Page 54 ON TRAVEL: «TRISTES TROPIQUES» 04, 2004
  Source: Lévi-Strauss, Claude, *Traurige Tropen*.
Page 55 ON TRAVEL: «TRISTES TROPIQUES» 08, 2004
  Source: Lévi-Strauss, Claude, *Traurige Tropen*.
Page 56 ON TRAVEL: «TRISTES TROPIQUES» 05, 2004
  Source: Lévi-Strauss, Claude, *Traurige Tropen*.
Page 57 ON TRAVEL: «TRISTES TROPIQUES» 06, 2004
  Source: Lévi-Strauss, Claude, *Traurige Tropen*.
Page 58 ON TRAVEL: «TRISTES TROPIQUES» 14, 2004
  Source: Lévi-Strauss, Claude, *Traurige Tropen*.
Page 59 ON TRAVEL: «TRISTES TROPIQUES» 20, 2004
  Source: Lévi-Strauss, Claude, *Traurige Tropen*.
Pages 60/61 ON TRAVEL 048, 2004
  Source: Schumacher, Eugen: *Die letzten Paradiese:
  Auf den Spuren seltener Tiere* (Gütersloh:
  C. Bertelsmann, 1966).
Pages 62/63 ON TRAVEL 053, 2004
  Source: Schumacher, Eugen, *Die letzten Paradiese*.
Pages 64/65 ON TRAVEL 055, 2004
  Source: Schumacher, Eugen, *Die letzten Paradiese*.
Pages 66/67 ON TRAVEL 025, 2003
  Source: Lindgens, Dr. Arthur, *Afrika aufs Korn
  genommen*.
Pages 68/69 ON TRAVEL 108, 1998
  Source: Yongnan, Shi, Wang Tianxing (ed.),
  Famous Places in China.
Page 70 ON TRAVEL 102, 2004
  Source: Richter, Walter, *Blüten aus Tropenfernen*
  (Radebeul/Berlin: Neumann, 1953).

the household; the other is entirely devoted to the grain that has been malted. Georg Schweinfurth, *The Heart of Africa* Meanwhile we kept sinking into the ooze more and more frequently, deeper and deeper; the insatiable mire would suck at us; and, wriggling, we would slip free. Cook kept falling down and crawling, covered with insect bites, all swollen and soaked, and, dear God, how he would squeal when disgusting bevies of minute, bright-green hydrotic snakes, attracted by our sweat, would take off in pursuit of us, tensing and uncoiling to sail two yards and then another two. Vladimir Nabokov, *Terra Incognita* It is dark and still. Rain sifts through the trees with a whisper. The horse is dead, the ass gone. There is no sound from Johnson. Mungo is

Page 71 ON TRAVEL 110, 2004
Source: Grosier, J.-B., *Die Welt des alten China* (Geneva: Editions Minerva, 1972).
Page 72 ON TRAVEL 084, 2001
Source: Reisigel, Dr. Herbert, *Blumen-Paradiese der Welt*.
Page 73 ON TRAVEL 090, 2001
Source: Brybycin, Georg, *Our Fragile Wilderness*.
Pages 74/75 ON TRAVEL 096, 2004
Source: *Paradiese auf Erden* (Künzelsau: Sigloch Edition, 1977).
Pages 76/77 ON TRAVEL 119, 2001
Source: Yongnan, Shi, Wang Tianxing (ed.), *Famous Places in China*.
Pages 78/79 ON TRAVEL 002, 2004
Source: Berger, Dr. Arthur, *Belauschte Tierwelt: Ein Bilderwerk mit Text aus dem Leben der Tiere* (Berlin: Deutsche Buch-Gemeinschaft, 1930).
Pages 80/81 ON TRAVEL 022, 2004
Source: Ulrich, Ursula, *Löwen waren unsere Nachbarn* (Radebeul: Neumann, 1964).
Pages 82/83 ON TRAVEL 024, 2003
Source: Lindgens, Dr. Arthur, *Afrika aufs Korn genommen*.
Pages 84/85 ON TRAVEL 073, 2004
Source: Paturi, Felix R., *Die Alpen* (Stuttgart/ München: Deutscher Bücherbund, 1984).
Pages 86/87 ON TRAVEL 075, 2004
Source: Roedelberg, Franz A., Vera Groschoff, *Ernte im Garten Eden*.
Page 88 ON TRAVEL 068, 2004
Source: Trenker, Luis, *Goldene Bergwelt*.
Page 89 ON TRAVEL 121, 2003
Source: Wyss, Max Albert, *Zauber der Berge*.
Page 90 ON TRAVEL 044, 2004
Source: Curry-Lindahl, Kai, *Knaurs Tierleben in Steppe und Savanne*.
Page 91 ON TRAVEL 087, 2003
Source: Preuß, Horst, Hering Hans, *In der Schorfheide: Streifzüge zwischen Havel und Grimnitzsee* (Leipzig: F.A. Brockhaus, 1975).
Page 92 ON TRAVEL 070, 2004
Source: Trenker, Luis, *Goldene Bergwelt*.

Page 93 ON TRAVEL 126, 2004
Source: Richter, Walter, *Blüten aus Tropenfernen*.
Pages 94/95 ON TRAVEL 100, 2004
Source: Roedelberg, Franz A., Vera Groschoff, *Belauschte Wildnis*.
Pages 96/97 ON TRAVEL 046, 2004
Source: Roedelberg, Franz A., Vera Groschoff, *Belauschte Wildnis*.
Pages 98/99 ON TRAVEL 093, 2004
Source: *Paradiese auf Erden*.
Pages 100/101 ON TRAVEL 037, 2004
Source: Kümmerli, Walter, *Der Wald*.
Pages 102/103 ON TRAVEL 105, 1998
Source: Boerschmann, Ernst, *Baukunst und Landschaft in China*.
Page 104 ON TRAVEL 085, 2004
Source: Preuß, Horst, Hering Hans, *In der Schorfheide*.
Page 105 ON TRAVEL 086, 2004
Source: Preuß, Horst, Hering Hans, *In der Schorfheide*.
Pages 106/107 ON TRAVEL 040, 2004
Source: Höhn, Reinhardt, *Seltsames aus dem Reich der Pflanzen* (Lucerne: Reich, 1977).
Pages 108/109 ON TRAVEL 009, 2001
Source: Ullrich, Wolfgang, *Afrika einmal nicht über Kimme und Korn gesehen* (Radebeul: Neumann, 1962).
Pages 110/111 ON TRAVEL 017, 2001
Source: Berg, Bengt, *Mit den Zugvögeln nach Afrika*.
Pages 112/113 BARLEY, 2004
Installation view, Museum zu Allerheiligen, Schaffhausen, 2004. Interior view, detail: ceiling perforation (inspired by face paintings on photographs in: Lévi-Strauss, Claude, *Traurige Tropen*). Photo: Jürg Fausch.
Pages 114/115 BARLEY, 2004
Installation view, Museum zu Allerheiligen, Schaffhausen, 2004. Interior view, detail: book (Barley, Nigel, *The Innocent Anthropologist*) and chicken claws. Photo: Jürg Fausch.
Page 128 ON TRAVEL 058, 2004
Source: Dolder, Willi, *Tropenwelt*.

lying supine in the ooze of the forest floor, naked as the day he was born, broken it seems in any number of places, and feeling very weary indeed. Very weary of exploring, very weary of Africa. And very weary of being alone here in the dark, defenseless and afraid. He props himself on his elbows, wincing with the effort, and looks around. Nothing. The dark is so absolute and inpenetrable it's as if the earth has been turned inside out. But what was that? A movement in the bush, a rustle of leaves. T. Coraghessan Boyle, *Water Music* At first glance, one might have thought that these houses were of the same type as the local Brazilian dwellings. Actually, they were quite different in design, since the area enclosed by the posts supporting the high,

End flyleaf *The Englishman, fright figure of the Nicobars*
  Source: Kramer, Fritz, *Verkehrte Welten: Zur
  imaginären Ethnographie des 19. Jahrhunderts*, 2ⁿᵈ ed.
  (Frankfurt am Main: Syndikat, 1981), p. 109: ill. 7.
Backcover ON TRAVEL 111, 2003
  Source: Grosier, J.-B., *Die Welt des alten China.*

***

Technical data about the works

ON TRAVEL 001–130, 1998–2004
  Series. RC print, acrylic glass, wood.
  178 × 178 cm / 218 × 160 – 180 cm / 160 × 240 – 300 cm.
  Courtesy:
  Kunstverein Schaffhausen
  Galerie EIGEN+ART, Berlin / Leipzig
  GalerieUrsMeile, Lucerne

ON TRAVEL: « TRISTES TROPIQUES » 01–20, 2004
  Series. RC print, glass, wood. 87 × 67 cm.
  © for the photographs in «Tristes Tropiques»
  Claude Lévi-Strauss, 1955/2004.
  By kind permission of the author and the publishers
  Editions Plon, Paris.
  Courtesy:
  Kunstverein Schaffhausen
  Galerie EIGEN+ART, Berlin / Leipzig
  GalerieUrsMeile, Lucerne

BARLEY, 2004
  Rémy Markowitsch in co-operation with
  Philipp von Matt, architect, Berlin. Installation.
  Wood material, paint, beer bottle, book, chicken
  claws. 226 × 226 × 306 cm.
  Craftsmanship by: Schmid & Vollenweider,
  Furniture Workshops, Lucerne.
  Chicken claws: mount prepared by
  Marcel Nyffenegger, Schaffhausen.
  Courtesy:
  Kunstverein Schaffhausen
  Galerie EIGEN+ART, Berlin / Leipzig
  GalerieUrsMeile, Lucerne

The collected quotations were reprinted
with the kind support of:

F.A. Brockhaus AG, Mannheim
The University of Chicago Press, Chicago, USA
Diogenes Verlag, Zurich
Duke University Press, Durham, North Carolina, USA
S. Fischer Verlag GmbH, Frankfurt am Main
Editions Gallimard, Paris
Sabine Groenewold Verlage, Hamburg
The Johns Hopkins University Press,
Baltimore, Maryland, USA
Melanie Jackson Agency, LLC, New York
Mohrbooks Literary Agency, Zurich
University of Nebraska Press, Lincoln, Nebraska, USA
Northwestern University Press, Evanston, Illinois, USA
Penguin Group Inc., New York, USA
The Random House Group, London
RCS Libri SpA, Milano, Bompiani
John Ryle, Chair of the Rift Valley Institute, a network
of regional specialists in Eastern Africa, www.riftvalley.net
Secker & Warburg, The Random House Group Limited,
Rushden, Northants, UK
Georges Simenon Ltd., a Chorion company, London
The University of Wisconsin Press, Madison,
Wisconsin, USA

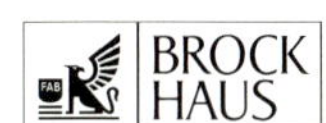
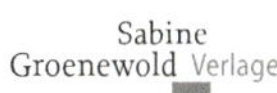
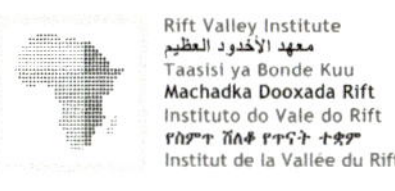

two-sided palm roof was smaller than the total area of the roof itself, so that the building had the shape of a square mushroom. *Claude Lévi-Strauss, Tristes Tropiques* It was considered a great joke when I asked why they had left off the normal spikes that protect a house-dweller against witchcraft. Everyone knew that a white man was not subject to attacks from witchcraft just as everyone knew that he must live in a square, not a round house. My own house was consequently built square and, instead of witchcraft remedies, an empty beer bottle was placed on top. *Nigel Barley, The Innocent Anthropologist* In front of the hut a spring bubbled with classical water. Indoors was the hearth, also a settle, and a large cheese kettle. On the wooden walls

ACKNOWLEDGEMENTS

I'd like to thank all my fellow travellers who supported my *On Travel* expedition: I thank Markus Stegmann, Director of the Art Department at the Museum zu Allerheiligen, Schaffhausen, for the idea and the invitation to set off on my *On Travel* journey on behalf of the Kunstverein Schaffhausen. Together with Claudine Metzger, exhibition curator, we travelled through many climate zones, and I am grateful to both of you for alternately cooling my fevered brow and providing vital human warmth when I faced hypothermia. Thank you both for working so closely with and alongside me. My thanks also to the Museum zu Allerheiligen and its director, Roger Fayet; to the town of Schaffhausen, the Kunstverein Schaffhausen and its President Walter Stählin, and to Hortensia von Roda, of the Sturzenegger Foundation, Schaffhausen, without whom this publication would never have seen the light of day. I thank the Erna and Curt Burgauer Foundation, Zurich, and the Fuka Fund, Lucerne, for their support. I'm delighted that *On Travel* is to travel on: I thank Ellen Seifermann, curator at the Kunsthalle Nürnberg, for her invitation, and look forward to our joint venture. – Yet what would my travels have been without my "informants"? I owe my travels – and this book – to them and their books. Countless photographers, authors and their publishers guided me along twisting paths. I thank Claude Lévi-Strauss for the permission to publish as trans-illuminations in the series *On Travel: « Tristes Tropiques »* his photographs of the Caduevo, Bororo, Mundé and Nambikwara in the Amazon region and in the Matto Grosso, all of which first appeared in *Tristes Tropiques* in 1955. 'Ethnographically' the best informant has been Thomas Kissling, graphic artist in Zurich: I'm indebted to him for Nigel Barley and his rectangular hut from *The Innocent Anthropologist*; for T.C. Boyle's frightfully beautiful *Water Music*; and for Bouvier's *The Scorpion-Fish*. Rolf Bismarck wisely prescribed the correct dosage of Stephenson's *Diamond Age*, Christoph Doswald Steub's *Alpenreisen* and Todorov's *The Conquest of America* while Edith Jud sent me for a booster of Keller's *Pankraz der Schmoller*. I am grateful to my brother Guy Markowitsch for our many conversations, and for Viktor Segalen as well as Derrida's *Of Grammatology*; to Bea Moser for Bellow's *Henderson the Rain King*; to Irene Müller for Maugham's

The Moon and Sixpence, *The Trembling of a Leaf* and Waugh's *A Handful of Dust*; to Thorsten Platz for Fichte's *Homosexualität und Literatur*; and to Katja Richter for Frisch's *Homo Faber*. My longest and most beautiful journey has been life with Maya Roos. To her I owe Thoreau's *Walden* and Sterne's *Tristram Shandy*. Roland Scotti, curator at the Kirchner Museum Davos, knew about Fletcher's *Isles of Illusion*; Ellen Seifermann recommended Vonnegut's *The Sirens of the Titan*; I also thank all those who sent me vast supplies of information, and apologise if I have not listed their names individually. The gripping online reading sessions with Thomas Schwarz and his Robert Müller home page were crucial, as was Angelika Jacobs's *'Wildnis' als Wunschraum westlicher 'Zivilisation'*. Special thanks to Stephan Fiedler and Thorsten Platz, Berlin, for the layout of the travel images and expert guidance along this journey: *On Travel* is now the third work to be published with Berlin's all&slothrop, after *Handmade* and *Bibliotherapy* with Stephan Fiedler. It is thanks to Elisabeth Stofer and Wolfgang Krebs, at Apostroph Übersetzungen&Beratung, Lucerne, that "the foreign" was made accessible to us readers, at least at the language level; I am grateful for their kind sponsoring, and the perfect management from Janette Steudler and Stephen B. Grynwasser, who translated for Apostroph those excerpts that were not available in English. *On Travel* was conceived under a tent with Maya Roos, and I'm grateful to her for her editorial guidance and research work in the jungle of books and the swamps of the www. After the huge project management task with *Bibliotherapy* I am indebted to Antje Weitzel, Berlin, for the editorial overview, the scientific handling of the sources, and the refreshing input. My thanks to Lala Minou Möbius, Berlin, who not once went under while swimming in the sea of copies and books; to Loredana Markowitsch, who coolly transcribed the quotations and looked after her own family and job; and to Robert Roos, Horw, who supervised the copy and added his own distinctive linguistic sheen. I thank Jörg von Bruchhausen, Berlin, for the photographic transilluminations of the book pages; he is a master at rendering colour tones and shades of grey. The 13×18cm slides were scanned and interpreted to perfection by Günter Hansmann, Berlin, Licht&Tiefe.

key frames, several pans, milk buckets and such like. It has been remarked upon hundred of times that culture leaves its mark everywhere, and so there was also Saxon earthenware, and cups with views of Saxon Switzerland or the Rhine. In a corner there was a small crucifix with sundry pictures of saints all around it, hinting at a small family altar. Various paintings were also affixed here and there, for the sake of embellishment. Ludwig Steub, *Alpenreisen*   We were suspended in hammocks, with beer within reach all the time, sweating as though sweating was our purpose in life, incapable of coming to any decision, quite contented actually, because the beer there was excellent, YUCATECA, better than the beer in the uplands. We lay suspended in

I thank Philipp von Matt, architect, Berlin, for our fourth
venture – on a tiny scale by his standards; again I have
benefited from his friendship, conversation and unerring
instinct: For my exhibition *you're not alone* 2004 at the
Kirchner Museum Davos – (*you are not alone Vol. 1 und
Vol. 2* looks at regulations and alcohol, 2004, at the
Galleries Eigen + Art, Berlin, and Urs Meile, Lucerne)
– we reconstructed Ernst Ludwig Kirchner's living room,
where he spent his last few years, addicted to the morphine
derivate *Eukodal*. For *On Travel* we developed *Barley*,
a "modernistic primeval hut", which through Barley's
The Innocent Anthropologist: Notes from a Mud Hut gave
me the idea for the self-quoting "Barley Hut". I am
indebted to Martin Schmid, Schmid & Vollenweider
Furniture Workshops, Lucerne, for his sponsoring and his
fine workmanship. The wooden frames for the *On Travel*
photographs and *Barley* itself were created in his workshops. The Swiss chicken claws – arranged by Markus
Huber, curator at the Museum Stemmler, Schaffhausen
– which firmly grip Barley's *The Innocent Anthropologist*
inside the hut are the work of Marcel Nyffenegger,
taxidermist, to whom I am most indebted. The creative
audio output for the Museum zu Allerheiligen has become
a tradition: After *Schaschlik*, 1997, for the exhibition
Animaux et Animaux, under the curatorship of Markus
Stegmann and with literary inspiration from Stefan Hardt's
Tod und Eros beim Essen, Hanspeter Dommann, Lucerne,
has now produced my *On Travel* reading. I thank
Hanspeter Dommann, sound engineer, for the expert
recordings and digital post-editing. Without Judy and Urs,
i.e. Gerd Harry Lybke, Gallery Eigen + Art, Berlin, and
Urs Meile, Galerie Urs Meile, Lucerne, my expeditions
would too often have become bogged down in the
quicksand of sad reality – I thank you! My thanks also to
Kathrin Becker, Esther Bühlmann, Miou, Davix,
Clementine Deliss, Shahram Entekabi, Sabine Fleck,
Felix Stephan Huber, Urs Stahel and David Thorp for
exciting discussions, ideas and recommendations.
My warmest thanks to my parents Nina and René
Markowitsch, for their generosity and delightful reading
weeks on the "happy islands". – I thank the publishing
companies for sponsoring the quotations in my compilation.
I also thank Editions Plon, Paris, and Barbara Angerer for
the *Tristes Tropiques* commitment; Sylvie Nerisson, Paris,
for advice and assistance; and Annette Scherer, Verlag
für moderne Kunst Nürnberg, for putting me right so many
times. I am grateful to André Stutz and the Stutz Foto
Color Technik AG, Bremgarten, for the generous
sponsoring, and to his team for such good co-operation
always. A special thanks to René Linder for his brilliant
interpretation of sample prints and digital data; to Astrid
Linder for the digital handling of the *Tristes Tropiques*
series; and to Christiane Sep for her dedicated print
exposure work; hers is a profession that has become all
too rare in today's digital world. As a laboratory technician
she specialises in large-format analogue prints, working in
darkrooms with enlargers and negatives to expose photographs on to paper that is even shorter-lived than we are.
– Thanks to Peter Küng's skills the photographs do fade
less quickly; he and his team seal the photographs air-tight
with silicone and UV-resistant acrylic glass against the
air's polluting effects. I thank B+T Bild+Ton AG, Ebikon,
for sponsoring my video installation *Mr. Herbert*, made
possible by Andreas Brennwald. My thanks to Roger Duss
of B+T, for the faultless execution of my digital AV requests.
Two of the few common denominators we share with the
people from earlier worlds we still read about include a
penchant for intoxication and a love of enjoyment. Beer is
one of those cultural achievements to which people of all
continents and cultures have readily subscribed over so
many centuries, and my warmest thanks go to the Brauerei
Eichhof, Lucerne, for its beer culture in *On Travel* and
Barley, in particular its director Werner Dubach and
Franziska Weissen. Beer has a legitimate place among
intoxicants. – It is also under the influence, albeit literary,
of Avital Ronell's *Crack Wars – Literature, Addiction, Mania*,
again recommended by Antje Weitzel, that I conclude
with a quote: "There is no culture without a drug culture,
even if this is to be sublimated to pharmaceuticals."

Rémy Markowitsch, Berlin 2004

our hammocks and drank, so that we could sweat better, and I couldn't think what we really
wanted. Max Frisch, *Homo Faber* But when in the future someone will be asked whether he has ever
been to the Tropics, he will say: "The Tropics? What for, the Tropics! I'm the Tropics!" Robert Müller,
Tropen *Let us first separate, "tropics" from "exoticism". The further I go, the more I realize how
indispensable it is to my friends and to me that I write my Essay on Exoticism. I told you I had
been happy in the tropics. This is violently true. During the two years I spent in Polynesia, I could
hardly sleep for joy.* Victor Segalen, *Essay on Exoticism* The white man possesses a quality that has
enabled him to make his way: *disrespect*. Disrespect being empty-handed must fabricate. The

This book is published to coincide with the exhibitions

Rémy Markowitsch · On Travel

5 September to 7 November 2004
Museum zu Allerheiligen / Kunstverein Schaffhausen
Baumgartenstr. 6, CH-8200 Schaffhausen, Switzerland
www.allerheiligen.ch
Director, Art Department Markus Stegmann
Curator Claudine Metzger

3 February to 3 April 2005
Kunsthalle Nürnberg
Lorenzer Str. 32, D-90402 Nürnberg, Germany
www.kunsthalle.nuernberg.de
Director Ellen Seifermann

On Travel

The original idea for the exhibition and book was conceived by Rémy Markowitsch and helped on its way by Museum zu Allerheiligen / Kunstverein Schaffhausen, Switzerland.
The quotations and excerpts were compiled by Rémy Markowitsch and Maya Roos.

Barley

Concept: Rémy Markowitsch in collaboration with Philipp von Matt, architect, Berlin.
The exhibition in Schaffhausen features the Multiple *Barley* created by Rémy Markowitsch and Philipp von Matt, architect, Berlin, published by Edition 5, CH-Erstfeld, www.edition5.org.

On Travel is sponsored by

The Sturzenegger Foundation, Schaffhausen
The Canton of Schaffhausen
Schaffhauser Kantonalbank, Schaffhausen
The Town of Lucerne, Cultural Department,
FUKA Foundation, Lucerne
The Erna and Curt Burgauer Foundation, Zurich
Apostroph AG, Translations, Lucerne
B+T Bild+Ton AG, Ebikon
Brauerei Eichhof, Lucerne
Stutz Foto Color Technik AG, Bremgarten
Schmid & Vollenweider, Furniture Workshops, Lucerne
Hanspeter Dommann, Sound Recordings, Lucerne

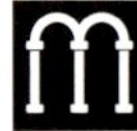 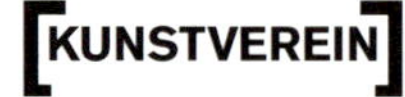 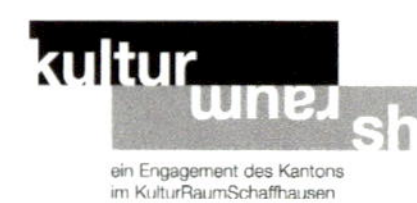 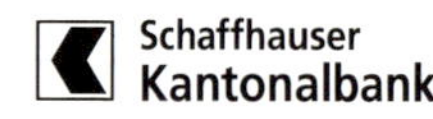 

Hindu is *religious*, he feels that he is connected with everything. The American has hardly anything. And even that is too much. The white man does not allow himself to be hypnotized by anything. Henri Michaux, *A Barbarian in Asia*   It was very simple, and at the end of that moving appeal to every altruistic sentiment it blazed at you, luminous and terrifying, like a flash of lightning in a serene sky: "Exterminate all the brutes!" Joseph Conrad, *Heart of Darkness*   Just as the individual is not alone in the group, nor any one society alone among the others, so man is not alone in the universe. When the spectrum or rainbow of human cultures has finally sunk into the void created by our frenzy; as long as we continue to exist and there is a world, that tenuous arch

Publishing details

Editor
Markus Stegmann, Schaffhausen
Editorial team
Maya Roos, Antje Weitzel, Berlin,
and Claudine Metzger, Schaffhausen
Assistant
Lala Minou Möbius, Berlin
Proofreading
Apostroph AG, Translations, Lucerne
Translator
Stephen B. Grynwasser, for Apostroph AG,
Translations, Lucerne

Reprographic transilluminations
Jörg von Bruchhausen, photographer, Berlin
Exhibition photos
Jürg Fausch, photographer, Schaffhausen

Design and typesetting
all&slothrop,
Stephan Fiedler and Thorsten Platz, Berlin
Scans
Licht & Tiefe, Berlin
Printers
H. Heenemann, Berlin
Bookbinders
Lüderitz & Bauer, Berlin
Edition
German edition: 1,400 copies
English edition: 400 copies

© 2004 Verlag für moderne Kunst Nürnberg,
Kunstverein Schaffhausen, Rémy Markowitsch
The authors and lenders have been identified
as the holders of the copyrights to the texts and
illustrations cited.
Despite intensive research, we were unable to
ascertain the name of the author with certainty
in every case. We look forward to hearing from
you accordingly.
All rights reserved.
Printed in Germany.

ISBN 3-936711-33-X (publishing edition)
Verlag für moderne Kunst Nürnberg

ISBN 3-907066-55-3 (museum edition)
Museum zu Allerheiligen, Schaffhausen, Switzerland

Distributed outside Europe by
D.A.P. / Distributed Art Publishers, Inc., New York,
155 Sixth Avenue, 2nd Floor, New York, NY 10013,
phone +1(212) 627-19 99, fax +1(212) 627-94 84

Bibliographic information published by
Die Deutsche Bibliothek
Die Deutsche Bibliothek lists this publication in the
Deutsche Nationalbibliografie; detailed bibliographic
data is available on the internet at http://dnb.ddb.de.

Rémy Markowitsch is represented by:
Gallery EIGEN+ART, Berlin/Leipzig
www.eigen-art.com
GalerieUrsMeile, Lucerne
www.galerie-meile.ch
For more information on the artist and his work visit:
www.markowitsch.org

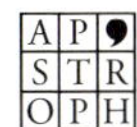
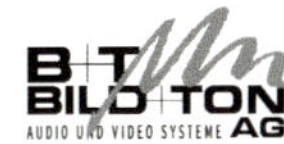
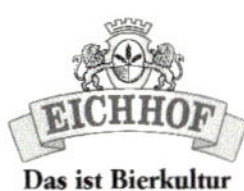
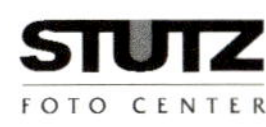

Schmid & Vollenweider
Furniture Workshops, Lucerne

Hanspeter Dommann
Sound Recordings, Lucerne

linking us to the inaccessible will still remain, to show us the opposite course to that leading to enslavement; man may be unable to follow it, but its contemplation affords him the only privilege of which he can make himself worthy; that of arresting the process, of controlling the impulse which forces him to block up the cracks in the wall of necessity one by one and to complete his work at the same time as he shuts himself up within his prison; this is a privilege coveted by every society, whatever its beliefs, its political system or its level of civilization; a privilege to which it attaches its leisure, its pleasure, its peace of mind and its freedom; the possibility, vital for life, of *unhitching*, which consists – Oh! fond farewell to savages and

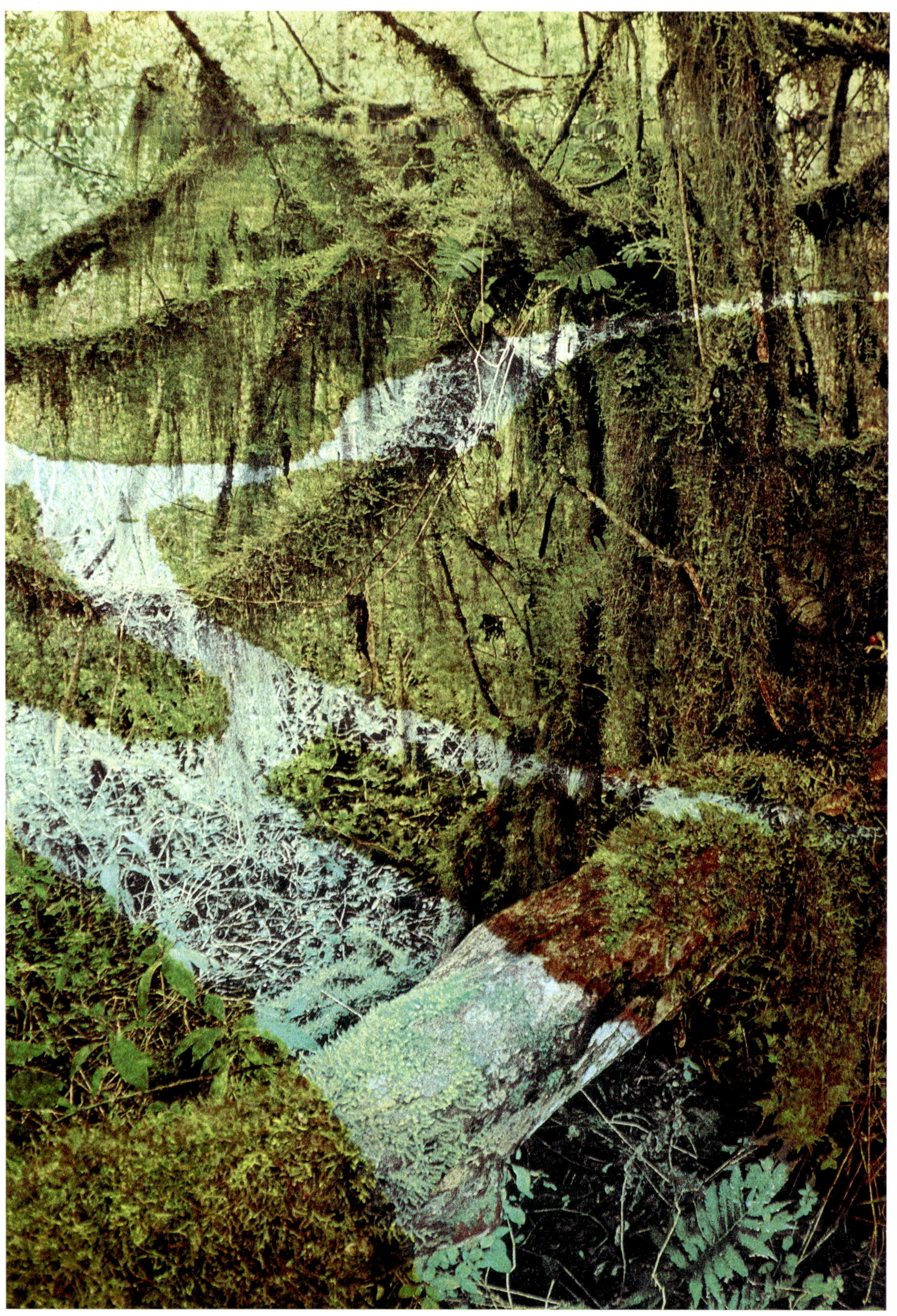

explorations! – in grasping, during the brief intervals in which our species can bring itself to interrupt its hive-like activity, the essence of what it was and continues to be, below the threshold of thought and over and above society: in the contemplation of a mineral more beautiful than all our creations; in the scent that can be smelt at the heart of a lily and is more imbued with learning than all our books; or in the brief glance, heavy with patience, serenity and mutual forgiveness, that, through some involuntary understanding, one can sometimes exchange with a cat. Claude Lévi-Strauss, *Tristes Tropiques* "Avoid irritation more than exposure to the sun. Adieu. How do you English say, eh? Good-bye. Ah! Good-bye. Adieu. In the tropics one

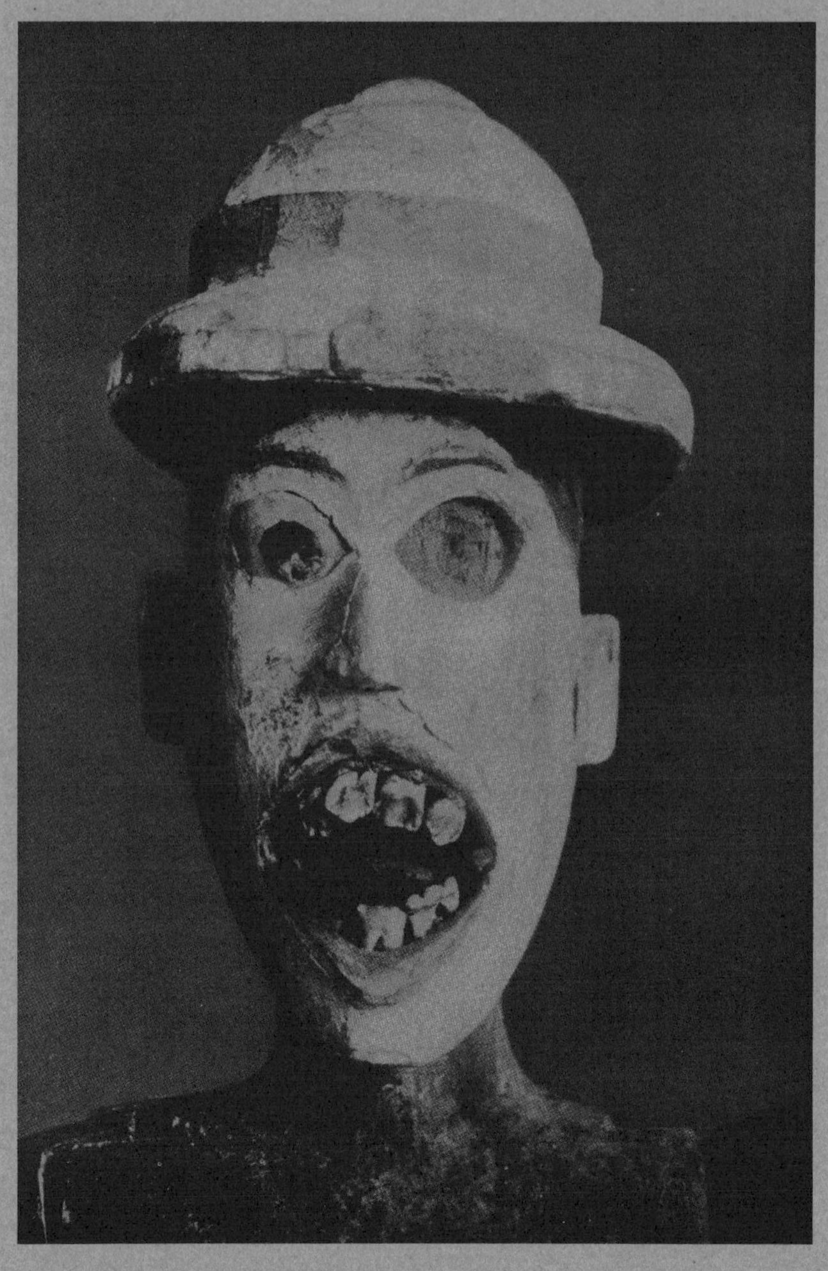